Crete
on the
Half Shell

Byron Ayanoglu

Crete
on the
Half Shell

A Story About an Island,
Good Friends, and Food

Toronto · 2004
Harper Perennial Canada

First published in hardcover by Harper*Flamingo*-
Canada, an imprint of HarperCollins Publishers Ltd,
2003. This paperback edition 2004.

HarperCollins books may be purchased for educa-
tional, business, or sales promotional use through
our Special Markets Department.

HarperCollins Publishers Ltd
2 Bloor Street East, 20th Floor
Toronto, Ontario, Canada
M4W 1A8

www.harpercanada.com

Line drawings by Olga Ryabets

National Library of Canada Cataloguing in
Publication

Ayanoglu, Byron
Crete on the half shell : a story about an island,
good friends, and food / Byron Ayanoglu. –
HarperPerennial Canada ed.

ISBN 0-00-639160-5

1. Crete (Greece) – Description and travel.
I. Title.

DF901.C8A92 2004   914.95'90476
C2003-905658-9

RRD 9 8 7 6 5 4 3 2 1

Printed and bound in the United States

for Aristedes Pasparakis,
the world's greatest chef
and Crete's most valiant son

Acknowledgements

Great thanks to:

Karen Hanson, the Angeloglu family, Minas Ayanoglu, Eleni Eliadis, Stephanie Fysh, Androulla Haalbroom, Jörn Heitmann, Hertz Rent a Car, Rod Morrison, Amnon Medad, Mara Meimaridis, Rachelle Naubert, Olympic Airways, the Orfanoudakis family, Pandelis Photo, the Sutherland family, Jane Vavak, and all the kind people of Crete.

In Search of My Greekness

The snow is falling in dime-size lacy jewels, covering the earth, shading the evergreens' branches, and painting the landscape white. The snow is so thick I can barely see in front of me. Familiar landmarks have become chimeras of their original shapes.

The Bay department store is to my left; I can see only an outline, but I know it's there. I'm in the middle of Phillips Square, which in summer is a midtown flower market but which has now become a slippery expanse that I have to cross to reach Place Ville Marie, where they are waiting for me. Montreal in winter is pedestrian hell—far too cold, far too slippery, and far, far too wet. If the snow doesn't drench you, then some nasty motorist will swoosh by, spraying you with waves of slush.

A car with a total rogue at its wheel—yellow parka and Italian sunglasses resting in his gel-slick hair—is driving straight for the puddle near me. He's laughing. I can see he means to spray me. I jump to the side to avoid the imminent slush, lose my balance, and fall.

Now I'm lying face down in the snow. I'm frozen to the core, more so than I should be. It's as if I'm nude. I look down at myself and in horror discover that I'm outdoors in deep winter in my swimsuit and flippers.

My limbs are going numb. I panic. I try to stand up and run for cover. But I cannot. Every time I'm almost upright, I fall and bury myself deeper in the soft snow. A very loud noise startles me. Then a flash of lightning blinds me. Thunder and lightning during a snowstorm? Another blast, like a truckful of exploding gunpowder. It shakes the house. It wakes me up.

I was safe in my Marioú home. I was in bed, still very much in Greece, inside my delightful hillside home on the sunny southern coast of Crete. It had all been a dream. A cold-wet and horrible dream. I chuckled with relief. But there was an unusual chill in the room. And the light filtering through the curtains was dull. It thundered again. And a strong wind howled. Damn! The bad weather had returned. We had had ten straight days of sunshine since Christmas. I had hoped that we had gone over the hump. Apparently not. There was a storm brewing out there. I could feel it. But at least I couldn't hear any rain.

My room-mate, the photographer Algis Kemezys, returned from his morning walk. His face was flushed, his shoes sodden, and there was suspicious wet white stuff on his jacket and hat. I thought I was imagining things, a lingering vision from my dream. I blinked to make it go away. It didn't.

There was another clap of thunder as Algis walked to the double balcony doors in front of my bed and drew the curtains. "Look," he said cheerfully.

I looked, I froze, I shut my eyes. "No-o-o!"

"Oh, yes!" nodded Algis. "Now it's snow."

Montreal-style, puffy, insistent snow was quietly covering the landscape in an alpine blanket, tinting icy outlines in the olive grove, brushing white patches on the hills, wrapping my prized view in winter fog. I could no longer see the sea!

In the last week, I had found diversion in the recklessness with which the Greeks celebrate the arrival of the New Year. I witnessed a repeat of the newly adopted Christmas shebang, with its endless parties and *Ayios Vasilis* (Santa Claus) and expensive presents, for *Protochronia* (New Year's Eve), which had always centred on lavish parties and a gift-bearing deity, the white-bearded, red-suited St. Basil. This made Greeks the only people on the planet to have two Christmases within a week of each other when they could ill afford even one.

Then the holidays were over. My great chef-friend Theo had finally called to reassure me that he had changed his mind about suicide, but that he could no longer tolerate the cheerfulness of Crete, and wasn't coming back in a hurry. Algis had once again postponed his return to Canada, because he was onto something new and exciting photographically, but it meant he would be outdoors in the hills all day long. Left to my own devices, I had diluted my lifelong anxieties in sunshine and *Protochronia*.

But it was disheartening, nearly impossible, to readjust to a life of ordinary food and to the possibility of a world without Theo and his cooking. The bare truth was that I was going to have to find my own fulfilment and learn to enjoy my own company. I had been prepared for this when I had originally made up my mind to move to Crete from Canada, but the bleakness of my situation was now coming into focus. I wasn't sure what to make of it.

Everyday life has a sameness and a predictability wherever

one happens to be. The greatest challenge facing us well-fed, highly spoiled individuals is to stave off boredom, a boredom that derives from being part of an affluent, insouciant society, and that tortures us with anxiety unless we feel we are being useful. Sadly, our usefulness has only one true gauge: money. And the pursuit of money is the most boring of all our activities. I once wrote, *"cash flow is the cockroach of human existence."* I've never found any evidence to the contrary.

On the other hand, everything about my own life had, up to that point, been demonstrably satisfying, despite being boring. My childhood was both loving and privileged, leaving me with little to carp about in terms of unresolved abuse or repressed inner children. My young adulthood could have been problematic libido-wise since I was overweight (well, fat), but luckily I persevered and discovered that there are multitudes of thin, sexy people out there who actually prefer corpulent lovers. I married first at nineteen, then three more times later on, and have had several relationships on the side, even though I don't mind being unattached: I find I sleep better alone.

I had never made a lot of money, but always enough and without trying very hard. I had gained a modicum of fame with my food writing and my stage plays, so that important people usually returned my phone calls. I had a collection of getting-older ailments—stomach ulcers, joint stiffness, a bad back, shortness of breath from years of smoking, and a life-long fight with excess fat—but I could cope uncomplainingly.

Really, the only thing missing from my life was this Greekness, which I had used as my pretext for coming to Crete. What I hadn't counted on was that being Greek was no simple matter, even if one was born Greek. It involved a tremendous backlog of rules and traditions, and I guess I had lived too long in North America to relate to it in any real way.

Real Greek life, outside of small pockets of sophistication in big cities, notably central Athens, is predicated on the family, on unquestioning faith in the Orthodox Church, on the unassailable authority of men and the uncompromising subservience and labour of women, and on the ongoing struggle to earn a living in the cockfight of the Greek marketplace. On previous brief trips to the homeland it had all seemed quaint and slightly exotic. Now, embedded in it, engulfed by it, desiring to be it, I was dizzy, almost nauseous with the reality of it. It was becoming painfully obvious how very un-Greek I had become.

I had successfully been staving off discovery of my non-Greek self by borrowing cheer from the early January sunshine—until the snowstorm of the century, as it was to be called: a freak of nature for people who had never seen snow in their homeland, the first snow to have stuck to the ground in the Marioú area in sixty-five years.

I watched the storm all day, and it was like no Canadian storm at all. It came in fast-moving waves, with thick layers of the white stuff accompanied by thunder and lightning as if it were rain, only to pass and reveal the sun, the view clearing so I could again see the sea and the snow-patched olive groves. In a few minutes a new wave would follow—the same thick snow with the view fusing into whiteness, my little Mediterranean world seemingly transferred to a mountainous northern location. And a half hour of punishment later, a new clearing, sun, view.

This went on all day, and despite myself I enjoyed it, punctuating my storm-watching with treats, such as boiled chestnuts, that Algis had risked his life to walk to the village and purchase.

At the end of this insanely variable day, the sunset dissolved the most ferocious of the snow waves to grey, bringing on instant darkness and freezing temperatures. I settled down with the rest of the chestnuts to watch the bedlam of Athens-under-snow on television. Athens suffers adversity like no other city on earth. Chaotic and under-functional at the best of times, with the most fragile infrastructure in the Western world, the capital breaks down at will. Mere rain is enough to paralyze it. Now, under a blanket of snow, some two feet of it—a soupçon in a snow-ready town like Montreal—it had become a disaster area, with all transportation at a standstill and essential services in great jeopardy.

The consequences of the snowstorm occupied over an hour of the newscast, illustrated by interviews with its many victims. A housewife whose kitchen was at the other side of a ten-pace exterior court wailed that there was no way she could cross the snow to reach her kitchen and cook, and she, her husband, and their three children would surely starve as a result. And, even more typical of the Greek mentality, an elderly woman, who was loudly furious, cursed the government: first the euro, which had recently replaced the drachma as the national currency, now the snow, and all this on top of the untimely death of her favourite singer, Stelios Kazantzidis.

I had bit into the last chestnut and was wondering which of my books I should read to pass the time when the electricity died. The lights, the TV, and, most injurious of all, the electric thermostat for the oil heating ceased to function. The room—my pride and joy, my warm room with the fabulous view—became a dark, forbidding icebox in no time, with all of the built-in safeguards that kept it cool in summer conspiring against me.

There was nothing to do but go to bed fully clothed under a mountain of blankets. I tried to fall asleep, though I was not in the least sleepy, hating the clammy feeling of condensed body heat under so many layers and the icy cold that froze my face and head and especially my bald spot.

I woke up grumpy and miserable, colder than I'd been since one night long ago when I had unwisely decided to camp out on a Swiss meadow in the so-called summer of the Alps, and had woken in the middle of the night with icicles formed on my moustache. I threw open my curtains fully expecting to see a white landscape, though I could tell it was sunny outside.

The snow had disappeared, the sea was calm and blue, the olive groves were back to their grey-green with no trace of white. The terrible storm that had thrown all of Greece into a tizzy had melted away with a few hours of morning sunshine as if it had never happened at all.

The electricity returned by noon, and I was once again master of a warm room, with a million-dollar view and only the usual Greek worries, like "What's the use of life," "What can the government do for me," and "Where's my next cup of coffee."

And just as I was feeling comfortable enough to restart the investigation of whether I could ever become a real Greek again, a new disaster struck: my landlady Erato came up, all flustered, to ask me to turn off my heating and use it only in the evening. The one-day storm had created a fuel shortage on the island, and there was no telling when we would get a refill of our diminishing oil supply.

Great! Just great. Why should anyone want to be part of a culture where one can't even have an identity crisis in some sort of comfort? This was too much for me. I decided to defer to a higher authority, someone who could put it in perspective for me.

I called on Niko, Erato's husband, back from mending his sheep shelter, which had come undone during the storm. All his animals had survived, and to celebrate he had brought a huge turkey to slaughter and had had a few drinks. I could smell the *raki* on his breath from ten feet away.

"So, what do you make of all this, Kirie Niko?" I asked him. "One day the snow, then a night of ice cold in my lonely bed, and now some sunshine, okay, but no more heating for who knows how long, because the oil companies are hoarding the fuel so they can raise the prices."

"Really? And all that happened while I wasn't looking," he said. "Now stop complaining, and listen to this *mantinada*." He sang:

> *I can no longer bring myself to utter I-love-you,*
> *because I said it once, and it covered me in painful*
> *sores, I was wounded to the core.*

He allowed a few seconds of silence for the song to settle in the air. "Now, *there's* something to fret about," he winked.

"Or how about this one?" He sang the next *mantinada* very close to my ear, practically singeing it with alcoholic fumes.

> *I've loved you more than anyone could ever love you.*
> *More even than your mother, who gave you life.*

I couldn't figure out the relevance of that to my own predicament, but Niko couldn't care less. He repeated the chorus, relishing it, getting louder with each reprise.

"And now, listen to the best one. The inimitable Xilouris wrote it when his son died." Niko's eyes watered. His face saddened. His voice faltered.

The wind put out the candle I was clutching in my hand.
And now my life is darkness, all night and all day.

Part I **The North**

Chapter 1

The Arrival

The long trip back home was down to its final leg. Soon a routine forty-minute flight from Athens would transport me to Crete, the birthplace of all that is Greek. I was on a mission to restore, in some measure, a Hellenic destiny interrupted by four decades in the Diaspora. I had been born a Greek in Constantinople and lived there until my family emigrated to Montreal when I was twelve years old. Now I was an aging Canadian, nearly arthritic after too many sub-zero winters, looking for a way to be young again, and soon.

This "soon," however, was taking its sweet time. My mind and spirit were already on that plane—heck, they were already on Crete, in a delightful, flowery cottage with a view of the warm sea. But, my body—as well as my three suitcases, iBook, mini tape recorder, international-access Fido, emergency supply of Earl Grey tea, six credit cards, and passport—was sitting in an airport-bound taxi that had managed to progress only two blocks from my hotel in ten minutes.

Madhouse Athens and its permanent traffic jams were no strangers to me. In the past, during vacations, I had never minded much. However, today, nearing the culmination of a lifelong ambition to return and live in the homeland—today it would have been decent, not to say fair, if the cars and trucks and buses had just parted and let me sail into my future.

It would have also been kind if the excitable citizens of the metropolis had decided to call a truce today. Instead there were no fewer than six simultaneous demonstrations on Syntagma Square, paralyzing the core of the city and causing massive bottlenecks.

Everyone, from fourth-graders furious about their slashed lunch allowances to underpaid judges, neglected veterans, and disenfranchised Albanians, had stepped out to plead their cases *al fresco*. Also present were domestic flight baggage handlers, whose strike had forced me to find a private cargo company to transport my suitcases—hand luggage only, the airline had stipulated. So I now found myself stuffed in a taxi that was stuck at a traffic light. Green, yellow, red— green, yellow, red—over and over again.

And then there was the matter of my cabbie. Athenian taxi drivers consider it their professional prerogative to talk—nay, to orate—at will to their captive customers. This guy, a wiry fellow with permanent stubble and eyebrows that met in the middle like a Chinese brush stroke, had a lot to teach me, especially about the pathology of road rage.

"The fault, sir, the responsibility, the HEART of the matter lies with the government. Am I right? Well? Can you deny that? Of course not. It's obvious. And yet, you are wrong! It's not true, because the government is helpless. It is lame. A parasite. So if not the government, then WHO? The big corporations? Don't even think about them. Greeks DO NOT support big corporations. We all take our kids to McDonald's, why not?!" A McDonald's was directly to the right of where we were stuck in traffic. "It doesn't mean I support them, or believe in them. No, sir! Then, who? The Church? Not on your life! Please. Don't make me puke. I go to church every Sunday, and on all holidays. All Greeks do. But trust me: I wouldn't let a clergyman into my cab if mine was the last car on the road and he was late for his own funeral. No, sir. They are perverts, those monks. They disgust me." A small breath, and then: "The middle class? Ouf! They don't know if they're coming or going. They are useless. They walk into my cab, her with her big hair and him with his ill-fitting suit, and they tell me to step on it because they are late, and the sister-in-law is very fussy about time. What step-on-it? As if I wouldn't STEP ON IT the moment the road was free. As IF I would want to spend one extra minute with these people in my car if I could help it! Hah!"

He paused to take a deep breath, then he screeched, "DID YOU SEE THAT! What a *malaka*! Bloodless, gutless MORON!" He was aghast, pointing menacingly at a car three lanes away that had missed a fleeting chance to change lanes, which would have allowed the two cars to our immediate and far left to move over one spot, giving us the leeway to steer around the truck in front of us and jockey for a better position deeper in the central, most polluted part of the congestion.

He stuck his head out of the window and hurled a highly expletive comment at the offending car, with zero probability of being heard by the criminal at its wheel. He turned back to me, livid. "That man has no right to be on the road! No right! I'm so . . . ANGRY, I could VOMIT!" Instead of vomiting he lit a cigarette, instantly filling the tiny car with billows of harsh smoke.

But he was back in a moment: "And on top of everything else, Panathinaikos sold out yesterday. They took a useless penalty five minutes from the whistle. And trust me, that penalty was poorly struck, and our goalkeep should've saved it. But did he even try? Not on your life. Crooks. They threw the game, a European Cup quarter-final with Inter Milan. We had them on the ropes. I'm so angry! They threw the game, because somebody in London or in Las Vegas paid them big money to lose and rake in the gambling profits. Yes, you're damned right I'm angry. I'm so angry, I could VOMIT on someone!"

Since I was the only one near enough for him to vomit on, I kept my opinions to myself, and in any case, I was finding him kind of soothing. He was so agitated about so many things that he made my own worries seem petty. He continued talking, arguing with himself, answering his own questions, all the way to the airport—all seventy-five minutes of the gruelling ride that was meant to take less than thirty. As his meter whirled through drachmas like a dervish, I heard him out on everything—from how the treacherous Japanese were undermining the economies of their former WWII enemies by over-pricing their cars, thus making it impossible for him to buy a new and safer vehicle with brakes that actually worked, to that putrid Foskolos, author of Greek TV's most-watched soap operas, who was such a terrible writer he was single-handedly obviating two and a half millennia of Greek drama. His tirade was peppered with frequent outbursts of verbal abuse against every other driver on the road, for offences ranging from going too slow to picking one's nose while abruptly changing lanes . . . until finally, FINALLY, the car stopped in front of the domestic wing of Athens's brand-new, conspicuously Europeanized El. Venizelos Airport.

I took the last available table in the airport café, and sat down with an espresso and my John le Carré. It was one of his recent paperbacks, not his best, a far cry from gems like the Smiley trilogy and *The Perfect Spy*. The book was enjoyable nonetheless, and I became so engrossed in the story of a righteous banker—an oxymoron if I ever heard one—and his twisted father, that I didn't notice someone had taken the chair opposite me. I looked away from the book to take a sip of my coffee, and found myself the recipient of a bemused smile.

He was an average-looking man—short hair, clean shaven, glasses, ordinary clothing that could have used better ironing—my age, maybe a bit older, indistinguishable from many others like him at the terminal except for a bright, charismatic glow.

I took a sip of my espresso, avoiding his eyes and deliberately lowering mine to the page, determined to pretend that I understood no language of any kind if he did start speaking. He let out a howling laugh that startled me.

"So, what is this, Montreal? You don't recognize your old friends anymore?" he exclaimed in a mixture of accents. And he laughed again.

I peered at him. And somewhere underneath all the normalcy, I perceived Theodoros: the legendary Theo, eccentric chef and restaurant genius of several continents, who had started his career overnight by suddenly abandoning academia (he taught applied physics at the University of British Columbia) to open his first restaurant in Vancouver's Kitsilano district—Electra, named after his daughter.

I had met Theodoros in the dizzying late sixties on the Canadian West Coast, when he used to ride around in a vintage convertible Mercedes-Benz, dressed in ceremonial black like some warlord from Crete, with a fringed head scarf and knee-high calfskin boots. He lived very high in those days following the immediate success of Electra, opening restaurant after restaurant, money flowing through his hands like liquid.

Theo expanded to Calgary and Toronto, where his restaurants, Emmanuel's and Koutouki, revolutionized Greek cooking in those cities, and then to L.A., then London, until eventually, like all other expat Greeks, he returned to Greece. I had heard that he had arrived broke, having spent his fortune faster than he had made it, but that he had found backers and quickly opened several restaurants in a row. He burned a gastronomic swath through the Athenian dining establishment, with serial successes. He was lionized by the media and developed a cult of devout fans, much as he had done everywhere else he lived.

I had run into Theo many times since our initial acquaintance three decades earlier, and I had witnessed so many incarnations of this heroic, rather mythical man that nothing much about him could surprise me anymore.

In the past, he had always stood out, in any crowd. Today he seemed to be blending in. He looked like anyone else going back home to Crete after a short visit to Athens. Was this a genuine transformation, or just a phase?

"I've moved to Crete," he announced. "I live there now. I can't take Athens anymore. It reminds me of Panama City. Not that Panama City was all that bad. There was one time . . . Have I told you about the time that the Russian circus was in town, and there was this Colombian prostitute? Her name was Teresa. Her father had been a coke king in Bogotá, but he was gunned down, and she escaped death by a fingernail. She walked all the way to Panama. No stroll down the Parade, I assure you. Some thousand kilometres of jungle. And she ended up on the sidewalk outside my hotel—"

"Why Crete?" I asked, interrupting him.

"Why Crete?!" He was astonished by my question. "Crete is the epicentre of the Earth, that's why. It is the beginning and the end of life. Do you realize that Crete has never been subdued? Conquered by just about every marauder who ever sailed the eastern Mediterranean, but never vanquished! No, sir. Crete is eternal, and it's sublime. The most beautiful place I've ever seen, and I've seen them all. Crete is the home of our best people. Both the Minotaur and Zeus were born there. Also Kazantzakis the author, Venizelos the founder of modern Greece . . . Hey, El Greco, the painter. He was from Crete. Tra la la. And I am from Crete!"

"You?! Come on, Theo! So far you've claimed to be Canadian, South African, English, American, and Athenian."

"Well, it turns out, I'm really from Crete, and I proved it in Vancouver with my outfit. Remember my black outfit?"

"Who could forget?"

"Yes. That outfit is the traditional dress of my village, Anógia. The last village in the foothills of Psilorítis. We are a tough bunch, you'll see . . . You are bound for Crete, aren't you?"

"I hope so."

"Yes. In this country you must have hope, and you must also have faith. So far those two items are still free. Of course the best thing about Crete is the food. The food in Crete is so great that people are refusing to die just so that they can keep eating it. It has been publicly proclaimed. The diet of Crete is the healthiest on the planet. They did a major study in The

Hague." Theo settled back in his seat. Though not a big man, he had the ability to occupy a big space.

"Well. The Hague," I smiled. "I'm not going to argue with anything that is proclaimed by The Hague."

"It's quite a town. I spent a night there once."

"The Bulgarian Opera Company was there, and they featured a live sex act?"

"Wrong. Actually there was nothing going on. That was the funniest thing. No one at all was there. The whole Hague was deserted. It was the longest night of my life."

"So what's the secret of this diet? What makes it so great?"

"Always the curious one, eh, Byron?" he said. "All those years of living in Montreal, I guess."

"Well? Do you know?"

"Of course, I know," he scoffed. Theo had never been known to buckle under any challenge. "It's many things. First of all it's the greens. There are more than one thousand kinds of wild edible greens that grow in the hills of Crete. All the greens are special, and there is a specific, time-honoured recipe for each one. Some are steamed and served with stewed broad beans. Some are served raw with oil and lemon. Some in pies. Then there are the raw milk cheeses. Have you ever tasted *tirieftis*, the fresh cheese of pregnant goat's milk? Or *anthogalo*, the full-fat ewe's cheese fermented just until the piss smell has turned sweet? Then the vegetables. Oh, my God." He threw his hands up in the air as if paying homage to the gods of vegetables. "Organically grown, vine-ripened jewels, available all year long. The unfiltered, day-old olive oil, with its scent of jasmine and orange blossom. The hand-fed suckling pig. The dark peasant bread, baked into soft husks. Yogurt so thick, you cut it with a knife. And honey so splendid, you can name every kind of flower the bee sipped. What makes the food of Crete great? The climate, the tradition, the right soil, the right altitude, lots of hard work, centuries of overlapping cooking styles, and not the least of all, palates like ours to appreciate its greatness. Are you still fond of food?" Theo's twinkle was friendly but mischievous.

I shifted my three-hundred-pound frame. "Well, I am on a diet, Theo. It's a new concept, my own invention. Far as I know, I am its only practitioner. It involves eating as much as I want of my favourite foods, and hoping to get to swim afterwards to work it all off."

"You're lucky. October is an excellent month to swim in Crete. You're staying the month, I hope."

"I'm planning to stay for much longer than a month. I'm going to Crete to find a place to retire."

"RETIRE?" Theo spat out the word. "Are you CRAZY?"

A very loud announcement saved me from defending my sanity. The flight to Heraklion was ready for boarding. Suddenly all the waiting passengers got up as one and rushed to the gate. And we, though provided with reserved, numbered seats, followed suit, springing from our seats to join the melee.

"I'll keep doing my food writing. I'm on to a new play, I'll write that. But I'm tired! Okay? I'm fifty-five years old. My body creaks all over. I have just enough money. I think retirement is a good option!"

"Nonsense!" Theo shouted back. "I'm older than you. If you're ready to retire, what am I supposed to do? Die? Well, I'm not ready to die, and you're not retiring. That's all there is to that!"

"And if I'm not retiring, then what am I doing?" I chuckled, narrowly escaping a major concussion as an industrial-size ghetto blaster was passed hand to hand overhead for an elderly lady, whose carry-on luggage it was in addition to her two canvas bags full of Athenian delicacies.

"You're going into business with me!"

"Oh? What business?"

Theo ducked to dodge a parcel that had air vents and seemed to be jiggling, and that smelled suspiciously of wet goat. "I can't discuss business under these conditions. Suffice it to say that it'll revolve around food, and fun, and it'll be a bit of a kick on your butt. Retire? And then what? Live on a budget for the next fifty years? On Crete, my people think of retirement only after the age of one hundred. At your age, at my age, it's business. The best age for business! Now that we know so much, and we can still click our heels. Oh, I have just the place for you. You'll pee in your pants when you see it. In Fodele, not far from Heraklion."

"And after I dry off, what am I doing in Fodele?"

"I'll tell you about it during the flight," he yelled from ten feet away, having seen an opening to get closer to the ticket taker. "I'll go on ahead and get us seats together." And then I lost sight of him.

The flight was overbooked and several passengers were denied access. We were lucky to get seated at all, let alone together. Details of Theo's business plan would have to wait until we landed. I tried to read more of my book, but the excitement of nearing my destination was getting the better of me. The chance meeting with Theo, the most Zorba of all the Greeks I've known, added just the right amount of spice to my upcoming retirement . . . er, adventure . . . whatever. Suddenly, I was ready for anything.

I stared out the window and watched the gentle Aegean

glide past, until the promised island in all its mountainous majesty came into view. There she was: Crete. A pink mirage of interlocking peaks, descending steeply into a ring of emerald sea. The water was so clear I could see the bottom from the sky.

Chapter 2

The First Supper

"I have a suite in Fodele," declared Theo. "We'll go there directly after the market." I heard him with half an ear as I collected my luggage and picked up the hire car. It was small, the better to negotiate the narrow roads of Crete, and now it was loaded to the gills with all my gear, and with the two of us snugly in the front.

Theo had automatically assumed the driver's seat. "You don't know the roads—I'd better drive," he had said, afraid, I suspected, that I would lose it in Greek traffic and get us into an accident. He's mortal after all, I thought to myself.

He raced out of the airport, weaving around slower cars like a car jockey in need of the bathroom, and lunged into traffic, passing three cars and two trucks on a blind curve. "Don't worry, I never take chances," he said. "I've had only three collisions in my life, and none with someone else's rented car." He let out a roar and floored it, the tiny engine straining to keep up with his commands.

"I'm happy you have room for me in Fodele," I said to take

my mind off his driving. "I can't wait to settle in and take a shower."

"Oh, you will. Right after the market."

"What market?! Aren't we driving straight to Fodele?"

"Relax, will you? We're going shopping first. It won't take long."

"Shopping?"

"I promised my landlady a meal tonight. My place has a kitchen. She's opening a restaurant and I need to show her some samples of my cooking. It'll mean a nice job for us. Setting the menu of her restaurant."

"Menu? Restaurant?"

"Yes. On the ground floor of the hotel. You'll love it!"

"Love it?"

Theo took a sharp left turn off the highway, across opposing traffic, and headed the wrong way down the one-way on-ramp.

"I hate the normal exit," he said by way of apology. "It leads to a ten-minute delay. This ramp empties right where I want to be." He manoeuvred around two oncoming cars, neither of whose drivers seemed surprised to have to dodge a car coming from an illegal direction. "Don't worry. We all drive the wrong direction when we need to. Thing is, the market closes down in twenty-five minutes, and I have no time to waste on traffic rules."

And thus we entered Heraklion, named after the mythological strongman Hercules (Heracles), who many Hellenes feel should come back to life and raze the city to the ground.

Heraklion is an uneasy collection of Venetian castles, stiflingly overcrowded Ottoman neighbourhoods, and three-storey fifties prefab apartment houses—the kind middle-class Greeks prefer because they are new and clean—all haphazardly superimposed and set on a hopelessly disconnected network of permanently bottlenecked streets. The city is nevertheless instantly likable entirely because of the pace and the high-voltage, rather expansive personalities of its inhabitants. Nowhere in the city is the outgoing nature of the Herakliots more in evidence than in its Central Market. Spanning several blocks smack in the middle of the city's most crowded quarter, the market is an ode to the citizens' dedication to old-time gastronomy. Stalls of all food-persuasions spill generously out onto the sidewalks, selling fresh produce, dry goods, meats, fish, and seafood with an abundance and an exuberance that belie our constipated times.

Tucked into the market's crevices are shops with the delicacies of Crete's most select and exactingly traditional producers: goat's- and ewe's-milk cheeses from Vorízia; thick, aromatic yogurt from Anógia; fruit and chestnuts from Chania; olive oil from Sitía, red mullets from the southern coast's Libyan Sea; suckling pigs from Lasíthi; grain-fed chickens and roosters from Ierápetra; and wondrous breads, buns, and cheese and spinach puffs concocted from Muslim recipes since 1827 at Toulis Bakery.

Theo, pressed for time or not, naturally sought out only the best purveyors of each of his many needs, zigzagging the market, improvising his menu as he went, enlarging it to four courses from the original two. I struggled to keep up, carrying my laptop and briefcase, which I had refused to leave in the car with the rest of my luggage, parked as we were in a very suspect, indeed, totally illegal spot. "I'm NOT wasting valuable shopping time to look for a better spot to accommodate your LUGGAGE," Theo had barked. "If it were up to me, you would chuck all this garbage into the sea, and free yourself!"

To better free himself for the exigencies of his shopping

spree, Theo kept dumping plastic bags full of his purchases onto my already overloaded arms. Soon I resembled a walking shopping bag, with live shrimp jumping out of their cramped quarters to attack the delicate innards of my iBook. As was bound to happen, Theo lost count of what he was spending, and he turned to me. "Give me 10,000 drachmas. Oh, cut out the face, it's only thirty euros. I need to buy the rooster and the rabbit!" he thundered. Theo is one of those people who know you can't deny them anything if they ask for it loudly. I gave him the money, and he rewarded me with some rest. He installed me at a café table and ordered me a Greek coffee, medium sugar, while he delayed the closing of the butcher shop opposite the café to deal with his meats.

"I don't have proper knives at my place," he informed the hapless, cackling butchers. "I have to debone and slice the meat here." I sipped my coffee, watching him carve and chop and remove offensive bones from a golden-fleshed free-range rooster and a milky white rabbit.

The meat properly prepared and packaged in plastic bags, the shopping was finally over. Theo actually considered dumping these last bags onto my hands, then humanely conceded that he could carry them himself, and he led me back to the car, which had been neither towed nor ticketed. "They went on a rampage of ticketing illegal parking last month," chuckled Theo. "Now they'll leave us alone until after Christmas when their coffers will be empty."

A leisurely twenty-minute drive, with peaks towering to our left and cliffs plunging steeply into the turquoise sea to our right, brought us to Fodele. Theo, no longer pressed for time, chatted freely all the way—something about random selection and benevolent chaos, a theory from physics with its origins in Aristotle. "If you set out to create an idea or an object, be it in the arts or sciences, you're bound to fail," he informed me. "The surest way to achieve nothing is if you decide you must achieve something. The only road to success is to allow events to take over and concepts to enunciate themselves, trusting your own knowledge and experience to sift out the gold from the debris. Ordinary mortals find it impossible to follow this simple rule because they are insecure and they feel they must control their own destiny. And so they fail in life, never quite knowing what they did wrong. Even I suffer from insecurity occasionally, but then I remember the golden maxim. It can be applied to all human endeavour, and all the arts, especially the culinary."

Much as I wanted to listen to him, I felt muggy and sticky and my mind was fixated on water. A swim, for example—for which I knew Theo would never allow me the time, there being so much cooking to be done—or at least a nice, hot shower.

"Ah, a shower," said Theo smiling. "The Canadian solution to the problems of the world." I smiled too. Sniffing the air in the car, I mused that a shower wouldn't be a bad idea for him either. I could detect a pungent combination of fried fish, cigar smoke, tarragon, oregano, goat cheese, and a generous helping of garlic.

Fodele, a prosperous marketplace for the surrounding farmlands since the Middle Ages, is best known as the most probable birthplace of the painter Domenikos Theotokopoulos, also known as El Greco. He found fame, fortune, and immortality in the sixteenth-century court of Philip II in Madrid, and eventually Toledo, without ever returning to Crete. The historical near-certainty of El Greco's origins is widely celebrated in Fodele, especially at a reconstructed house and an adjacent Byzantine church, lovely to behold in all their interlocking geometrical features, situated about a kilometre away from the modern-day centre of the town. El Greco brings the foreign visitors to this village. The Greeks, especially those from Heraklion, come here to enjoy the rusticity, the fresh foothills air, the river that trickles through the centre of the village, and the countless orange trees that decorate its periphery like bearers of ripe suns setting on dark green leaves.

The residential part of Fodele is on the right bank of the river, while the left bank is devoted to a commercial street ringed with restaurants and shops selling the region's renowned embroideries and macramés.

The whole lot of it—the orange trees, the charm of the village, the murmur of its river, the nature lovers' path, the fat swan-like ducks floating on the water, the several busts and tributes to El Greco, the widows in their shapeless all-black clothes busily doing needlework on their riverside perches— left me unimpressed. My only motivation to proceed, to keep breathing, was to get inside this famous suite of Theo's and take my shower.

The hotel was on the upper floor of a two-storey stone building inside a leafy park. On the ground floor was a dishevelled warehouse—the premises, I guessed, of the future restaurant. Theo's suite was a two-room affair, with many windows, comfortable beds, a good-size balcony, and a toy kitchen with hardly any counter space and two smallish elements fed by a tank of propane gas.

"You're going to cook on that?" I asked.

Theo looked at me patronizingly. "I've yet to meet a kitchen I didn't want to cook in, just as Don Juan never met a woman he didn't want to seduce. Go take your shower so I can concentrate."

I rummaged through my luggage and located fresh clothes, which I laid out on my bed. I retrieved the large, soft towel I had brought all the way from Montreal along with a down pillow—home comforts I find essential in countries that take pride in their tiny, punishingly unabsorbent towels and their rock-hard pillows—and headed for the bathroom.

Theo looked at me pityingly. "I hope you enjoy cold water," he said.

"Why?!"

"I've been running the hot, and, well, there doesn't seem to be any."

I frantically cranked the hot water in the shower, and all it gave me was ice cold. "I forgot," shouted Theo from outside. "They're fixing the solar-heating system. They've been at it since last week, before I went to Athens. I was hoping . . ."

It looked like I was stuck with a cruel, frigid downpour, as Theo continued his conciliatory lecture: "Actually, we're lucky to have water of any kind. Water is this country's most precious commodity. It isn't all that long ago that in a hotel like this we would've had to go to the river and bring water back a bucket at a time."

After less than ten seconds I jumped out of the ordeal, no cleaner, if involuntarily refreshed. I shivered into my fresh clothes and reported for duty in the kitchen. I couldn't have been gone longer than eight minutes all told, but the place already looked as if a tornado had hit. This was Theo's favourite way to cook. Create & Slash, his co-workers used to call it, which meant that he cooked while they cleaned up after him. Since I was the only co-worker around, cleaning up was obviously my domain.

And thus we spent a fascinating three hours preparing a feast for the landlady of the hotel, in an effort to impress her with Theo's prowess in the kitchen. Attempting to impress anyone from a kitchen such as this was beyond me, but then again I was no Theodoros. This man did not cook, he created. He used what he found around him to concoct random miracles in a prandial chaos. He had tales of feeding a hundred high-powered guests using a single wood-burning fire and a medium-sized frying pan. Now, with two adjustable fires and several cooking implements, he appeared unstoppable.

In between dancing around him to clean up sink, floor, counter, and dishes, I watched him throw in a bit of this and lots of that, taste sauces, season and reseason, marinate greens, sauté meats, grate cheeses, and restructure genetic signatures of foodstuffs to draw out of them the last iota of their essential tastes. Peeling fruits and shelling fragile shrimp he assigned to me, claiming his fingers were too thick to properly perform exacting tasks, though I suspected he simply couldn't be bothered with the boring stuff.

The preparations were all done by six-thirty. As the October sun dipped behind the mountain, the sky turned a watercolour pink and the evening breeze transformed the edgy heat into a warm caress. We set the table for our guest out on the balcony, and I cleaned up the kitchen once more while Theo lit a victory cigar. All that was left to do now was last-minute stuff—rewarming, adjusting sauces, and decorating the plates.

Instead of at eight, she arrived at a quarter to nine, fashionably late for a country lady—in Athens she'd have come closer to ten. A beautiful woman, a grandmother at forty-eight, Eftihia—Greek for "happiness"—was a mega-entrepreneur with four retail stores, plus the hotel and the imminent restaurant. Nevertheless, she was first a Greek wife and mother; she was late because she had to feed her husband and her younger, unmarried daughter, whom Theo had pointedly not invited since their tastes began and ended with meat and potatoes.

We indulged in a few minutes of pleasantries and a taste of her homemade wine, a bright red with a distinct taste of cloves and an excess of alcohol, before Theo and I popped in and out of the kitchen to serve the many courses of the complex meal.

First off the fires was a tasty, garlicky sauté of shrimps and oyster mushrooms on a bed of seasoned wild greens, the bittersweet *yaloradiko* and the bearded, sweet *papoules*, two of the many leafy reasons Crete's diet promotes a long life. All three of us cleaned our plates with much lip-smacking.

Next up, a succulent fry-up of rooster nuggets in a sauce of mustard, lemon, and oregano, garnished with steamed mustard greens. The crunchy bit on this plate was a wedge of potato *roesti*, composed only of grated raw potato browned in a non-stick pan with no oil whatsoever. Theo was in the process of designing a line of foods "fried" without oil: his contribution to healthy eating. "It tastes fried, but it isn't," he declared to Eftihia. "A little Zen for your degustation." It was doubtful that Eftihia understood "Zen," but she swayed in appreciation nonetheless.

The spectacular third offering left me breathless, while Eftihia poked at it with next to no appetite. It was too unusual for her tastebuds, which though evolved, were still very much Greek. It was a stew of rabbit in a sauce of rosemary and the sweet muscat wine of Sámos, accompanied by a bulgur wheat–grated carrot–minced onion pilaf enhanced with melted *tiro-malaka* cheese, whose unripe sheep-meadow flavour blended with precision into the other tastes on the plate.

We were too full to even move, but Theo wasn't quite finished teasing our palates. "It is exactly when you are no longer hungry that you can enjoy delicacies," he said. "I never eat when I'm hungry. Eating is one of life's greatest diversions. Better than sex." He winked at Eftihia, who nodded knowingly. "It is only when you don't need it that it arouses you."

The delicacy with which he aroused us to continue eating was his own version of Crete's favourite dessert, *bougatsa*, a filo-dough pie with a sweet custard filling, a sort of *galaktoboureko* without the heavy syrup.

Theo's version had a semolina–goat milk custard, flavoured with vanilla and cardamom, rounded out with thinly sliced fresh pear and apple. The custard was enveloped in a thick, Chania-style filo, and slow-fried in ewe's-milk butter until golden brown. His sauce featured drunken raisins, soaked in the local eau-de-vie *raki*, added to warm honey and cooked until just steaming, with some of the alcohol left in the raisins.

The meal-in-itself dessert was so rich and otherworldly that we relished it in total silence. Stars had covered the clear sky, and we sat back dazed. Theo and I, in any case, were content. Eftihia, who had managed only some obligatory "oh, very good" and "oh, splendid" comments during the meal, sipped the last of her wine, and rendered her judgment: "The dessert was excellent and I loved it, but that's not unusual, because I'm a big fan of *bougatsa*. And the best part of it was that it wasn't overly sweet. The shrimp and the rooster I congratulate because they were not oversalted. I find most chefs use too much salt. You made me very happy."

It was the kind of compliment that would have left most chefs unsure they had been complimented. But Theo was pleased. He had made her happy, and there is no feat more worthwhile for a Greek than to make a woman happy.

Chapter 3

Into the Hills

The next morning, a Sunday, as the memories of the previous night's delicious meal lingered on my palate, I wondered with some chagrin how long it would take for the conservative palates of Crete to appreciate someone as innovative as Theo. He had pleased Eftihia mostly by his moderation of salt, but had totally failed when he contravened the sweet-salty limen with wine from Sámos, a rival island.

The singular recompense for the expensive, labour-intensive adventure appeared to be that Eftihia had been made happy. But despite the fact that making women happy has been man's primary usefulness on earth since the famous incident under the apple tree, there really was no discernibly bankable reward for that happiness. Eftihia's restaurant was months away from completion, and therefore from needing a menu, and, bottom line, all she would need on that menu would be the same old roast lamb and overcooked noodles that everyone expected, be they summer's foreign tourists or winter's weekend Herakliot punters.

Theo, on the other hand, marching to his own tune as

always, woke up singing a rousing mountain melody from his native Anógia, absolutely convinced that we had scored big-time with Eftihia, and that both he and I would imminently be receiving mighty offers of kitchen partnerships from her.

Barely able to contain his excitement, he became grandiose and generous, suggesting a swim to start my day and then a drive into the mountains to Teménia, where an acquaintance's restaurant had chickens that laid eggs with yolks so orange they seemed red—the ideal brunch after a dunk in the sea.

I couldn't have been happier about the prospect of a swim because the morning sun was quickly burning off Fodele's night dew and raising the mercury to summer levels, somewhat surprising in October even for this sunbelt location.

A mere twelve minutes from Fodele, on the other side of the hill, is the holiday town of Aghia Pelagia. Once just a sandy cove at the bottom of a cliff, it has become a fully articulated beach resort with a multitude of sunny hotels spread among the farmlands in the dips and valleys of the hillside. A three-mile hairpin road down from the national highway culminates in a pleasing former fishing village that brims with holiday-makers in summer, petering out in the early fall to summer-worshippers who refuse to believe that their favourite season is over, and later on to absolutely no visitors at all.

The fine weather of this October Sunday had driven a large number of summer-fanatics to the beach, but only as observers. Greeks have a love affair with the sea that has flourished unabated since antiquity. They like to be near it, watch it, smell it, enjoy it at all times of the year. However, bathing in it they tolerate only during the hottest months.

Much like well-mannered gentry who wouldn't dare to wear white shoes or short-sleeved shirts after Labour Day, Greeks wouldn't dream of swimming in the sea after the last day of September, whatever the weather. They fear catching laima, an incurable sore throat, one of many typically and exclusively Greek ailments; this one is a result of post-seasonal swims or of drafts at any time of the year.

Theo, as true a Greek as was ever born within inhaling distance of the sea, joined his fellow sufferers at a beachside café table with a double unsweetened Greek coffee. Meanwhile, the sea, emerald green with turquoise highlights and warmer even than in summer, stretched languidly, rippleless, into the fabled Aegean, a model for swimming pools worldwide and a source of more swimming pleasure than all those billion swimming pools combined. And best of all, I had it all to myself.

Exhilarated and refreshed, I could have stayed in the water all day, but I kept it to thirty minutes, sensing Theo's restlessness. It is unwise to keep someone as intense as Theo waiting. Especially since he had just promised me the best eggs in Crete.

We drove very fast for an hour west towards Chania on the safe and comfortable national highway before turning south to head into the challenging roads that lead to the Lefka Ori (white mountains). These high mountains, named for the winter snow on their summits, are home to some of the most treacherous roads in Crete and are dotted with tiny white-washed villages clinging to their faces as if suspended by celestial strings. One of these villages is Teménia, near the tourist attraction the Samarian Gorge.

The morning's fine weather had become scorching, even in the relative cool of the mountain. Theo, afraid of catching laima from the draft, enforced a closed-window policy, turning my little car into an oven. Neither of us had had the courage to bathe in cold water that morning, but at least I had

had my swim in the sea. Theo was emitting a loud combination of the many flavours of the previous night's meal, most prominently rabbit and rooster, but also, subtly, rosemary, thyme, Sámos wine, and lemon, as well as the inevitable garlic and cigar smoke. It was overwhelming, but also soothing, like being inside a gourmet kitchen.

The drive was taking much longer than promised, the tricky and relentless turns forbidding any sort of speed. I was beyond worrying if Theo would get too hungry to enjoy the distant eggs because by now I was famished. Theo had prevented me from eating breakfast so as to get a faster start, and nearing noon, after a good swim, all I could think of was lunch.

Relief came in the form of some luscious blackberries about a kilometre outside the village of Prasés. We had just driven through a series of gut-wrenching mountain passes, which my map indicated were to continue indefinitely all the way to Teménia. Picking blackberries, a sport best practised by bears, can be a thorny, painful pastime. Theo was soon covered in blood, and I let him continue picking, not seeing the necessity of both of us suffering. My contribution to the berry picking was to locate a plastic bag, which Theo filled in no time with at least a kilo of the sugary treats. He returned to his driving seat elated.

"Forget Teménia and the fried eggs," he announced. "Your brunch today will be a Crete *caltzouni* with a blackberry topping. I need a couple more things and an oven, and we're in business!" He let out a ringing laugh and floored the gas.

A remnant of the Venetian culture that occupied Crete for several centuries (AD 1212–AD 1669), *caltzouni* descends from *calzone*, which is a piecrust encasing either a savoury or a sweet stuffing and which is still served in Italianate locales, especially in New York City pizza parlours, where the stuffing echoes the dressings of a pizza, with tomato and cheese as its base. In Crete, where it is often known by its diminutive, *caltzounaki*, the stuffing is sweetened fresh cheese with an egg mixed in for additional texture, and it is served with a honey dressing on top. For its proper deployment, Theo needed the fresh cheese and egg, as well as flour, yeast, and milk for the crust, mint—his own enhancement to the stuffing—and local honey from thyme flowers. No other kind would do.

Just outside Prasés a woman was knitting on her porch. Theo slowed down the car and accosted her: "I need some *armexia*. Where can I find it?" *Armexia* means "milking," and it is the fresh cheese made from milk that is curdled as soon as the goat has obliged. It is meant to be eaten the same day.

"I don't have any," she apologized. Then, cheerfully, "But Mihalis always has some. You can find him in the white house with the blue door." Crete is an island awash with blue-doored white houses, but Theo drove up to the exact house unerringly. A man was sitting in a pickup truck in front of the house, his engine running.

Theo propelled our fragile car in front of the truck, cutting off Mihalis's exit. "Are you Mihalis?" he asked the man. "I need some *armexia*!"

Mihalis chuckled. "I have some, but my wife needs it for supper," he said.

"Your wife wouldn't know what to do with it," exclaimed Theo with imperious impatience. "Sell it to me!"

Very much to my surprise, Mihalis got out of his truck and meekly went in through his blue door. There is obviously some kind of Crete code between men that overrides the need of wives for freshly made cheese.

Mihalis returned with a cheesecloth bundle, whey still dripping, the contents warm. The cheese couldn't have been curdled much more than an hour before. "You won't find fresher in the entire prefecture," he said, beaming. "How much of it do you want?"

"All of it, of course. I'm making *caltzounis* for my friend. He's from outside and has never had it," said Theo, motioning in my direction.

"Well, in that case," whispered Mihalis, with a sympathetic glance towards me. He retreated through the blue door and returned with the cheese packaged on a plate, now free of its cheesecloth and smelling of the fall flowers the goat had grazed. Mihalis had placed three just-laid eggs on top of the cheese. "You'll need these," he said as Theo nodded enthusiastically.

"How much do I owe you?" asked Theo nonchalantly. Mihalis lowered his eyes in embarrassment. "Nothing at all," he exclaimed emphatically. "It's for the *xenos*," gesturing towards me.

Xenos, a mixture of "stranger" and "guest," makes up the business end of the word *filoxenia* (hospitality), which is at once the most revered and the most unbreakable rule of the Greek sensibility. It was a moot point that Mihalis had spoiled his wife's supper plans by parting with the *armexia* because it was for me.

Our next quest was for mint. "All the housewives grow mint on their front yards. They like the smell when they sit in the evenings with their coffee," remarked Theo. And true enough, the lady next door to Mihalis's white house had some in front of her own white house. She tore off a bundle of the aromatic herb and handed it smilingly to Theo, "For the *xenos*."

"Now to find a little store and a kitchen," said Theo, as we parked in the heart of wink-and-you've-missed-it Prasés. There was no restaurant in this village, but there was the indispensable coffee house, a prerequisite of any congregation of Greek society: a place for men to drink coffee and *raki*, complain about life, play cards and backgammon, watch TV, and hide from their wives once they've given away all of supper's armexia.

The café had no real kitchen, only a tiny gas burner for making Greek coffee and an ancient waffle maker that had toasted its last grilled cheese sandwich a good twenty years earlier.

Miraculously, the waffle maker turned itself on once its dust had been wiped off and its dangerously frayed cord plugged in. "We'll cook the *caltzouni* on this silly contraption," Theo said. "This has never before been attempted, which means it's bound to work."

We quickly occupied the café. Five old men, the regulars, watched Theo's antics adoringly, while the owner, his wife, and their teenaged son scurried to follow the great chef's orders. In no time, flour, yeast, and milk were purchased and a bowl was found for mixing the dough, while the boy was sent a kilometre away to his beekeeper uncle to fetch a cup of the proper honey.

Theo mixed the dough ingredients and covered the bowl with a cloth to let the dough rise a touch. He demanded another bowl, in which he whipped up the cheese with the eggs and the mint. He tasted this and let his eyes roll back in bliss. "Sweetest cheese on earth," he proclaimed. He shaped his dough into a big flat slab and piled as much cheese into its middle as would fit. Then he folded it over and invited me nearer to admire his creation. "The best damn *caltzouni* you're ever likely to eat," he smiled with pride.

He carefully lifted the pregnant pie and lowered it onto both sides of the waffle maker. "We'll have to turn it when the first side is done. It'll be tricky without a spatula, but we'll simply have to manage . . . And WHERE is my honey?" he hollered at no one in particular.

The boy ran into the café just in time, panting and carrying the precious jar. Theo emptied the thick amber-coloured nectar into a small pot and added a little water to dilute it. He heated it on the coffee-making flame until it came to a boil, forcing the honey to relinquish its texture and become liquid. He bellowed for yet a third bowl, but there was no need to yell: the café owner's wife had already brought it. Theo transferred the berries into it and poured the hot honey over them.

He returned to his *caltzouni*, and using a plate and a fork, he flipped it onto its uncooked side, spilling a messy dollop of the melting cheese filling on the floor. The café wife instantly got on all fours to wipe up the mess as the rest of us gasped in awe at the rosy brown colour of the cooked side.

"The second side takes less time," Theo assured me, understanding that my hunger at this juncture knew no bounds. He stirred the berries in their honey sauce, causing purple-blue streaks to fuse with the golden syrup.

He turned the now fully cooked pie onto a platter—another contribution from the lady's kitchen—and decorated the top with the berries, letting their thyme-perfumed sauce drip around the edges. He cut big chunks onto plates and spooned berries and sauce over each portion. He gave me the first plate. Finally I had food in front of me. It was so beautiful, I paused a moment before I took my first bite. Everyone else—

the café family, the five regulars, Theo himself—was served a portion, but they all waited for me to dig in. And so I did, inviting the gentle flavours to explode in my mouth.

A life-affirming amalgam of tart fruit, cheese lively with a mixed aroma of goat and herb and mint, crunchy yeasty crust, and the eternal sweetness of mountain-thyme honey with its overtones of vanilla and nutmeg, its scent of the Greek summer. I gasped. It was so good, it almost choked me. The others nodded in unison and raised their spoons.

Chapter 4

On My Own

I woke the next morning to a rude shock. Theo was gone, and in his place was a quickly scribbled note: "I'm bored. I'm off to Athens. Enjoy the suite and pay the October rent, it's due: I'll pay you back. Cheers. T."

The Greek temperament, with its mercurial turnarounds, had reared its head just a mite too soon for my liking. My decades outside Greece had taught me to keep my own mental switchbacks in relative control. If I was to fit back into the society of my forebears, I absolutely had to be reacquainted with the foibles of my people as soon as possible.

I cranked the hot water faucet to maximum, stood under the shower, and in my anger forgot the essential tenet of Greek plumbing: *Athens wasn't built in a day, and hot water is restored only when the plumber finds time to come in from Heraklion.*

I turned the clock back to my Constantinople childhood, when taking a bath—which in cold weather we built up the courage to do but once a fortnight—meant heating water in the kitchen and dunking oneself with it somewhere near a drain.

My makeshift bath over, and cleaner by a few meagre degrees, I took stock of my situation. Basically I was back where I had been before the chance meeting with Theodoros at Athens airport. My official early retirement could begin this very day. I was in a beautiful village with adequate housing to serve as a base for the search for my ideal location. I even had a kitchen to cook my own breakfast and could thus avoid having to appear in public before I'd had a chance to wake up fully. My essential morning routine was to have fresh orange juice—no problem in this orange-rich valley—followed by a cup of tea and the all-important shower—preferably hot—then a little breakfast and a crucial cup of coffee, at which point I was ready for anything.

Since I had been fated to live in Fodele on my own, I needed to stock the larder with my favourite foods, local restaurants being not only expensive but also monochromatic in their repetitious grilled meats and fried potatoes. And so I drove the twenty curvaceous, well-banked kilometres back to Heraklion, bypassing the ceaseless turmoil of the capital's downtown and arriving directly at the market.

I revisited all the shops that Theo had shown me, culminating at the Anógia dairy outlet of Manouras for aged cheddar-like *kefalograviera*, sweet-sour unripened *anthogalo*, very ripe, sharp *anthotyro* for grating on noodles, and a good quantity of his full-fat sheep's yogurt, whose original culture, Manouras claimed, went back two hundred years in an unbroken line of yogurt-curdling.

My car full of enviable edibles and smelling nostalgically like Theo after a bout in the kitchen, I struggled through the traffic to get back on the highway for Fodele. There were two open-backed trucks parked near the entrance ramp. I could see cages stacked up inside both of them, and a very ripe

smell emanated into the open air. One of the trucks had suckling pigs in its cages, the other plump chickens and roosters.
Streams of stale blood near the trucks informed me what the
destiny of that livestock was.

The chicken truck also had egg cartons full of freshly laid,
chicken-shit-smeared eggs sitting on its open back flap. "You
can't get fresher eggs than these," boasted the master of the
mobile chicken coop, and so I bought a dozen.

Back home, I feasted on fried eggs with deeply orange-
coloured yolks, probably the next best to those in Teménia. I
finished my meal with a cupful of Manouras's historical
yogurt, sweetened with sugar instead of honey as per his
instructions. "Honey interferes with the taste of the yogurt,"
he had told me. "The ewe put her best effort into the milk that
became this yogurt. You owe it to her to savour it for itself."

Sometime in the late afternoon I strolled down Fodele's
main street to Eftihia's mother's shop to pay my rent. Seventy-
three-year-old Kiria (Mrs.) Melpo, as everyone called her,
hobbled along with the aid of a metallic walker, victim of a
bad hip and an even worse first hip-replacement operation.
Eftihia had told me that her mother was in line for a second
operation, but like everyone else in this age of first-come-first-
served medical miracles, she had been waiting for several
months with no relief in sight.

Kiria Melpo had spent practically all of her adult life
dressed in widow's black. She had married a sixty-year-old
man when she was twenty, and had had three children with
him in the next five years. Thirty days after the birth of her
youngest, Eftihia herself, the husband had died of bad *laima*
he had caught sitting drunk in a November cross-draft. And
thus began a lifelong struggle to raise her children, starting
in the post–World War II years in a Greece devastated by

the Germans and then torn apart by the Allies' fighting the Communists.

She revamped part of the ground floor of her main-street home into a handicrafts shop, which didn't start making money until years later when those same warring Germans, Allies, and Communists came back to Crete as tourists. Her survival income came from back-breaking work in the family orchards and gardens, whose vegetables, oranges, and olives required constant care and whose yield depended on the capricious rainfalls of this mostly dry land. It was a tough life, obviously, and it only succeeded because Kiria Melpo was a Greek mother of the most tenacious kind. The Mother is the mightiest force of Greece. There is no greater power than she, nothing more dependable, more eternal, more giving and generous and selfless and forgiving, nothing more intractable or intransigent or adamant, yet nothing more fragile and brittle—and absolutely nothing, nothing whatsoever in Greece or in the entire cosmos, that is harder, nay, more impossible to live up to or to deserve. It was difficult to believe looking at Kiria Melpo now, moving slowly, painfully, vulnerable and weak, that she once was strong enough to succeed in a society governed by men, steering her family on a course designed determinedly by her.

Her eldest son she ordained a scholar and put through university. Her second son she trained to take over the farms. Eftihia, her only daughter and youngest child, she forbade to continue school, even though she begged for it. She married her off to a young farmer at seventeen but then, perceiving that the girl had aptitude for making money, provided her with capital to go into business.

Kiria Melpo was proven right at every turn. Her eldest son

was now a university professor. Her younger son could be seen daily returning from the fields with truckfuls of organically grown and much-in-demand dandelions, carrots, and daikons. As for Eftihia, she not only became the most successful businessperson of Fodele, she was also an exemplary Greek mother, gracing Kiria Melpo with two granddaughters and four great-granddaughters.

When I arrived at the shop clutching my rent money, Kiria Melpo was in the residential part of her building overseeing the homework of her seven-year-old great-granddaughter, Ioannitsa, who smiled sweetly at me, a little shy but plucky, a miniature copy of Kiria Melpo. The aged matriarch left the young one to her own devices, and trudged back and forth to her kitchen to bring me treats, sugar cookies and tiny clementines, green skinned, but sunset coloured and sweet inside.

The weather remained gloriously hot for several more days. I drove to the beach faithfully to swim in the clear, multi-blue waters, witnessing the gradual shutdown of Aghia Pelagia as its many restaurants, shops, car-rental agencies, and suntan-oil kiosks closed down. It was a ghost town in the making, an entire world of pleasure put on ice, awaiting the spring and the return of the holidaymakers. Meanwhile, my hot water was restored, and I took steaming showers with a vengeance.

Ablutions aside, my life, much like that of all Greeks with nothing-much-to-do, became a bottomless cup of coffee. Coffee is not just a drink and a stimulant in this country. It is the definitive lubricant for all manner of social occasion and the ultimate consolation for being stood up, horny, depressed, lonely, broke, or any of the other million Greek reasons for being sad. Conversely, it is the celebratory libation for any success, joy, or bit of good news.

Greeks like all coffees. For years they revered Nescafé, which they prefer *frappé*: shaken, with an inch of foam. Now they have discovered espresso and filtered, which one can find even in tiny villages. The coffee of record, however, now as it has always been, is the Greek.

A replica of Turkish, which is a copy of the Middle Eastern, Greek coffee is a strange brew. It is the only coffee—save for the "ranch" style of the Wild West—that retains its grounds in the final product, making for a nasty surprise to the uninitiated when a mouthful of sludge invades the palate in lieu of the final sip.

In order to make it settle to the bottom, the coffee is stone-ground to the consistency of talcum powder. A heaping teaspoon of the grounds is mixed with the desired amount of sugar and a demitasse of water, then boiled together in a *briki*, a small coffee pot with a long handle.

The sugar content is the true variable of Greek coffee, and it can range from none (*sketo*) to half a teaspoon (*pikro*), one teaspoon (*metrio*), two teaspoons (*gliko*), and many teaspoons (*vari-gliko*).

The tricky aspect of Greek coffee making is the chemistry involved in boiling solids in water, which results in boiling over. This not only makes a mess on the stove, it burns the coffee and robs it of the very important *kaimaki*—or *crema*, as they call it in espresso-speak—that appetizing, richly brown foam that reveals the darker potion underneath it as one takes the first few sips.

Espresso's *crema* comes from the machine's jets of steam, which create the foam as the hot water is forced through the grounds. Greek coffee's *kaimaki* is created during the boiling of the coffee, and it is at its best for only one or two seconds when the water reaches its boil but hasn't yet had a chance to boil over. To get it right, the experienced coffee maker stands over the stove watching intently as the critical point is reached. If the *briki* is removed from the fire too soon, the drink will have *kaimaki* but will be gritty with uncooked coffee grounds. If it's removed too late, it will over-boil and become undrinkable.

It has never been calculated, but the number of hours involved in watching Greek coffee to prevent its over-boiling, let alone the endless hours spent sitting at cafés and at home waiting for the coffee, drinking it, and digesting it with a few cigarettes, must be monumental.

During one particularly coffee-heavy day, when I sat down for the magic drink six separate times, I mused that had all those coffee-related hours been invested in productive work, Greece could long ago have climbed out of its Third-World status instead of having to sell its soul and its beaches to the European Union.

But then again, what kind of a nation and what kind of Greekness would we have had without the perfect *kaimaki* on a *metrio*, sipped at a seaside table, waiting hopelessly for a lover who will never show up, moaning audibly at the iniquity of a lonely life that is spent in sunshine where the only thing that matters is the elusive pleasure of the moment?

All Greek men stay babies all their lives. They require constant care, while their minuscule attention spans demand a new diversion hourly. They have no management skills, especially when it comes to money or time. The money thing is easily solved—they let the women deal with the cash flow. Time is something else again.

Passing the time entertainingly is a Greek man's only preoccupation. In the summer this is an easy chore. The weather, particularly the silken caress of the night, provides Greek men with an infinite array of possible diversions. The favourite is sitting at an outdoor table until the wee hours kibitzing with other men and creatively coveting every attractive woman passerby. This sport is known as *kamaki* (harpooning), and it helps to kill off big blocks of time satisfyingly.

In the winter, or rather, the less than ideally warm weather that normally passes for winter in Greece, this pastime is more difficult. For one thing, women are harder to find on the streets. Foreign women are no longer around to be ogled, and Greek women find winter a good opportunity to spend time at home balancing the books, worrying about the education of the kids, and doing the laundry.

Laundry, much more than money and time combined, is the greatest obstacle Greek men face. If modern Lysistratas wanted to force their men to obey them, refusing to do their laundry would be a more effective method than denying them sex as their ancient counterparts did. Laundry, as Canadian performance-artist Margaret Dragu has always claimed, is sacred. In Greece, it is even more than that. It is the pinnacle of civilization, and women are its high priestesses, the possessors of its infinite secrets. The electric washing machine, modern laundry's holy temple and a staple of every Greek home, is strictly the property of women. Men are forbidden from even approaching it, let alone using it.

Whatever they may think of the ineptitude of their men, Greek women would never abandon their husbands, sons, and unmarried brothers unlaundered. Mothers have been known to follow their conscripted sons to their army barracks just to do their laundry, and also to slip them some allowance money.

Were it not for their women, Greek men would walk around penniless, dazed, and confused, their tender parts permanently chafed inside unwashed underwear.

It is with thoughts of this nature that I tackled my own laundry, by hand, perched over the kitchen sink, not really sure if sixteen rinsings were sufficient to get rid of the soapsuds.

I had been watching the workers from my balcony for several days. They were laying down flat stones on a walkway by the bank of the river, securing them in place with cement. Finally, on the tenth day of my solitary time in Fodele, the work crew and cement mixer disappeared. An announcement, made through loudspeakers that could be heard in all corners of the village, informed us that the nature walk was now ready, and invited us to partake of its pleasures.

In the late afternoon of that day all the matrons of the village, dressed in their Sunday best even though it was only a Thursday, with semi-willing husbands, also in their fineries, beside them, came out to walk the walk and inaugurate what seemed to be a pet project. From my balcony I heard them muttering, "Oh, beautiful, beautiful," and I couldn't resist joining them.

It was a well-tended path, with stones properly held in place, that hugged the river, past fig trees and the obligatory orange groves. It was some three hundred yards long, a safe distance to walk for middle-aged types like the matrons and me. It was indeed beautiful, and it gave off a wisp of what

Fodele must have been like centuries ago—that is, providing one could avoid glimpsing the modern homes across the river, where London-dressed affluent couples were watching the same river and its floating ducks with pre-dinner Campari sodas in diamond-ringed, manicured hands.

It was late October, and time was passing more slowly with every succeeding day. The weather was still warm, and I continued my daily swims, but the beach trips were briefer now since all of Aghia Pelagia had closed down and there was nothing to do there after the swim.

Maybe Theo was right. Maybe I wasn't quite ready for retirement yet. The point was brought home in all sobriety during an attempt I made to while away an afternoon drinking *raki* at a sidewalk bar by the river. Thing is, I've never been any good at drinking; alcohol gives me a bellyache, and instead of making me happy or giddy, it makes me sad. I was on the verge of tears when church bells began a dolorous pealing, and all traffic, both vehicular and pedestrian, came to a standstill.

The air was filled with the sickly sweet smell of frankincense, and a procession was coming down the main street. At its head was the priest in black robes and tall hat with the mortarboard on top. Behind him the deacon was swinging the incense burner, to the left, to the right, and straight ahead, to chase away the devils and open up the way to heaven.

The heaven-bound one was in his casket, being carried by eight very old men in suits and tightly wound ties, seemingly on their way themselves, if for no other reason than because of the noose-like knots around their necks. And snaking behind the casket was the entire population of Fodele, paying their respects. The relatives, with tears in their eyes, were up front, and all the way at the very back were people who barely knew the deceased, on parade out of duty.

I considered joining them, but decided to stay put and ordered a coffee to counteract the *raki*. I needed some inspiration. I needed someone to save me. I needed something to do.

Chapter 5

A Visit to Zeus

Early, around eight a.m. on the thirtieth day of my stay in
Fodele with no sign of Theo on the horizon or anything
more interesting to wait for than the itinerant fishmonger
with his very fresh if somewhat expensive baby red mullets
and tiny octopuses (the former of which are the best frying
fish in the universe and the latter sweet and flavourful simply
boiled and dressed with some wine, vinegar, capers, and
olive oil), I was woken by a phone call. It was the photographer Algis, about to board a flight for Heraklion from Athens
airport. He would be in Crete in about an hour, and could I
tell him how to find me.

Suddenly rejuvenated, I offered to be at the arrivals' lounge
to greet him, almost afraid to ask him what had made him look
me up, or, come to think of it, what made him head for Crete
off-season in the first place. I was worried he might change his
mind and cancel his flight if I gave him a chance to think
about it. He reminded me that we had made a date the previous summer to meet in Crete in January to work on a newspaper travel article together. He had decided to come early since

44

he was in Europe on assignment and wasn't due back in Canada until the following week.

Preoccupied with my efforts to restart my life on Crete, I had indeed completely forgotten about this arrangement. But I couldn't be happier that Algis had not. I expedited my morning routine by skipping breakfast and drinking my coffee en route, and I made it to the airport with five minutes to spare.

He stepped out of the arrivals' gate, lean and trim, all blond hair and blue eyes, boyish grin in place, smelling of the fresh Canadian outdoors in autumn even though he had just been working under heavy lights in Milan and Paris. Algis, a photographer of all callings, had a personal preference for exotic locations, returning to them as often as his bread-and-butter work in society and style photography allowed. His photographs of India, focusing on its fetish for holy cows and its technicolour sadhus, were a landmark of image-making on the Subcontinent.

A light traveller, Algis showed up with the obligatory camera case and a compact shoulder bag, both of which he had been allowed to carry on board. Two pairs of pants and four shirts, and he was all set. I had to admire a guy who circles the globe with fewer clothes than I need for a weekend, but instead of responding to my compliment he excitedly told me about The Idea.

In the highly competitive business of travel writing, The Idea is everything. Journalists have been covering Crete ever since print was invented. To sell a story about such a popular destination we would have to have a fresh angle. Algis had chanced on an art show in Paris based on the legend of the Minotaur. Separately, in Milan, he had photographed a fashion show with a Greek pantheon theme, which had closed with a giant Zeus in a replica of the Mount Idi cave where the god was supposed to have been born and raised. Since both the Minotaur and Zeus are part of Crete's mythology, Algis had combined the two into a story idea—something to do with the divine and labyrinthian allure of Crete for visitors and invaders alike for five millennia.

I drove us towards Heraklion, eager to participate. "Let's get back to Fodele so you can relax, and then do Knossos tomorrow, and Zeus," I started to say, but he stopped me in my tracks.

"I know it sounds crazy, and not all that professional, but I was hoping you'd agree to try to do it all today. I mean, start with the Archeological Museum in Heraklion right now. So we can get inspired a bit, you know? Then get to Knossos—I understand it's just outside the city . . ."

"Then go to Fodele to relax, and do the Zeus thing tomorrow," I added, hoping.

"No. Do Zeus right after Knossos," said Algis with Canadian determination. "What is it? An hour away, ninety minutes? I checked it out on the map . . . Thing is, I've got only four days, five max. And I want to trek, for the fun of it, and also take some shots for this outdoorsy magazine . . ." He trailed off. I guessed he didn't want to sound too pushy.

I laughed and told him it would be tiring, and a handful, but it was possible, why not. Anyway, I knew from experience that it was counterproductive to try to change a North American's travel plans. If he was willing to go back five thousand years into history and then drive up a nine-thousand-foot mountain on the same day, who was I to interfere? And it would provide me with a far better way to pass the day than sitting in Fodele waiting for the next funeral procession.

☾ ☾ ☾

I've never been too big on archeology, even in a museum as airy and entertaining as the one in Heraklion. I enjoy a good myth as much as the next fellow, but I soon reach my saturation point when I'm faced with room after room of painstakingly reconstructed pottery and the glassed-in tchotchkes of an ancient world.

To give the Minoans credit, they did keep pretty busy in the arts during their fifteen centuries in power (2600 BC–1100 BC), from Neolithic times to well into the Bronze Age. They rivalled neighbouring Egypt for hegemony of the region, worshiping bare-breasted female fertility figures and decorating fifteen-hundred-room palaces with as-yet-undecoded concentric circles and curlicue-winged griffins, laying out geometric motifs that artists have been imitating ever since.

The rulers of those ancients had the run of this open orchard of an island, and they must have had a whale of a time. Crete is a benign garden, where nothing life-threatening hovers and where foodstuffs take turns ripening in sequence throughout the calendar year. The many deep-sea bays provided an ideal conduit for a seafaring nation to develop its thalassocracy, which thrived in Crete's crossroads-of-three-continents location.

The extravagant natural phenomena—the dramatic skies, sudden sea-storms, overpowering sun, and topographical hyperboles—became the symbols of the rulers' self-attributed divine powers. Since they claimed to control all of nature, they took credit for its extreme conditions to better manipulate the awed, cowed, subservient masses.

Patterns emerged as we strolled from one section of the chronologically arranged museum to the next. The Minoans, an integral part of the origins of Western history, appear to have been a devout, civilized people, with a concentrated interest in cooking implements, libation vessels, jewellery, clothes, miniature art, and hairstyling. It was an accessorizing, well-groomed, well-fed culture, a fitting progenitor to European civilization, which would eventually make of those same concerns its greatest contribution to the human race.

Algis was particularly impressed with the upraised-bull-horns symbol that pervades Minoan iconography. It is replicated everywhere, from the raised arms of the high priestesses as seen in sculpture to the parapets of fortified walls. For Algis this was an echo of, and probably a homage to, the holy cows of India, and he became convinced that the ancients of Crete must have had contact with the Indians, whose own civilization goes back even deeper into the past.

As if by magic, with a bit of a short drive we leapt from the controlled environment of the museum to the epicentre of the action: the meticulously excavated, partially rebuilt Knossos. Knossos was the largest and most important city of the Minoans, the seat of their empire, the city with the most magnificent of their many palaces in Crete—and, one would have to suppose if one believed it existed at all, the home of the Labyrinth.

There is no clear evidence that the Labyrinth and its most famous resident, the monstrous, virgin-flesh-eating man-bull Minotaur, were in the least real. It is theorized that they were fictions perpetuated by the Minoas (the Pharaoh-like hereditary rulers of the Minoans) as a deterrent against disobedience in their empire and as an adornment to the mystique surrounding the man-god status they assumed.

Algis refused to let historical authenticity dampen his enthusiasm. For him the Minotaur was a reality and the virgins arriving from Athens under the leadership of Theseus could still be seen disembarking in sheer terror from their black-sailed ship, while the Labyrinth twisted deep into the underworld via passageways under the palace—where, in fact, lay storehouses and the jails where the Minoas would have housed unfortunates who had dared to challenge their authority.

While Algis poked around in the crevices of the palace looking for evidence of the ancient Labyrinth to photograph, I sat under the shade of a magnolia tree in full flower. There are few floral perfumes to outdo that of the magnolia. It intoxicates. I envisioned an army of Minoan soldiers, slender waists, strong thighs, and assertive faces marching in step down the cobblestoned mall, leading slaves from Athens and Sparta and Thebes who were pulling cartloads of ivory and gold from Africa, lapis and rock crystal from Asia Minor, livestock from Cyprus . . . And then Algis nudged me. I had fallen asleep. He was ready to push on. Zeus was waiting for us up in his cave.

The road to the god of gods is arduous from the start. The gateway to the cave is Anógia, hometown of several prominent Crete citizens, including Theo. Anógia, which translates as "the upper earth," is the town at the end of civilization. Beyond is unfriendly mountain terrain with plateaux for grazing sheep and goats, and steep roads for nutty tourists in search of thrills.

Crete is shaped like a long, thin rectangle, with three mountain ranges equidistant from each other dominating the landscape west to east. In the middle range is Mount Idi (Psilorítis, the "tall peak," in modern Greek), the highest and most awesome of the three. Zeus, a mighty god who as a teenager would have to slaughter his child-devouring father, Cronos, to survive and claim his inheritance, needed an appropriately remote birthplace. His mother chose Idi as the place to hide him from his father until he was old enough to tackle his own destiny.

The long, thin road that climbs to Anógia from sea level twists and turns much like gift-wrapping ribbon to which an expert hand has given a sharp stroke with the flat edge of a knife. I was almost delirious from the drive, mostly because I had had nothing to eat all day.

It was early afternoon, with a strong sun and a wispy breeze. This was a perfect lunch moment, and Algis, hungry himself, had to admit that stopping for food was a good idea, even though he was yearning to get to the cave now that he was almost close enough to smell it.

Theo had told me of a restaurant called Falcon, owned by a cousin of his—not surprising since just about everyone in Anógia is related. Falcon specialized in *ofto*, the highlands' signature wood-flame-baked lamb. The meat is carved flat, rubbed with the traditional lamb seasonings of lemon juice and oregano, and skewered into a butterfly shape. It is slow-baked along the sides of a tandoori-style oven with a high-burning wood fire in the middle, simulating the fare cooked for shepherds in the fields during wool-shearing operations in the spring. The result is a smoky succulent meat second to none in the generally succulent world of lamb.

We accompanied mouthfuls of the juicy meat with olive-oil-fried potatoes and steamed baby red-leafed dandelions, a special green of the mountains in spite of its colour. Though full, we were induced to sample another of Anógia's native dishes: overcooked spaghetti finished in sheep's butter and topped with shaved *anthotiros*, the ripened sheep's cheese aged to rival the best romano from Italy. Despite the quality of the cheese, the noodles are so over-boiled that this pasta dish is best left to those who love it because they grew up with it.

Over coffee, Manolis, the restaurant owner, clowned for us, framing his face in the hole of a highly decorated and hard-glazed wedding *kouloura* (round bread). Sculpted with symbols of plenty, love, and happiness, like birds, flowers, and olive branches, the *kouloura* is inedible and meant only for display by the wedded couple for good luck. It is a showy reminder that these well-fed people have food to spare.

Somehow it was now four o'clock, and the sky had sprouted ominous clouds. I was so comfortable, with a belly-ful of melted meat and obliterated noodles, I would have gladly skipped the half-hour drive to the cave had Algis not yelped when he noticed the time, and jumped out of his chair.

The wispy breeze had evolved into an alpine crisp wind, and soon after we climbed into the endless mountain switch-backs of the road to the cave, the sky turned into a grey-black mantle that seemed to be descending to engulf us—or were we ascending to be engulfed?

The final straw for me was the puffy grey fog clouds sweeping across the road, reducing our visibility to zero and creating an eerie sensation of travelling through cotton wool. I steered the car fearfully, desperate to get myself out of this dangerous predicament.

"These things usually clear up," said the steely-nerved photographer. "Anyway, you'd be crazy to attempt a turn-around here. If anyone is coming at us from either direction, we would be pushed right off the road into the cliff."

Frustrated and anxious, I snail-paced the car forward, and, amazingly, the cloud drifted off the road as rapidly as it had drifted onto it. The sun peered through a bank of fleeting clouds high up in the sky, and a golden beam lit up the plateau beneath us. A multitude of sheep were grazing, and in the distance was a white structure, a sort of lookout, with a solitary pickup truck parked to its side.

The lookout building was an abandoned café-hotel at the end of the asphalt road. A scraggly, uneven dirt path was at the edge of its parking lot, with a little sign that translated roughly as "Zeus this way, 500 metres." By now it was close to five, and the sun had disappeared yet again into the darkening sky.

"We should walk from here," suggested Algis.

"It's late. Let's drive up," said I, too lazy to be wise.

We climbed maybe two hundred metres up the practically impassable path to the first curve to find a large rock dividing the road into two equally unattractive sections. I didn't see the lethally sharp protrusions of the rock face, and decided to drive over it. The bottom of the car moaned painfully as it scraped over the rock. Ignoring the probable damage, I drove on for another hundred metres, this time into loose ground on one side and a steep rise on the other.

"You were right," I conceded. "It's time to walk, but you're on your own. I should get this car back down, and I'll wait for you."

Algis sprang out of the car and bounded up the hill, fighting against time to catch some of the fast-diminishing light. I didn't even attempt to turn the car around. I backed down, scraping the bottom yet again on the jagged rock.

"Goddamn Zeus and your bleeding cave!" I started to curse, but stopped. There was a bright, sharp lightning bolt straight ahead of me, and a loud clap of thunder right after it. I shuddered, and for one moment of weakness I feared that I had offended the big guy. I giggled nervously and dismissed the thought.

I managed to steer the car backwards down to the asphalt, and parked it facing the rolling plateau. The sky was almost black, and I had no idea what sort of photographs Algis would be able to take. I prayed that he had brought a flash.

At that moment the sun peered through a crack in the clouds at the horizon. There—Algis's flash, I mused. The shepherd was packing his truck, getting ready for his climb down. The grazing this plateau afforded fattened his sheep and aromatized their milk, the better to serve the various cheeses for which Anógia is famous.

However, the excellence of local cheese was far from my mind at present. Algis was taking his time; night would descend with its full dark force the moment the sun set into its mountain horizon. It would get cold, and the shepherd would be gone. I was feeling much more secure while he was still here.

Algis finally returned, happy. He had used the surprise sunbeams, obviously a gift from Zeus, for some unusual shots. He had taken them as a sign from the king of gods. Also elated that the mission was complete, I turned on the engine and put it in reverse so that I could get the heck out of this forbidding place.

The engine made a small noise, like a sickly complaint or a mechanical death rattle, but no effort whatsoever to propel the vehicle. Alarmed but not yet defeated, I sought refuge in a forward gear. The same noise, the same lack of response.

"Let's try pushing it," I said.

Algis got out and pushed while I tried several amateur tactics to bring the gearshift back to life, such as pumping the gas, and shifting gears suddenly as if to surprise the mechanism into working order. Nothing.

At that awkward moment the shepherd made his appearance, driving his little truck perpendicularly off the cliff face onto the asphalt. We flapped our arms up and down to make him stop, but we must have scared him with our urgency. He drove around us in a hurry and sped off onto the first switchback, soon out of sight as if he had never been there.

"What a creep! What a *malaka*!" I yelled. "I do believe we're stuck," I said smiling, refusing as yet to accept that such a thing could possibly be happening to me. "We're stuck. And it's cold. And we'll freeze to death," I added, still smiling.

"Nonsense," said Algis. "I'll go and find a way to get into that building."

"It's deserted, and it's locked up."

"I'll get in," repeated Algis with the intrepid certainty of youth that admits to no misfortune, only adventure.

I stayed in the car while Algis fought the increasingly cold mountain wind, scaling walls and trying rusty doors to no avail. Serious lightning and thunder followed, and then a driving rain. Algis rushed back into the car shivering. "At least it ain't snow," he muttered.

"It does snow on this mountain, you know," I started to counter, but I was drowned out by some bullet-like noises. Golf-ball-sized hailstones, of the kind I was to discover later hadn't been seen on Mount Idi for forty years, were descending machine-gun-style, bouncing off the roof of the car as if from the clubs of Tiger Woods.

"Well, it still ain't snow," grinned Algis, but I could see that his confidence was quickly waning. I started the engine again, and turned the heat to full. If I were meant to freeze on this mountain top, I wanted one final blast of warmth before I went.

The hail, as well as all other forms of precipitation, quit falling. A strong wind carried off the deadly clouds, revealing a star-filled sky. We opened the car doors and sweepingly frigid air blew in at us. We shut the doors and sank into despair. In the clear night there was only one ray of hope, and it was driving away from us at a steady pace: the high beams of the shepherd's vehicle reflecting off the cliff as he sped to the safety of Anógia.

Then, as if by Jovian benefaction, the light beam came to a standstill. It fluttered as if being turned around, and finally, mercifully, as if to reward our unassailable Canadian optimism, it began to shine its way back towards us.

The shepherd must have had a *crise de conscience*, or maybe a Grecian surge of *filoxenia*, and he came back for us. There was room for only one in the cab up front, so we put Algis and his luggage in the back, in the open among bags of wet hay, while the shepherd moved his rifle and other shepherding necessities out of the way so that I, the older and more vulnerable—being too fat to be in good health—could sit in comfort.

The shepherd played music for me on the radio, and even offered to turn on the heat. I would have enjoyed the heat, but he already smelled of several varieties of ripe cheese, and I knew that the smells would sharpen exponentially if heated. I declined the heat for the sake of my nose.

We reached Anógia and helped Algis down. He was stiff from the cold but as grateful as I to be back in a town. I rang the car hire company, and they agreed to send a tow truck and instructed us to wait at a café. We chose the church-side coffee-house of the widow Marika, another cousin of Theo's, a much-battered, life-wrinkled woman who ran a tight ship in her all-white little place, which was toasty warm from a wood fire.

The tow truck, manned by an able ex-marine called Konstantinyos, fit our little car onto its flatbed up at Zeus and picked us up in Anógia on its way back. Konstantinyos drove us to Heraklion airport, flying down the now pitch-black ribbon of sharp curves at top speed.

We drove back to Fodele in our new car, stopping for souvlaki on the way. It was warm at sea level, and we slept with the windows open, as if nothing unusual had occurred during this over-long day.

Chapter 6

The Business Meeting

"There is no god as generous as a well-fed god, and nowhere are gods better fed than in Crete." Theo punctuated his statement with a sweeping hand gesture, an open-palmed arc over his head in acknowledgment of the Ones above. "It has for a long time been my job to feed the gods of elsewhere, and now I make it my job to feed the gods of Crete," he said as if talking about any ordinary dinner guests. "Food. Cuisine. The combination of the products of this rich earth and the ingenuity of the culinary imagination is a timeless construct. We have had sixty centuries in which to develop our traditions, to habituate our palates to certain tastes, textures, and flavours. We believe that we have done it. That the job is complete. That we can go on like this forever. That we can offer soggy french fries with a messy tomato-paste sauce around unattractively butchered goat meat. That we can broil pork chops to death until they resemble old shoe leather. That we can dress exquisitely sun-dried cherry tomatoes with rancid oil and pretend we have enhanced them." Theo made a sour face. "My God, we live in a land sodden with the finest low-acidity virgin oil on the planet. Why use the rancid? Give the rancid to the pigs. Dip throwaway stale bread with that awful oil and give it to them. They'll love it. They'll lap it up. I, on the other hand, and all my gods, will abhor it. And I'll hate all who are responsible for trying to make me eat rancid oil. It's time, it's HIGH time—actually, it's beyond time—that we begin to dignify what we have here. To exploit it. To prepare it with love and intelligence. To present it properly. To appreciate its value and its quality, and of course to charge for it. To charge big money for it. There is an army of gourmets poised to invade us. They're coming with bottomless pockets full of DOLLARS: European, US, Australian, Canadian—you name the dollar, they're bringing it." Theo paused to let the money signs sink in. "They're coming here to eat because they've read and they've heard that we have the healthiest and the most tasty foods of the endlessly tasty Mediterranean. Can I help you to put it all in order? Can I help you make up a fabulous menu and then teach you to cook it? Can I lend you my name so that gourmets worldwide will rush to come here and eat? Yes. Yes. Yes. You bet your last about-to-be-defunct drachma that yes, I can." Theo took a sip of peasant wine and looked around the room impishly. Impishly, yes, but also belligerently.

He had shown up in Fodele unannounced in a four-wheel-drive vehicle the day after my Zeus tribulations. It was mid-morning. Algis had just taken off on his trek, setting out on foot south up the hill behind Fodele that leads back to the Mount Idi area. I was having my coffee, still a bit dazed by my close call the previous day. To console myself, I had toast with honey and *myzithra*, the ricotta-like sheep's-milk cheese that is reportedly the reason the teeth of Crete are so white and cavity-free.

Theo had waited impatiently for me to finish eating, helping himself to a large chunk of the *myzithra* while I dressed. He was in a hurry to get to an appointment with Christos, a hotelier who was completing construction of an expensive nature-tourist installation in the foothills north of Anógia. The trend-setting resort away from the beach was to feature deluxe accommodation with spectacular views, casual trekking and horseback riding, and mostly leisure and clean air. It meant to attract the kind of tourists, middle-aged and moneyed, who wouldn't consider any kind of trip unless it offered fine dining. Many of them would be the types lured to Crete mainly by its organically grown, traditional foodstuffs that demonstrably promoted longevity. But they weren't going to come merely to admire the produce or to eat the boring recipes of Crete. They would want good cooking, and that's where Theo meant to enter the equation.

He had been recommended by some of the heaviest hitters of Crete's hospitality hierarchy, and he felt secure that he would be hired to put a menu in place, with me as supporter-fan-helper, at the highest possible fee.

This new deal had become necessary because of sad news from Eftihia. Theo informed me that the much-suffering Kiria Melpo had been diagnosed with a heart condition to add to all her other woes. This had rendered her hip-replacement operation dangerous, and now she needed more care than ever. Eftihia, as the only daughter, was in charge of that care, on top of all her many ongoing businesses. She simply had no time left over to go ahead with her proposed restaurant.

Theo had aggressively and accurately negotiated some of

Crete's most challenging roads (thanks to the unerring road-worthiness of all four of his powerful wheels), and now here we were in important company, sitting in the rustic, food-laden dining room of the visionary hotelier's private quarters.

A wood fire was raging in the fireplace, tempering the autumn chill of the foothills; the surprisingly fine wine was going down easy, mellowing the mood of the company; and Theo was berating the lavish if badly cooked and messily pre-sented meal, personally put in place by Lisa, the wife-business partner of the rich man.

Theo's bravado was pegged on the utmost respect with which his talent was regarded by the other three guests at the table: Yorgo, president of the tourist federation of Crete, and the journalist–cookbook writer–Crete chronicler couple Antonis and Katerina, who had become great fans of Theo's during a recent trip to Barcelona, where they had gone as the official team representing Greece at a symposium on Mediter-ranean cooking, with Theo as their chef. There the Great One had distinguished himself splendidly, winning top prize for Greece with his updated and personalized Crete recipes.

Yorgo, Antonis, and Katerina were the culinary hierarchy of the island. Normally whatever they decreed became reality. They were also best friends of Christos and Lisa. They had arranged this meeting hoping that Theo could be persuaded to design a much-needed menu for this ambitious, pioneering venture, with its state-of-the-art New Mexico–style guest vil-las, spectacular setting, and ample kitchens, but no menu. What they hadn't counted on was the forcefulness with which Theo needed to establish his position.

Installing a menu in someone else's kitchen, something that Theo had often accomplished before, is among the most thankless chores in the restaurant business. It requires total domination and absolute authority in the kitchens, even though those powers usually belong to the one who is paying the fee, not to the fee earner. It's like asking a rich and powerful person to pay big money in order to hand a pet project over to an outsider to do with as he pleases. As disagreeable as this sounds to the capitalist, it is the only way it can work. A kitchen genius like Theo can't possibly be subservient and mince words if he's to be effective in performing a near-impossible task.

Just how impossible the task would be was shown by the entrance of the latest guest, Lisa's poor cousin. She walked in timidly, flabbily. A seasoned home cook who had never worked professionally, Agnes was the proposed head chef of the hotel. She took in the terrifying sight of Theo orating at full gallop, and almost burst into tears. She managed a weak smile instead and sat at a corner of the table, blushing.

"Poor Theo," I gulped inaudibly. I gulped again when Christos informed us that one of his own poor cousins, the equally unprofessional Agatha, would back up Agnes. The two of them were an adequate team, he trusted—well, he was convinced—to feed the fifty-sixty hotel guests, plus another fifty or more day trippers from high-rolling and equidistant Heraklion and Réthymno.

"You'll have a third person for them. To chop a last-minute onion, to wash dishes," I piped uneasily, not really believing that anyone could simultaneously be that rich and that naive.

"Well, no. We're buying a dishwashing machine," said the richly naive Christos.

"That should take care of the dishes," laughed Theo. "Maybe a last-minute-onion machine can take care of the rest."

The company laughed along with Theo, turning away from

me as if I were a fly in their soup. I could see that there wasn't any real future in this job proposition, and I gave up even trying to participate. In any case I was kept plenty busy chewing the overly tough giant pork chop I had foolishly allowed Lisa to load on my plate.

Yorgo, the diplomat who had been elected to keep the peace among all the disparate, idiosyncratic, and strictly profit-motivated hotel and restaurant owners of Crete, proved his mettle by changing the subject seamlessly. He agreed that a small team was indeed viable—as long as it was the right team, and properly trained. As his example he pointed to Theo himself and his exploits in Barcelona. There, working with a sous-chef, and a gopher who chopped onions and washed the pots, Theo had cooked for three hundred exclusive, highly critical guests. His menu had been a simulation of a Crete wedding, with the infamous *gamopilafo* (wedding rice), which involved the fat and meat of several goats and about a bushel of short-grained rice, as well as an oversized *Chaniopita* (Chania-pie), a circular puff of pastry and spiced meat, two metres in circumference, that used thirty kilos of meat, twenty of onions, five of condiments and spices, and a donkey-load of freshly rolled *sfoliata* (thick filo dough) to produce a feast of heroic proportions.

"That's what we need," voiced Christos and Lisa as one. "Heroic proportions to reflect the landscape, mirror the free spirit of the local people, and accentuate all that is enviably and inalienably a part of the interior of Crete. We need you to train Agnes and Agatha to do just that. How long would you need? Two days? Not more than four, I assure you. They're very capable, you know."

Theo eyed Christos wearily. "A month," he hissed without smiling. "To start. Then a weekend here and there throughout the winter, and another month before the summer for the warm weather dishes and the foreign tourists."

"But they're expert cooks," objected Lisa. "They have cooked for five weddings. Each with two thousand guests!"

"They're wonderful, both of them, I'm sure," scoffed Theo, unfazed. "But a restaurant is not a home, and it's not a village wedding. It has different rules and different procedures."

"The best restaurants are those that feel just like a home," remarked Katerina. "Antonis and I always strive for the feel of a home kitchen when we write a cookbook."

"Your cookbooks are meant to be used by home cooks," Theo reminded her.

"But," intervened Yorgo, "let's get beyond how long it would take to train Agnes and Agatha. What are we training them to cook?"

"Aah, the menu," sighed Theo. "It will be entirely of the surrounding region. Crete will be its middle name, maybe its first, BUT its surname will be Theodoros!"

"What do you mean by that?" Lisa was on the verge of being caustic, finally about to take revenge for Theo's earlier insults to her cooking.

"I mean that there will be variations, embellishments, signatures. All the tastes will be recognizable, but none of them will be ordinary. And," Theo smiled knowingly at me, remembering Eftihia, "none of it will be oversalted."

"Give us an example, please," demanded Lisa.

"Fine," said Theo. "I will."

I feared the worst. It was obvious he was about to implode.

"Roast suckling pig," started Theo. "Something you can

get anywhere in Crete. At Drossiá, for example, what we used to call *Yeni Kahve*. Same pig, but served with a chutney of watermelon and ginger."

"What's a chutney?" asked Christos.

"Duck," continued Theo, ignoring Christos. "Another of our common Crete foods. Practically a staple on our winter tables. But served Chinese-style, with pancakes and hoisin sauce."

"What's hoisin?" said Christos, meekly.

"Rooster. A fixture of our Sunday family lunches whatever the season. Served Mexican style. With *mole*!"

"What's *mole*?!" Christos was getting frustrated.

"A sauce of chocolate and chilies," said Theo, and Christos, Lisa, and Agatha recoiled in unison.

"And Mexicans enjoy that, do they?" asked Lisa.

"So do the Greeks. It's the biggest seller on a menu I just premiered in Athens."

"This isn't Athens," said Christos, as if revealing a state secret. "A lot of the clients we're hoping to attract will come from Crete."

"Herakliots' tastebuds are just as adventurous as the Athenians'," interjected Antonis, Katerina nodding vigorously in a unified pro-Heraklion-sophistication stand.

"But—chocolate and chilies? With rooster!" Lisa was aghast, visibly nauseous.

"Then we have the Thai influences," Theo continued mercilessly, knowing he had nothing to lose by being outrageous. "Lemongrass, curry leaf, coconut milk, shrimp paste, squid extract, the hottest chilies on earth—"

"All of them indigenous to Crete," laughed Yorgo, trying yet again to reclaim normalcy. "But be serious, Theo."

"I can't, unless I have a cigar," said Theo petulantly. "I've run out."

Christos, in proper host mode despite the breakdown in negotiations, sprang out of his chair and reached for a humidor full of aromatic Cubans. He offered the box to Theo, who chose a fat Cohiba.

"Castro's favourite," Theo smiled. "I hear his doctors forbade him to continue smoking them. Mine haven't, mostly because I've refused to go see them in the last ten years."

Theo felt the length of the cigar for moisture and, refusing the clipper, chewed off just the right amount from the mouth end. He accepted a match, turning the cigar in to the flame to light it evenly. He savoured a puff and blew out a billow of smoke, then washed it down with a large gulp of wine.

"Perfect cigar, and very good wine," he conceded to his hosts.

"Our own," chirped Christos and Lisa, once again masters of their own house. The brief spell of handing the reins of their kitchen to Theo was quite over.

Several attempts by Yorgo, Antonis, and Katerina to reopen the discussion led nowhere, as Theo changed the subject at every turn, relating anectodes from his travels to all corners of the world, always with a pointed attack against stupid people who just couldn't see how much smarter than they he really was.

Suddenly, Theo had had enough. He sprang from his chair, the half-finished stogie glowing expensively in his mouth, and manhandled me to my feet in the middle of a cloying bite of Lisa's syrupy baklava. He hurried our goodbyes and hustled me into the car.

"It's no use," exploded Theo almost as soon as the car had

started moving into the twilight. "They're such dumb Greeks, it hurts."

"You didn't give them much of a chance," I tried to reason with him, though I too had perceived problems.

"They need me so much it's ridiculous. They should be kissing my behind. Instead they want me to train the dullard cousins in two days. Imagine!" Theo would have been speechless had he not so much to say. "I'll tell you what they really want. Listen and WEEP, my friend. The smartarses! They want to use my name in their publicity, pretending that I invented the crap they intend to serve. It burns me up! And sorry I got you involved. Really, I apologize."

Theo was humbling himself, a stretch for him, but I was in no mood to be grateful for small mercies. "You did your best," I said.

"Well, you heard them! The jerks! They'll take you for all you're worth, and give you nothing." He shook his head and manoeuvred a tricky turn far too fast for comfort. "Do you know why they were insisting only *two* days, at most *four*? So that they could offer me such a paltry sum that they could trust my *filotimo* [self-respect] to refuse payment outright. To accept barter. Terrible meals cooked by Lisa, and maybe a weekend in their stinking hotel, in exchange for my genius. Hah!"

"It's a nice hotel," I said, shrugging.

"Yes, it is," chuckled Theo. "It would have been fun."

An old, wise Alexandrian Greek once confided in me, "Greeks will always buy you a drink, but they'll never feed you if they know you're broke and hungry, so as not to offend you."

Utterly unoffended, our filotimo intact, but absolutely frustrated and pissed off, stomachs cringing at the prospect of having to digest the heavy supper, we drove the many tedious kilometres back to Fodele mostly in silence. I wondered if any of our business plans would pan out. If not, what exactly was I going to do now that mere retirement wasn't even remotely interesting to me? And what would Theo have to do to stay on in Crete profitably instead of continuously rushing off to polluted, overcrowded Athens? Our only comfort was the ember of the Cohiba's even burning and its heady faraway aroma.

Part II # The South

Chapter 7

Room with a View

It was in Marioú, one of those whitewashed villages that Greeks like to perch on steep hills to the sea. It was a large room with many windows and a huge bright balcony. The view was something like this:

Straight ahead stretched a rolling carpet of olive groves punctuated by farmhouses and adobe chapels. The groves were flanked by twin hills with monasteries at their peaks. Nestled between the hills was an emerald bay of the Libyan Sea, crowned by Plakiás, an erstwhile fishing village whose main reason for existence now was the three months of tourism in the summer.

To my left and my right rose more hills with thyme-purple faces and jagged points like petrified eyes, noses, mouths, as if they were embedded Ancients forever waiting the right moment to return to life. Beyond the hills was the rest of the shore and an expanse of blue sea, its semicircular horizon broken only by ghostly outlines of distant islands.

Behind me were desert-coloured mountains, arid and un-inviting, with unlikely trees and wily goats the only residents.

Low-flying clouds hopscotched on the mountains, sweeping over their tops, bringing sudden mists through which the sunlight shone on an unbroken rainbow like a brightly painted halo around the insular universe of Marioú.

Beyond the mountains, out of my view, were two gorges carved out of the land by prehistoric tectonics, a massive earthquake, and millions of years of erosion. These gorges were the only accesses to Marioú.

The middle of southern Crete is at the bottom of cliffs, with most destinations reachable only after multiple hairpin turns from awesome heights. The area around Plakiás is an exception. Here the cliffs have parted into gorges, awesome passageways with deep scars that are rivers in winter and with tall walls of loose rocks that could be dislodged at any time.

Living on the other side of end-of-the-earth gorges that could collapse at will and isolate the whole area lends a touch of danger to one's existence; potential disaster governs and dictates one's every move, colouring daily irrelevancies in the palette of the rainbow. When driving down a twisty road through magical landscape to get a cup of coffee could be the last ordinary thing one will ever do, that coffee tastes like no other coffee has before.

I ended up at Marioú because the tectonics of my own life were shifting listlessly, threatening to hurl me into terminal boredom. Theo had left Crete for Athens immediately after the futile meeting with the hotel couple. In his wake he left a void that Fodele couldn't possibly fill. I spent an uneasy week, drinking much coffee and glass after glass of freshly squeezed clementines, which the villagers kept pressing on me by the bagful as if to console me.

All tedium evaporated with the bubbly return of Algis Kemezys. He entertained me with wondrous tales of his eight-day walk through the island, including to Zeus's cave. I couldn't for the life of me imagine actually climbing Mount Idi on foot, but he had done it, to experience the cave at leisure and in full daylight.

He had been rewarded with a series of mystical revelations, and he was now convinced that Zeus was an extraterrestrial. He had persuaded himself that this was the only viable explanation for the otherworldly aspects of the Zeus legend. "Legends aren't born at random," he explained. "They are always based on some sort of fact."

However the Zeus-ET was no cuddly pink creature in search of a mother-surrogate as in Spielberg's movie, but a ferocious being, tall as a mountain, wide as a storm cloud, and powerful beyond our comprehension. Algis's Zeus had fires emanating from his fingertips—the bolts of lightning observed by the Ancients—and eyes of molten lava that flowed in golden waves to scald the earth and carve the razor-sharp mountains around fertile plateaux. He exhaled fragrant gusts that howled through the canyons to settle in valleys, cooling the lava and drenching the soil. In his hands he held a giant spade and fork with which to till the ground and chisel the landscape. He was all life, all power, all giving, never forgiving. He was Crete.

Algis had recorded his cave visit in eerie photographs of rocks and driftwood. In the photos, he had discerned dreamlike visions of Zeus's face, images that could not be perceived by the naked eye but that came through on the film, much like the imprint of Jesus' face on the Shroud of Turin. Subsequently he had continued his trek, entrusting himself totally to the will of the god. And Zeus had guided him through glen and dale and forest and cracked cliff, all the way to the south coast and this particular room-with-a-view in Marioú.

He had come back to Fodele to see if I would leave the over-commercialized north behind and move to the south, share the cost of the room, and explore the area with him, in search as ever of the idea for our travel article. His return to Canada would have to wait.

It took no effort at all to persuade me to pack, load up the car, and get moving. It was a sunny mid-November morning and a pleasant drive, first due west to Réthymno, and then south from there through rolling hills and farmlands reminiscent of England on a summer's day. It seemed familiar and gentle, but Algis kept saying "Wait, wait," as if saving a surprise for me, some little secret between Zeus and him.

The surprise was the unannounced entrance to the gorge. The gentle countryside came to an abrupt end, giving way to a skinny road that wound through a crack between two hulking cliffs, the mountain seemingly crushed and torn by a merciless trampler of enormous proportions. I drove slowly in childlike wonder, an insignificant ant heading to its destiny on the other side. The gorge ended as abruptly as it had begun, revealing a panoramic view of the little villages, the carpet of olive groves, and the glorious sea that laps Crete on this side and North Africa across the way.

The house was on a hill surrounded by olive trees. It was a new construction, designed to let in maximum light. It had room to move around, a workable kitchen, and a clean bathroom with lots of hot water but the usual plastic, prone-to-breakdown plumbing that plagues all of Greece. I suppose it's fitting, if ironic, that Crete should suffer from imperfect bathrooms since it was the Minoans who invented indoor plumbing.

I positioned my writing desk beside the double balcony doors, giving me a splendid view at all times. I watched a band of eagles, nine of them, the leader with a wingspan of some seven metres, fly around in fragmented formations, circling a doomed prey, lending their fleeting shadows to the textures of the land. Larger shadows raced across the landscape, darkening the foliage to blue-grey when speeding clouds obscured the sun, and back to brilliant emerald greens when they had passed.

With Algis's prompting I spotted anthropomorphic rocks on the protruding hills: Zeus, his wife Hera, his sister Aphrodite, the dour Apollo, a snoozing dinosaur, a weeping cat, a screeching monkey, a man with a moustache, a young girl with a frilly kerchief. In the jagged rocks of this vista seemed to live the complete family of Crete.

And every evening, the sunset. Right into the sea in the middle of our view. Every evening a different golden-plumed show played as if to the strains of a lovingly plucked lyre, performed exclusively for us.

Our Marioú room-with-a-view came complete with a family. They were the owners of the complex. The titular head of the clan was Niko, the father. He was in his fifties with greying hair, an easy smile, and a jolly voice. He was a singer and a philosopher. Despite his relative wealth from olive oil and guest houses, and despite his station in life as one of the pillars of the community and an elder of the church, he was a man of the land, a farmer, happiest when picking wild mushrooms in his secret spot or when drinking with his cronies and then snoozing.

Erato, named for a muse, was the mother. She was in her forties, a capable woman, practical, obedient, and without a doubt the power of the family—its accountant, its brains, its organizer, its hardest worker, its defender, its soul. She was the kind who pampers others without ever pampering herself except with the inner conviction that they owe it all to her.

There were two sons, both of them in their early twenties, tall and handsome, athletes, warriors. The younger, Gregoris, was the playboy, with long, comely hair and a pad of his own. We didn't see much of him. The elder, Stamatis, lived right next door to us with his girlfriend, a down-to-earth Catalan of twenty-five who had come to Crete from her Costa Brava home, met Stamatis, and stayed. She refused to marry him, though she claimed to love him, and the parents accepted the arrangement even if in their time it would have been unthinkable. I never found out her real name because the Greeks had dubbed her Arete (virtue) as a gentle induce-ment to forgo her modernist objections to holy matrimony, settle down with Stamatis for good, and grant Niko and Erato some grandchildren.

Almost three weeks after we moved to Marioú came December 6, the feast day of St. Nikolaos and therefore the year's most celebrated day for anyone named Niko, short for Nikolaos. Every common Greek name is derived from a saint's, and every major (or minor) Greek Orthodox saint has a dedicated day. It is customary, even mandatory, for bearers of the name of a particular saint to observe the ordained day as a personal holiday in which to treat friends and family to as lavish a banquet as they can afford, and to get blind drunk.

Fortunately for me I'm named for the poet-warrior Lord Byron, who is not a religious hero-saint but only a national one, having died for Greek independence from the Turks in the 1820s. As a result there is no St. Byron Day.

And so on December 6, our landlord—actually, his wife, Erato—organized a large party with an embarrassment of food, all of it from their personal stock, both vegetable and animal, to be washed down with a frightening quantity of their own wine. He invited Algis and me to attend.

The party was in full swing, with much melodious noise, by the time we showed up. It was five in the afternoon, with a pre-sunset golden light. The male revellers, Niko's cronies headed by Niko himself, were all quite drunk, singing *mantinades*, the witty rhyming couplet, haiku-style songs of Crete that address the vagaries of life—a suitable verse for any and all situations—set to mountain music played on the lyre. This afternoon there was no lyre player, so the men sang a capella in throaty-drunk harmony.

As is usual in village get-togethers, all the men lounged on one side of the table, while the women, far less drunk than their husbands, huddled on the other. This male–female segregation has existed since ancient times, and was reinforced by Crete's Muslim domination during the 230-year Ottoman occupation of the island (AD 1669–1898), which was bloodily resisted but highly influential upon language and customs.

I've never been comfortable with any sort of segregation, especially that of women from men. Humanity's genders have little enough in common—there is no need to widen the gap during social occasions. And so I headed for an empty chair in the women's section, while Algis, thanks to his blondness and his obvious *xenos* status, was instantly absorbed into the heart of the male contingent.

Erato misunderstood my intentions, interpreting my anti-segregationist gesture as a sexual one. She smiled knowingly, and firmly redirected me away from my chosen seat to a chair next to Niko, one usually reserved for a guest of honour.

My own secret reason for wanting to sit with the women

was to be far apart from Niko and thus to avoid the enforced drinking that was bound to follow from proximity to the celebrant. Greeks, who invented wine, take it for granted that the fermented juice of the grape is beneficial to the constitution, and beyond that they consider drinking a measure of one's manliness. Refusing a drink that is being proposed to someone's health and happiness on his name day is highly insulting. God help the man who betrays a lack of manliness, and twice help him who insults a name-day celebrant in whose house he is a guest.

Niko chose the largest glass he could find and filled it to the brim with his ruddy homemade wine. He set the glass in front of me, raised his own full glass towards me, and poked his chin in the air several times. All the other men raised their glasses at once, and shouting *"yassou, chronia polla"* (health and long life), they clinked Niko's glass, poised to drink.

No one took so much as a sip. All eyes were on me. Hey, look, I wanted to protest, I've proved my manliness endlessly—hitchhiking through Morocco, eating street food in India, bankrupting myself in order to mount stage plays about government corruption in Canada—but, no, manliness was not the main issue. Insulting my host—and landlord of such a fabulous room at such low rent—was. I picked up my glass, clinked Niko's and the others', wished Niko "long life," and took a sizable gulp, about a fifth of the contents of my glass.

Meanwhile, Niko and his friends open-throated theirs, banging the emptied glasses down on the table. Niko took a look at my nearly full glass and shook his head with sadness.

"You don't love me," he said. "You don't respect me." I became alarmed, but he was smiling. He sang a *mantinada*, a rhyming wail about a wasted life, wasted opportunities. He refilled his glass and the glasses of the other men. He peered at me through half-closed eyes and topped up my glass. He lifted his own again.

"This time I want to see *aspro pato* [bottoms up]," he warned me, smiling only faintly.

I puffed my chest to its maximum girth, swallowed hard, cleared my throat, gathered my courage, and said, "No, I can't. It'll make me sick."

Niko lowered his glass pityingly. "Ah, life," he sighed. "Nothing but adversity. A disappointment around every corner. There is no logic to it. No recourse. No good reason to keep up the struggle. It amounts to nothing, you know. It's like a big black hole where everything we do ends up and disappears. Sometimes I think that the only worthwhile thing we own is this very moment. That's all there is that we can touch and feel and know for sure is real . . . It'll make you sick, you say? In how long? How quickly?"

"In an hour or two," I admitted cautiously.

"Oh, an hour! Or two! Then there is no problem at all, is there? In one hour, let alone two, you and I can have more *kefi* [enjoyment] than most men in the world can in a lifetime. Listen carefully." His eyes twinkled. He sang to me in a boozy voice. It was a song about the sweetness of one hour's joy with a beloved that rendered death directly afterwards worthwhile in the extreme. The other men joined in the chorus: "Give me one hour, and kill me, one hour, one hour with you, and kill me, one hour of joy, an eternal paradise."

Was he proposing sex? No. He wanted me to drink down my glass, to honour him and dignify his traditions. "Bottoms up" was a foolish, immature way to drink, and I had hated it even in high school. But he had dismantled all of my defences. There was nothing to do really but to raise my glass, clink to his health, and then drink it down without pausing, tasting it, inhaling its clean perfumes—the vanilla, the plum, the apricot, the clear light of the sun of Crete. I banged my glass down a bit later than the rest of them, but with as much gusto.

Niko was beaming. "Now you make me happy. Now you must eat, so you don't get sick. Erato!" But she was one step ahead of him. She gingerly lowered a loaded plate in front of me.

It consisted of rabbit *stiffado*, hopelessly overcooked with melted pearl onions and muscat-grape vinegar, sweet and tart. And equally overcooked turkey with tomato and thyme. Lamb roasted far too long with lemon and oregano. Peach-coloured pumpkin flowers stuffed with rice and raisins, steamed mountain greens with olive oil, marinated baby garlic cloves and purple olives. Clean goat's-milk feta, white as marble. Fried zucchini and eggplant with yogurt-mint sauce, breaded fried wild oyster mushrooms picked by Niko himself, and peasant sourdough bread, dark and moist. I washed it all down with more wine, sipping it—no more bottoms up—and it didn't make me sad, it didn't make me sick.

The rest had unwisely moved on to Scotch, mixing cultures and sensibilities. Gradually the songs, the smiles, the homespun philosophizing, ground to a halt, and the *kefi* was replaced by an alcoholic pall, an introspection as foreign to Greece as Scottish freckles and constant bad weather. No one cared any longer if I was honouring them or not.

I quietly thanked Erato for the party and the well-intentioned food (no, I didn't tell her she had overcooked the meats), and took my leave. I retired to my bed and slept like a baby to the lingering tunes of all the *mantinades* I had heard.

Chapter 8

Of Rainbows and Honey

It started to rain the day after Niko's feast day, and it didn't let up until Christmas Eve. Almost twenty days of continuous rain is a remarkable occurrence anywhere outside of England; in Crete it is unimaginable. An aggregate of twenty rainy days a year is considered a godsend on this island, which some years is left bone dry.

And it wasn't just rain. It was cataclysmic. It was round-the-clock, biblically proportioned monsoons lashing down in violent sheets, drenching the earth, overflowing it. It resuscitated every known riverbed with gushing streams, and exposed bubbling brooks that no one knew even existed. Fast-falling cascades gushed down from every indentation of the cliff face into the deepest reaches of the gorges. The sands of the beaches parted under the pressure of water that rolled down from the hills, colouring the emerald sea yellow-brown with the runoff. The rain washed off whole segments of the unpaved paths and roads, and caused rocks to avalanche onto main arteries, choking them until bulldozers could be put to work.

It was the kind of extreme weather that managed to faze even me, a seasoned Canadian inured by months and months of meteorological adversity every year. It took all my good humour to agree with the Greeks that the annoying and destructive rain was something for which to be grateful as it provided sorely needed moisture to the olives and the orchards.

After the first few days I gave up all pretense of thankfulness—there is only so much I am willing to suffer for the good of plant life. I stayed indoors to cook local foodstuffs, particularly certain greens that sprout only during rains, such as *thalassidi*, a sweet-salty dandelion green that grows in beach sands, and the bitter-tart *lapsanidi*, a resident of low hillsides.

After a full week of rains and howling winds I surrendered. I became grumpy and irritable. I am Greek. I consider sunshine to be not only a birthright but an essential element of my well-being.

The locals, those with thirsty flora and those without, all became equally grumpy, as the whole population of Crete, and the mainland, complained bitterly. Every one of them was stricken with wetness-related illnesses such as bronchitis, rheumatism, and depression, losing faith that full sunshine would ever return.

I say "full" because despite the constant rain, there was in fact some sunshine every day. A quirky sun would appear through cracks in the ominous clouds and penetrate through sheets of rain to paint miraculous, brightly articulated rainbows on the hills behind my house. These were giant, almost solid versions of the fleeting rainbows I had witnessed earlier, and they mocked me with their cheerful colours as they framed Marioú under a proscenium.

To ease my discomfort and to replace the sunshine I

craved, I ate jar after jar of honey. Thyme-flower honey, the same amber-coloured nectar Theo had demanded for his *caltzouni* ages before, was also available in Marioú—no surprise considering the unlimited supply of cyclamen-coloured thyme growing on its hills.

And when I had had enough of dipping my fingers into honey, being awed by the big rainbow, and taking bone-chilling walks to admire the perturbed sea with frothy waves inconceivable during its normally caressable tranquility, I took refuge in visits to Réthymno. It is one of the prettiest towns on the Mediterranean, and only a half-hour drive from Marioú when the roads aren't made impassable by some rain-related damage.

Réthymno, on its naturally protected deep-water harbour, has a long past, stretching back to Minoan times, but the period of history that shaped and forever beautified it was the over four-hundred-year span of Venetian rule. Those seagoing, canal-dwelling folks who gave us gondoliers, risotto, and Canaletto were quite the empire builders in the Middle Ages, very much the terror of the Mediterranean. They took their turn at the helm of Crete, sandwiched between the Arabs and the Ottomans.

Crete's relentlessly colonized people don't seem to have minded the Venetians as much as they did some of their other conquerors. Fellow-Christian Venetians didn't antagonize the locals with religious harassment, and they repaid what they reaped from Crete with a wave of construction the island hadn't seen since the Greco-Roman period fifteen centuries earlier.

They built fortresses around the best harbours, and delightfully comfortable towns outside the walls of the fortifications. They did it at Heraklion and Chania, where they based their power; but they reserved their most charming legacy for Réthymno. There they built a stupendous town-sized fortress on the site of the ancient seafront acropolis, and on its periphery, like a garland around the beefy neck of a prizefighter, they sculpted a flowery set of connected neighbourhoods, with dainty, tall houses inside courtyards on a maze of narrow roads and alleyways. It was a functioning theme park of what life must have been like in pre-industrial days.

For me the attractions of Réthymno went well beyond the supremely pretty "old" town and the fortress that seemed to float on the azure sea. The "new" town that had grown out of the old offered all the services of the modern age, just like Heraklion, but with less traffic, less noise. There was shopping, professional photography processing, internetting (note: this is a new verb, "to internet," and you heard it here first), restaurants, movies, and some of the best *bougatsas* outside of Theo's kitchens: all the niceties of life that were missing from Marioú I could have in Réthymno.

And then the weather got worse. I couldn't quite believe it, but it actually *snowed*, briefly in Marioú, but substantially on the mountains behind the house, enough to stick to the ground and whiten the peaks. I reached for the honey jar, and when I had licked off the last fingerful, I put on whatever warm clothing I had brought from Canada (which wasn't much) and I got in the car for a solo escapade to Réthymno. Algis preferred to climb a mountain and reminisce about childhood skiing trips to Maine.

I sensed trouble as soon as I entered the gorge. The road surface was slick and slippery, which meant taking extra care to avoid local drivers, who were unused to frozen roads and drove as fast as if it were summer.

I was following a bouncy car from a safe distance, both of us whizzing by much faster than we should have been, when out of the blue—or rather, the grey—a thundering roll of brown death plunged at us from the lip of the cliff. Large rocks, loosened by the force of water, were crashing down at such speeds that it was useless to try to avoid them. Both the car ahead of me and I froze in our tracks and braked to sliding, uneasy stops. It must have been our lucky day, because only a smallish rock storm rattled off the roof of the other car, and nothing touched my car at all, even though a lethal mega-boulder landed within a couple of feet of my front end.

I hurriedly turned my car around and carefully steered through the stone-age obstacle course back to the safety of the open road. Grateful to the higher power that had spared me a crushing, I chose that very moment to get religion, a state I had rejected at age twelve and had lived without ever since.

I was born into a Greek Orthodox family, a member of a vestigial Byzantine minority in a city we still called Constantinople even though its new masters, the Ottoman Turks, had been calling it Istanbul for five hundred years. As a child I was force-fed religion, with coerced devoutness and obligatory church attendance, a kind of spiritual shield we as a community had adopted to resist assimilation.

Greek Orthodoxy is easy to reject since its operative language is *katharevousa* (formal) Greek that no one but priests understands anymore and its service is saddled with arcane procedures and ostentatious trappings more fanciful even than those of the Roman Catholics. All of it was meant to impress and awe into submission the vapid, uneducated faithful of the past, and therefore it appears ludicrous, even insulting, to a modern intellect.

I had put up with its silliness while I was still too young to do otherwise. But when my parents had had their fill of living in fear of the Turks and moved us to Canada, where the risk of assimilation is nil since the country is so fragmented and so libertarian, I instantly gave up the pretense and became a pre-teen sophisticate.

However, the near rock death in the gorge coupled with the rock assault on my car up at Zeus's cave was a scary enough sequence to supersede my sophisticated intellect with fear and send me rapidly to the Church for divine protection. My conversion was enthusiastically embraced by Algis, who had already visited all the churches of the area, not only to photograph them but to partake of their spirituality.

Born a Catholic to liberal parents, Algis had had a loosely religious upbringing, and as a child hadn't learned to be oppressed by churchly matters as I had. As a result, he was fascinated by religions of all persuasions, making a point of becoming immersed in them, all the more so if they were extreme. He loved the blood-infused Catholicism of Mexico, the antique Hinduism of India, the ethereal Buddhism of Tibetan-style monasteries in Nepal, and now the possibly extraterrestrial divinities of Crete's Ancients as well as the inalienable Orthodoxy of its Christian era.

It can be argued that it's impossible to be Greek without being Orthodox, just as it is to be American without being materialist or a chef without a well-tuned palate. For over four decades I had begged to differ, considering myself as Greek as a charcoal-broiled souvlaki even if I was as atheist as Lenin. And here I was in a moment of upheaval, having just escaped a gory death by a chance roll of rocks, attending any church I could find—and there were so many—starting that very after-noon and at every opportunity thereafter. I went at least three times a day, up to five times on Sundays. I crossed myself at every turn, right-to-left, not left-to-right like the Catholics, and with three fingers pursed together to recall the Holy Trinity. I knelt down yet again in worship of the frowning, white-bearded old man, our austere All-Powerful and His Son, the Crucified Christ suffering for all eternity as He rises out of the grave. I kissed the silver-outlined icons of saints who were tortured for their faith and for the sake of all the Greek Orthodox to come. I sat unfidgeting, as I could never do in my childhood, through the endless liturgy sung in a long-forgotten foreign tongue. I fasted to take communion— red wine to signify His blood, with sodden bread His all-enduring flesh. I breathed in the smoke of incense burning on charcoal in silver braziers that swung at the end of triple silver chains towards the sinful to make them dizzy, to make them give up resistance to the one true God, fight the heathen, believe, and never doubt.

I had immersed myself in a desperate state of grace, which I hourly prayed would prove temporary. If only the rain, snow, and cold would desist, and the sun sail on blue skies again!

Chapter 9

Ironed Shirts from Beyond

As if in answer to my prayers, in heavenly reward for my renewed faith and boundless piety, winter came to an abrupt end the day before Christmas. I woke on December 24 to bright sunshine and signs of early spring—birds chirping and an incandescent steam evaporating from sodden ground and well-fed foliage, melting into the white Greek light and the cloudless, clear blue sky.

It wasn't exactly warm outside—the light winds emanated ice-chilled from snow-covered mountains—but the strong sunshine had a therapeutic effect that warmed the heart, if nothing else. Algis had lined up several new churches for me to pray in this day, but I cancelled the lot in favour of a strictly secular visit to Réthymno to enjoy its charms. Algis agreed to join me, without hesitation. Slowly converting to a Greek, he too was overjoyed by the return of sunshine and the promise of heat, which has a spirituality all its own.

It had been only a week since my near-death-under-rocks, and I approached the gorge with a healthy amount of trepidation. There was no need. The fallen rocks had been cleared away, while their still-attached relatives appeared for the moment to be firmly cemented to the cliff face. We sailed through the gorge and the subsequent twenty kilometres to the outskirts of Réthymno.

At the top of the hill leading down to the city we were treated to an astonishing sight. To our left were the imposing Lefka Mountains, regal in thick white snow like the virgin brides of a visiting potentate. Straight ahead the red-roofed, whitewashed expanse of Réthymno descended sharply to its circular Venetian port and the aquamarine sea beyond.

The traffic into the town centre was thick. Last-minute Christmas-shopping fever had gripped the city, which was bedecked with festive lights and an obscene plethora of Santas, in the flesh and also in plaster replicas. A battalion of parents crazed with fear of disappointing their newly loot-greedy children was buying, buying.

In the old days, Christmas in Greece was a gentle religious holiday, a family occasion, a meat-eating celebration for the birthday of the most enduring god in the annals of Western religion. The observation of the holy event would start with a vegan fast—forty days for the truly devout, seven days for the less so—leading to a church service and holy communion to break the fast, followed by the fowl or lamb rewards of the Christmas Day lunch.

Christmas used to be a day of rest and warm feelings, of thanks for surviving the winter solstice, for turning the corner into jollier times, into the heart of winter that inevitably leads to rebirth. The boozy parties and modest gift exchanges were reserved for the following week, at New Year's Eve.

Now, however, thanks to globalization, Greece has been afflicted with the whole package of Anglo-Saxon Yuletide: the tree, the ornaments, the cards, the presents, the expense, the all-out effort to worship at the altar of merchandising for the sake of hyperbolic consumption.

With blasphemous anti-Christmas humbug tickling my brain, I escaped the commercial heart of Réthymno by ducking into one of the narrow passages of the old town. Here, in the toy-like streets where normal people carry on their normal lives as if they're living in a normal place, there were very few reminders of the season, maybe a small set of coloured twinkling lights, a tiny plastic Santa suspended by gold thread inside a window.

The quarter was eerily deserted and the sunshine spotlighted particular patina-dressed relics: the copper cupola of a Byzantine church, the metallic ornaments of a Venetian door. I was thankful for the tranquility. The snaking streets melded into even more twisting alleys, a maze that drew me deeper and deeper inside it with no specific destination at all. Algis had lingered in front of a long-forgotten Ottoman *hammam* (bathhouse) to photograph it, and I had lost him. Now I was entirely on my own, out of time in a timeless place.

There were childish squeals from a dead-end pathway where young boys played soccer with a bounceless ball using an overgrown gateway as the goal. I leaned on a stunted palm tree and watched them. I remembered my own childhood, when a game just like this occupied me for many blissful hours. But my reverie was short-lived. A piercing scream blew in from around the corner. The boys stopped their game. There was total silence for some long seconds, and then a torrent of excited voices.

The boys and I ran towards the source of the noise. There, in the middle of a cobblestoned street, was a middle-aged woman, her dressing gown half on, staring at the sky in tears, surrounded by her neighbours, who were all speaking at once, trying to comfort her and to get to the bottom of what had scared her so.

She moved somberly closer to her house, leaving a semicircle of onlookers around her with her ancient courtyard as a backdrop. She was like a tragedian at the acme of the drama taking the lead turn to address the Chorus, with an amphitheatre full of spectators glued to her every word. She spoke in agitated, halting, yet articulated tones:

"I promised on her deathbed. I promised. I swore to the Virgin. I crossed myself. I made a sacred covenant to take care of him. For her. She was a saint. I wouldn't have done it for him. He's a miserable sod. He doesn't lift a finger. For anything. For anyone. He's so spoiled. She spoiled him. She did it all for him. She would've died for him. He was her only son!"

She took several strophes, turning on the spot, to mark a division in her story. She raised her arms to punctuate her speech, to signify the more serious moments to come:

"She was my aunt. But more than that: she was my protectress, my mother. She raised me as her own after my parents died. I too would have died were it not for her. I owe it all to her. My life, my happiness. My marriage, my children. She made me promise to take care of him when she was on her deathbed, and I swore to her that I would. And I have. You all know I have. I do everything I can for him, and he never thanks me, he always demands more. Ooooh."

Tears and wails.

"You all know what abuse I take from him. No woman alive has taken such abuse, or done so much for a cousin, but I do it. Well, yes, I complain, I am human, and he is an animal. Who among us wouldn't complain? But I do what is needed. I do so much. I clean his house. I shop for him, I cook for him. I do his laundry! As if I don't have enough to do for my husband and my own sons, those slobs. All men are slobs, and yes, I complain, who wouldn't, I'm only human, I am only one and they are so many, so messy, so hungry. And he's the worst of all of them, and only a cousin, not a husband or a son or a brother, but I do it for him, I find the time, I do everything I can, I do his laundry!"

This was a saga about laundry—something I could easily appreciate. I was riveted to her every word, as was everyone around me. By now she had become breathless, spitting out her sentences half finished. Suddenly she shuddered; a shadow crossed over her like a crow circling for carrion. She crossed herself several times, muttering holy words and desperate exorcisms.

"Forgive me. Please, Auntie. Forgive me. I have complained, I know. I've shouted at him, I know. I've been harsh with him, I know. But he tries my patience so. He insults me. He belittles me. He knows what I promised you, and he takes advantage."

At that moment the sun hid behind a solitary cloud. The street was covered in darkness. She whimpered.

"I've not been well. I was in bed. Trying to recover from the *laima* I caught during the rains. Such a cough, such a sore throat. I was so sick. I was half asleep. And in my sleep, in my confusion, she came to me. My aunt's ghost came to me. She was so unhappy with me. Because I wasn't taking care of her son like I should, like I had promised!"

She broke down this time in a painful coughing fit. Her friends and neighbours, the audience, advanced towards her, to hug her and to nurse her, but she held them back with a firm, upraised hand.

"No, no. Don't. I am to blame. I admit it. And this is my punishment. I've been lax. I have not cleaned his house in two weeks. And I haven't been ironing his shirts. Not for several months. I admit it. But he changes twice a day. Who can keep up? I can't—" She started to break, but she recovered. "She was so real, so alive. Her hair loose and black like when she was young, and her widow's black kerchief over her head, so humble. So pious, she continues to mourn her dear husband even after death. She was so real. I could have touched her. And she wasn't cross with me. Not really. Just sad. She wasn't mean. She was good and kind. Like always. Her voice was a bit strange, a bit hoarse, almost like a man's, but considering where she's been, what do you expect? She didn't come in, she stayed outside, framed in the window, which I had left open to let the sunshine in, some warmth after all this rain. She stood very still, and called my name. 'Ismene-e-e-e. Ismene-e-e-e. Why are you going back on your promise, Ismene? Why? Why are you neglecting my son? Why?'"

She seemed lost in the remembrance. Moved.

"I heard the whole thing in a half sleep. Like a dream. Like a nightmare. No! A dream. I opened my eyes. And she was not a dream. I saw her! And when I tried to reach out to her, to touch her, she disappeared. She was no longer there. She had gone back to heaven."

Ismene's story was spent. The sun returned to scorch the scene in harsh light. She collapsed to the ground in slow motion, as if she had become disjointed now that she had confessed her failings.

Running footsteps broke the tension as a middle-aged man with fashionably long and flowing jet-black hair made his entrance. "Cousin, cousin," he was shouting, "what's wrong? Are you hurt?"

The crowd parted to allow the new player clear passage to the fallen woman. He rushed to her, he went down on his knees, he held her to his chest. He gingerly helped her to her feet as she clutched his jacket. She was weeping.

"I saw your mother," she whispered. "She came to me in my sleep and wouldn't let me touch her when I woke. She is cross with me."

"Sh-sh," whispered the man to her. "It's all right. It's fine. Nothing's wrong."

He walked her to her door, carrying her part of the way as she held on to him imploringly. She righted herself on her front step and kissed him on the cheek. "Bring me your shirts," she said loudly for all to hear. "I forgot to iron them."

"Don't worry." He kissed her back. "You can do them after Christmas." She kissed him again and went inside, shutting the door.

She had pulled his jacket and it was coming off his arms. He tried to correct it, but in so doing his hand got caught in the pocket. As he tugged to free his hand a black kerchief came halfway out, there for all to see before he could stuff it back in. He perused the crowd sheepishly, but they looked away as if they hadn't noticed anything. He walked away quickly to put an end to the drama.

I turned to the woman next to me with raised eyebrows. I had found the action a bit extreme even if it did revolve around such a sacred concern as clean clothes.

"He's unmarried," she confided to me. "Someone has to do his ironing, otherwise he'll look like a bum and no one will ever marry him and she'll have to cater to him forever. He needs to give her a push once in a while. It's for her sake as well as his."

Chapter 10

Another Christmas
for the Road

The weather not only held for Christmas Day, it improved. The chill breezes from the mountains were diverted by a southerly wind that blew in from Africa with a scent of the desert and a heat sufficient to awake the buzzing of the bees and the crickets, the chirping of the birds, the blooming of the flowers: a symphony of summer.

Algis and I started our day very early with a drive to the hilltop Preveli Monastery for Christmas mass, not so much because I still felt the need for divine protection as to gain the confidence of the locals, who would view me as a barbarian if I didn't worship at a church on this Holy of Holies.

Founded in the sixteenth century during Venetian times and renovated extensively in the last fifty years, Preveli sits on the highest peak of a spectacular promontory with a 270-degree view of the sea. These days it is reachable by a nicely paved road and is quite the tourist attraction. Not all that long ago, however, it was inaccessible by vehicular means, and thus afforded secure monasticism. It was this same inaccessibility that allowed several hundred British soldiers, on the run after losing the island to the Nazis in the Battle of Crete in 1941, to reach the monastery undetected. There the monks hid them and took care of them, risking certain death at the hands of the Germans. The monks proceeded to jeopardize themselves exponentially by leading the soldiers to an uncharted beach and onto English submarines to effect their escape.

We arrived at seven-thirty, late for a service that begins at five and ends at eight. We walked past the plaques and the donated fountain commemorating the wartime exploits of the brave monks, breathing in the perfumes of jasmine and mimosa, which were flowering again now that the rains had stopped. We went up the few steps to the well-worn walkway in front of the crumbling monks' quarters, the only untouched part of the original construction.

In the centre of the sunken square of the courtyard is the church of Preveli, with its recently plastered, smooth exterior and its ancient, incense-scented smoky interior, with icons of saints and the Virgin painted directly on its about-to-moulder walls: the decomposing, two-dimensional idols of the Orthodox church. My attention strayed to the gilded altar, the raised pulpit to one side and the elaborate throne for a visiting prelate on the other, the carved silver chandeliers with countless wax candles pointing their flames heavenward, and the Romanesque dome in the middle of the ceiling, where a painted image of Christ, the *Pantocrator* (Omnipotent), peered down at his flock, soothing us, washing over us with the prospect of eternal salvation.

The service over, the fasting worshippers lined up for Christmas communion, while the less devout stepped out into the open air, now glorious in morning light with a view of the infinite sea, for some gossip and a post-devotional cigarette. I hadn't fasted the last two days, but I had before that during my seven days of faith, so I stuck around for a sip of the blessed wine and a nibble of the sacred bread, in company with the lady baker from Lefkogeia, the butcher from Plakiás, the gas station owner from Asomatos, and Erato's sister Terpsichore from Marioú. Now everyone in the whole region would find out that I was, ecclesiastically speaking, an acceptable person, and maybe accord me the courtesies and discounts owing to a fellow Greek Orthodox.

On the way back, Algis got out of the car at the foot of a moist hill that Niko had told us about. It was his secret place for *amanites* (wild oyster mushrooms), big as a wrestler's hand and brown skinned, redolent of the definitive earthy flavour of the real thing (versus the pale hothouse taste of the commercially grown). Algis had optimistically brought a huge plastic bag for his mushroom hunt. I wished him luck and sped off to the beach.

The sea hadn't quite regained its swimming-pool stillness, but I could see the bottom through its southerly shivers and I was determined to dive into it as a special Yuletide treat after three weeks of deprivation.

The road west of Plakiás hugs the coastline for a few kilometres, ending in the beach frontage of the final restaurant on Soúda's compact bay. This restaurant, like all tourist-dependent enterprises, was closed for the winter, but I had adopted it as my beach place. I sat on a rock surrounded by roses in full bloom, projecting ahead to summer, when I would be able to hang out here all day, holding court at an outdoor table, punctuating my sociability with dips in the sea.

The place was deserted, so I took off all my clothes, the better to perform my Christmas baptismal. I walked along the water's edge to absorb some warmth from the sun and build my courage for the dip.

The violent rains had created rumbling temporary rivers that sliced through the sands with runoff from the hills. There was a scrawny waterfall down the rocks at the edge of the bay, with surprisingly powerful, though thin, jets of water thundering noisily into a frothing pond—fresh water to spare in a landscape that is as a rule dry, even parched.

The southerly wind died down for a reason all its own, and magically the sea became as still and transparent as the Greek sea is meant to be. I gave up all mental resistance and plunged in. The first shock of coldness was painful, but I refused to give up. I swam some agonizing strokes. It felt strange, like a delicious swoon, a taste of hypothermia.

I stayed in the water for what felt like an hour (actually, it was eight minutes) and came out into the sun. With the wind having died down, the air temperature had risen, sharpening the contrast with the water. A sensation of all-powerfulness swept through me. I raised my arms to the sun in metaphysical ecstasy, and loudly sang an extemporized incantation to Apollo.

Little giggles snapped me out of my naturist trance. Three young children, highly amused by my naked antics, were pseudo-hiding behind a palm tree, watching me while pretending not to. I covered myself as best I could with my hands, and ran to the car and the modesty of my clothes.

There was a double surprise waiting for me when I got back home. Algis had located the mushroom stash on the hill, and he had walked home with not only the bag but all of his pockets full of prize specimens, some as big as dinner plates. I had barely had time to voice my kudos when he pointed to a second surprise.

Standing heroically on my balcony, backlit against the

shimmering quilt of olive groves and shiny sea, was Theo, tapping his foot, impatiently waiting for me to return.

"Took you long enough," he said. "What're you trying to prove? That water's so cold it'll singe your feathers right off, like you were a chicken for the plucking."

I jumped for joy and ran to him. I embraced him, Greek-style, with painful slaps on the back. I didn't ask him banal details of how he had found my place: I had phoned to tell him that I was in a house on a hill near Marioú, and he must have figured out the rest. I wished him a hearty "Merry Christmas," which he rebuffed with, "Equally charmed, I'm sure."

I tried to formally introduce him to Algis, but it turned out they had met several years earlier in Marrakesh, when Algis was working on his Moroccan Mosaic photo project at the Mamounia Hotel, and Theo was there trying to relax after a three-day catering extravaganza for the King of Morocco in Rabat. Well, lah-dee-dah.

Theo had driven to Crete from Athens, via ferryboat, in a practically new Aston Martin. This was obviously the result of his recent menu job with a neo-yuppy mega-eatery, the sort of place that pretends to be in London or New York and charges shamelessly for misconstrued modern recipes—unless it's lucky enough to entice someone like Theo to design its menu, in which case it charges unabashedly for credible recipes.

He had filled his car to the limit with mythical edibles and had come to cook for me for Christmas. I would hazard that he had also come to get away from the hubbub of the capital, which becomes intolerable in its upmarket fashionable stratum, but I was flattered nonetheless.

"I think this'll be my last job ever!" he hissed. He continued with a series of obscenities, all of which added up to "I'm fed up with trying to feed the Greeks," as Algis and I unloaded his car to cart the goodies into the kitchen. "They adore the IDEA of the world's delicacies, the fusions, the fresh-market cuisines, all those innovations that are taken for granted in every civilized corner of the planet, but they're happiest when you give them what their mothers fed them, most notably *bifteki*!" He translated for Algis's benefit: "That's Greek for 'burger,' my boy. Jeez. I almost throttled the son of a mountain goat! It was regular, like clockwork. Every four hours on the button, every day for a month, he would burst into my kitchen with yet another burger idea. Meanwhile I'm working my butt off trying to teach his so-called chefs, a bunch of idiot drones, a complex menu for which he can charge the prices he wants to charge, and he's on his *bifteki* theme. He tried, though, I gotta give him that. He started out with a Thai burger on a galangal and lemongrass sauce, then he went on to Japanese-style with yakitori sauce, Indian with curry sauce and chutney, and finally—dig this!—a burger patty topped with Sevruga and crème fraîche. *À la Russe*, he called it." Theo snorted his disapproval, exhaling fire from both nostrils.

"So, did you give the poor man a *bifteki* on his menu, or what?" I laughed, struggling with a giant pumpkin that was obstinately stuck in the Aston Martin's trunk.

"Over my dead body," grimaced Theo, pulling out the pumpkin with a flick of his index finger. "Be careful with that," he cautioned when it wobbled precariously in my arms. It must have weighed nearly twenty kilos.

All the food was finally inside and packed away strategically, so that items could be found when needed in a kitchen that had become cramped and inadequate for the Theodorean largesse. And we got to work. We proceeded to cook continuously for the next thirty-six hours, pausing only to eat and sleep, up to the end of Boxing Day, taxing my tiny burners and small oven to produce dishes worthy of the better restaurants of London or New York.

It started with a sushi lunch, a Japanese affectation that couldn't be more foreign in this Greek setting, where raw fish is equated with instant death. The fish in question were fresh, still-breathing mackerel and red snapper that Theo had just purchased off the boat of a fisherman in Réthymno harbour, possibly the only fisherman in Crete to have gone out to sea on Christmas morning.

"He was probably working off his hangover from last night. Christmas Eve, like all birthdays, is an excellent reason to drink," observed Theo, as he added sugar and rice vinegar to the sushi rice and covered it with a wet cloth to make it sticky and ready to shape into the bite-size nuggets that become pedestals for slices of fish.

"I'm finding it hard to believe all this, Theo," I exclaimed. "Sushi in Marioú! And who knows what else to follow—I didn't take a close look."

"This is nothing," he scoffed. "This is easy. It went from the market to the car to your kitchen. I once brought a ten-kilo West-Coast salmon from Vancouver to a small village in Wales. The village was so small you had to walk the last five kilometres: they had never got around to making a road. It was for the relatives of a raven-haired Welsh beauty I had fallen in love with. No one in her village—some ghastly unpronounceable name—had ever seen a salmon that big, and no one had an oven big enough. I had to cook it wrapped in foil inside the embers of a fire on the beach. They laughed at me, but of course it came out succulently spectacular. And to punish them for laughing I made them eat it with really pungent Swedish-style honey mustard. They hated the mustard but they put up with it because they couldn't get enough of the fish. And another time . . ."

Theo rambled on about unforgettable food-transportation exploits while he cut exact slices of the pulsating fish flesh, a task of supreme delicacy and more taxing than usual as he had neglected to bring his sushi knife and had to perform with my dinky Swiss Army, the only sharp blade in my arsenal.

A precisely sculpted nigiri sushi with a mini fish filet that tastes of the sea, seasoned with the searing bitterness of wasabi radish, dipped lightly into the salty fermented soya, chased by a crisp vinegary sliver of pickled *gari* ginger: this is a perky combo that had aroused my appetite even in my most jaded restaurant-reviewing days. Here, in the monochrome of no-surprises Crete cooking, it induced a series of gustatory implosions. It brought tears to my eyes (though that could have been the wasabi shooting up my sinuses). I moaned.

"I achieved sushi perfection, much like this, in Toronto once. Some Canadian company was trying to suck up to Sony, or was it Toyota—whatever—and they wanted to impress the big guy from Japan, so naturally they hired me," reminisced Theo, puffing on his post-prandial Cuban, having eaten the meal wordlessly, as he was prone to do if the food was good. "I had a slew of fish flown in from Japan, all of them alive in special tanks, but what really got their goose was the sea urchin that I flew in from Chania. They couldn't get enough. Their sea-urchin caviar is called *uni*, and it's a greasy, yellow goo. Mine had a clean taste and a deep orange colour. Exquisite, actually. I invented a special sauce just for them. Chilies, ginger, lime juice, sake, and only a drop of soya. It gave them a new dimension. Well, several new dimensions all at once," he concluded, dreamily smacking his lips. "Tried to get sea urchin this morning. None to be had. Not one. Shame, really."

"Did you make out all right in Athens?" I asked.

"They gave me the Aston Martin," replied Theo testily, peeved that I had shattered his sea-urchin reverie. "It's used, but it works. I'm owed quite a bit of cash on the side, but I doubt I'll ever see any of it."

"So, isn't it time we settled down to a business together here on Crete? That was your idea, wasn't it? You got me thinking about it."

"Yes, I did."

"It's very sad that Eftihia's plans fell through because her mom is so ill. That's just misfortune, and there's nothing we can do about it. And those people at the hotel, well, they were something else again, but that was just a shot in the dark, wasn't it? Now, surely, we can do something else. Something that's our own."

"Yes. Surely." He pointed his cigar at me. "Obviously, yes . . . I meant to talk about that. It's one of the reasons I came to see you. Aside from the pleasure of eating with you, of course." He jumped out of his chair. "But not now. Enough chit-chat. Now we have to get to work. The goose, a sumptuous beast from Strasbourg, France, is ready for her Christmas close-up."

I followed him into the kitchen so that I could clear the sushi decks and prepare the counters for the goose. Theo loved to cook but he loathed to clean up. It was the same in his professional dealings, where, from what I knew, he combined extravagant creativity with messy financial arrangements. Theo was far too worldly and brilliant to have street smarts. He tended to jump into projects wholeheartedly and worry about the money afterwards: a formula that fed his imagination and artistic spontaneity but predictably cheated his pocket. Being a shrewd observer of human nature, he was fully aware of corruption and cruelty and the common attitude of those with money that they are the only ones who deserve to have it. Theo simply held himself above all that— except when it was time to replenish his Cubans and, counting his pennies, he'd realize that he couldn't even afford Dominicans.

He must have read my mind. "You'd think," he said with a twinkle in his eye, "that being the fall guy of rich *archidia* [testicles] who fancy themselves restaurateurs is a thankless life, but then again I take one look at the colour of this pumpkin—" he pointed at the innards of the leviathan I'd had to so carefully lug from the car, sunset with apricot highlights "—and I say: [expletive] 'em. Let 'em keep their money and croak on it. They never experience the glory of a freshly cut pumpkin. They get to see it only after I've cooked it and put it on their plate. I, on the other hand, feel and breathe this pumpkin. I know this pumpkin from seed to flower to twenty-kilo monster with rock-hard skin and sweet aromatic flesh that I can endlessly reinvent."

The pumpkin was boiled gently, puréed, and set in the strainer to drain out its excess water. Ginger, nutmeg, and a drop of sweet ewe's-milk cream were added, along with a tiny sprinkle of salt. The red cabbage was boiled and chopped. Tart apple, green onion, and fennel leaves were added, as well as a light dressing of cider vinegar and safflower oil. The potatoes were cooked and tossed with chopped fresh rosemary and arugula and a sweet butter from the same ewe's cream.

Meanwhile, quince was poached and added to dried bread,

raisins, chopped onion, slices of kumquat, sage, and goose fat to become the stuffing. As the goose roasted in the oven, Theo's patented watermelon-ginger chutney was dished out into a shallow plate to temper and reassume its subtle but meaningful range of flavours.

Algis and I juggled our chores around Theo, who was making our over-extended kitchen seem more unbearably tiny by the minute. We cleaned, fetched, put away—devotedly, selflessly, untiringly, motivated by hunger and a curiosity to find out if he would manage to pull it off. By sunset the wizard had indeed done it, and he served us a snowbelt, Teutonic Christmas meal in the sunbelt on the other side of a prehistoric gorge.

All his various flavours and textures blended together harmoniously. As every great meal should, this one offered a composition of distinct tastes that shone each on its own but became glorious in combination with the others: the subtle spices of the aromatic pumpkin, the lively dressing of the red cabbage, the array of sweet perfumes in the quince stuffing, the meltingness of the ginger-watermelon chutney, and, most of all, the rich mouthfuls of the prized goose and its deep meaty wine gravy.

I hadn't had such a Christmas feast since Edinburgh, some thirty-five years earlier, at the parental home of Sandy Richardson, a schoolmate from McGill. During that meal, his hospitable mother had introduced me to sherry-drunken grapefruit as an opening course and to the true taste of a homemade, ten-year-old plum pudding for dessert. In between those two revelatory dishes, she had served a main course, traditional sage-stuffed turkey, whose succulence I've been trying to replicate forever.

After dinner we got right back to work to make a giant fruit and custard *bougatsa* like the one Theo had served Eftihia back in Fodele. This time it was intended for some people Algis had befriended, foreigners who had set up house in the Marioú area.

One couple was Swedish, with three platinum-haired, pink-skinned youngsters, the other a transcontinental duo— an African woman and a French man—with two chocolate-coloured, curly-haired children. Our little household turned Christmasy in the extreme as the five kids, supercharged from an excess of sugar, chattered in high squeaky voices, excited to be with each other and absolutely oblivious to us. The volume was dizzying, but through the tumult I could hear that these multi-ethnic children were speaking Greek.

Theo and I registered our Greek approval, but beyond that we found it difficult to concentrate in all the noise. The parents of the children, as parents are wont to do, ignored the noise altogether. They wolfed down platefuls of our goose meal leftovers and then dug with abandon into the intoxicating *bougatsa* and its coconut-honey coulis.

The children eventually exhausted themselves running around and screaming at each other, and the parents took that as their cue to pack up and leave. Algis left with them to take a nighttime walk under the three-quarter moon, which shone bright in the cloudless sky.

Theo shot back a couple of *rakis* and eyed me solemnly. I perceived a "serious moment" approaching, but I was too bubbly to take it seriously. I should have.

"I'm at a turning point," said Theo. "I've become a plain meat stew with no herbs, no garlic, no flavours. I'm desperate for something real, some meaning, some spice. Anything! My entire life is a waste. And every new job confirms this. The unexpected health problem with Eftihia, the crap with those nut cakes and their hotel, the mindless fool that I'm dealing with in Athens." He shook his head in distaste. "That schmuck and his *bifteki*! Do you know that the reviewers were knocking down my door, and I couldn't keep them out even though I begged them to wait until I was ready? Do you have any idea what those *malakas* would have done to me if they had found any kind of *bifteki* on my menu?" Theo shuddered at the potential ostracism. "I'm competing with the most grotesque culinary poseurs in history. Athens is trying to catch up gastronomically with the rest of the world. But Greek cuisine is not equipped to accommodate renewals in a hurry. It took us two hundred years to accept mayonnaise. Now we have to assimilate totally alien, faraway Asian concepts within a month. The fancy restaurants of Athens are drowning, they are grasping at straws. It is ludicrous to read their menus. It's like a litany of every fashionable ingredient and sauce they've read about in magazines but which they've no clue how to use. It's a sham and a scam, but the public demands it, and the critics are on the warpath. Give them anything that doesn't need forty words to describe on the menu, and they'll dismiss you. Give them *bifteki*, and they'll tie you to the back of their chariot and drag you around the walls of Troy until you bleed to death. And yet the stupid idiot will not relax until I find a way to put his burger on my menu!" Theo laughed bitterly. I snickered uneasily, but he froze me with a stern look. "At the end of the day, I think suicide is the only viable alternative to the nonsense of my life."

Aah, those late-in-the-day Christmas blues! What a comedown after all the fleeting hours of joy and reclaimed wonder. What cruel punishment for the short respite from hopelessness and misery. What foul conditions in which to digest the indulgent meal! And to be Greek, on top of all that! Terminal

pessimism joined to the most deflating moment of the entire
year: those three hours between the Christmas dinner and
sleep.

"I come from fifteen hundred years of the middle class, ever
since it was invented in Byzantium as a celebration of the end
of the first millennium," I said, not really changing the subject. "My happiness is predicated on material comfort and a
concerted effort to ensure that tomorrow and all the tomor-
rows to follow I will be equally well provided for so that I
never need to suffer. The countless people who have no
money can't avoid suffering, and the lucky few of the rich
classes suffer because they're too rich to ever be content.
Only those of us in the middle who have enough, even just
enough, to be cozy are permitted happiness. I have earned
the right to avoid catastrophe. Therefore, I can't see it."

"Can't see what? Your own point?"

"My point is that suicide is a piss-poor solution."

"Only the middle class looks for points and solutions."
Theo shook his head at my narrow-mindedness. "It's not
even remotely in your nature to understand me, is it?"

"It takes two to understand, Theo. You're so full of yourself, so bloated by self-indulgence, that you don't have the
capacity, let alone the desire, to understand anyone besides
yourself."

"I was talking suicide, not mass murder," he remarked.
"All I need is to understand myself!" Theo took a victory puff
on his cigar.

"Why don't you move to Tuscany? Love to come see you
in Padua. Or even better, Sienna."

"I was thinking France, more," said Theo pensively.

"Well, don't go to the north. They're too grouchy, all those
Normands and Bretons. And don't go to some remote village.

If it's to be France, I must have a good-sized town. I need to be able to walk to a café, rather than drive to it. Aix-en-Provence I adore." I reached for a chocolate-covered marzipan imported from Germany.

"Yeah, it's a good town. I spent a weekend there once, and I met an Algerian. A beauty, she was pure fire. And earthy, like a sizzling field of wildflowers in early May . . ."

We woke up late on Boxing Day, and Theo went for a drive to visit someone he knew at Kokkinos Pyrgos, a seaside town some fifty kilometres away. Algis and I spent a few hours on the beach trying unsuccessfully to build up the courage for a dip. The wind had picked up substantially since the day before, creating ferocious crashing waves.

Algis went on a rock hunt and returned with miniatures of the big rocks that had fired his imagination on the edges of the cliffs. These ones were fist-sized and highly compressed, with many colours of marble and granite, sculpted into recognizable human features distorted with pain.

"Look at them closely," instructed Algis. "Imagine these to be residents of Crete a million years ago. Let's say, the very first humans to live here. See them in a sort of paradise, where they lived in total bliss with free food, and caves with indoor plumbing, and gorgeous beaches to swim in. Like in heaven."

"Like being on a permanent all-inclusive vacation," I offered.

"Yes. And now picture them growing mean and vicious, and corrupt and stupid," speculated Algis.

"Like the restaurant owners who are abusing Theo."

"Exactly," agreed Algis. "They became so terrible that they displeased Zeus and the other extraterrestrial deities, and were expelled into the farthest reaches of unsurvivable space. They perished. But a few of them escaped and hid right here in Soúda Bay, thinking they had gotten away with it. However, the monks of Preveli got wind of them and informed Zeus, and he found them and smote them, melted them into limestone, trapped them in the rocks forever in agony, exposed to the elements, as a warning to subsequent Earth-dwellers to, like, behave!"

"Good theory, Algis." I inspected the distorted stone faces more closely, overlooking Algis's anachronisms in mixing Preveli monks with Zeus and prehistoric extraterrestrials.

"Yes, it is, and when you've totally understood it, I'll tell you how it relates to Excalibur and to the Mayan calendar." He smiled enigmatically.

Back at home base we found Theo not only returned, but already hard at work. The kitchen was awash in Chinese ingredients that he had brought earlier, plus a kilo of prized sea bass that he had just purchased in Kokkinos Pyrgos, quite probably the very purpose of his drive.

He was examining the bag of oyster mushrooms that Algis had picked the previous day. "You got some beauties here, my boy. The plump big ones are the ones you want. These wild ones grow a thick skin, and the small ones are tough, a little bitter, and not juicy at all. We like 'em juicy, don't we gentlemen?" He was grinning ear to ear, in total contrast to the funk in which he had gone to bed the night before.

Once again he read my mind. "Don't get all middle-class optimistic on me, Byron. I feel just as rejected, dejected, and abused as last night. It's just that you took so long coming back, I had time for a shower, and a superior shower it was too. And maybe you were right about that one thing: a good shower is worth its weight in hot water, and I enjoyed it. Usually, and when I bother to, I have baths. But I think I'll switch."

He turned from me to address his ingredients. "For our final meal, and I don't mean 'final' casually, we're going Chinese. I am cooking a lo mein of wheat noodles with Algis's marvellous mushrooms, green onions, baby bok choy, and tofu. I am steaming these excellent fish—quite rare this time of year, believe me—lightly steaming them, and dipping them in my special sauce, which is a melting pot of the entire Szechwan canon: garlic, scallions, ginger, soya, chilies, Szechwan peppercorns, dried shrimp—everything, that is, except fermented black beans, which would take it over the top, AND, as you well know, I never take anything over the top. I come close, but I don't go over." Theo did a jig of jubilant restraint, and plunged into his no-holds-barred cooking with the kind of gusto I had not been able to muster earlier when contemplating a plunge into the roaring waves.

The meal, just like all the meals I have ever eaten from the hands of this chef, was an orgy of ideal textures, exploding tastes, and exotic flavours, with al dente noodles alongside chewy, earthy mushrooms, and a fish so fresh its every morsel burst with clean sea-water essence that readily married itself to the strong scents of the sauce. Were this to turn out to have been my final repast with Theo, at least it would have been a worthy one.

Chapter 11

Passion for Olives

Theo's urgent departure right after Boxing Day supper spelt devastation to my tastebuds, which now needed to return to normalcy after his exquisite, two-day pampering. That situation was dire enough on its own, but it was made much worse early in January by the record-breaking freak snowstorm and its subsequent electricity failures and fuel shortages. These various inconveniences had then led me to existential anxieties (thank you, J.P. Sartre!), and to mental anguish upon realizing how unGreek I had become after all those years in Canada. It was all too much for my highly spoiled, life's-a-party self, and by the end of the first week of the new year I had descended into a funk.

"You're hung up on small things," said Algis, punishing me for my negativity. "You're always on about the narrow doorways of the toilets, and the doors opening to the inside instead of the outside, forcing you to squeeze yourself in. I mean, is that really a problem? All you have to do is lose some weight and then you'd slip right in like I do. You complain about the heating. Far as I'm concerned, having any heating at all is a bonus. I used to freeze all night in Hardwar when I was there to shoot the sadhus of the Kumbh Mela, but in the daytime the sun would come out, just like it does here, and I'd forget all about the cold. I love the winter here. I think it's far better than summer, when you roast. And I love the food here. I eat a vegetable that I know so well, like a zucchini or a dandelion green, and it tastes like a brand-new thing. And what I really love is that the vegetables and the fruits come in different sizes and shapes, not like the standard supermarket stuff back home. Leeks are three feet long. Tangerines can be as huge as oranges or small like plums but sweet and juicy either way. Green peppers are tiny or big and taste like green peppers are supposed to, with a hint of paprika and an accent of cayenne. The chestnuts taste of sweet vanilla. The broccoli has overtones of cucumber. The tomatoes, even those grown in winter, are just the right blend of sweet and sour. I like it all."

"I like the food. I've nothing against the food," I protested. "But eating on its own doesn't make me Greek."

"It doesn't? From what I see, eating is a big part of being Greek."

"We are the people who invented Western logic, lifelike sculpture, mosaic painting, philosophy, drama, the Olympic Games, the alphabet, and egg-lemon-chicken soup. By that reckoning, food is only one-seventh of our achievement."

"It's a good place to start. That's all I'm saying. For me it leads to awesome discoveries. A good meal opens the eyes. Look at these photos." Algis opened one of his picture books to show me photographs he had been keeping secret. They were stunning images of rock sculptures that he had built all over the Marioú area from rocks found in each location. He had pointed them out to me, but they blended into the landscape so seamlessly I had imagined them to be remnants of art works from another time.

He opened another book of pictures and showed me a personalized vision of Crete such as I could never have imagined. He had found a way to distort the scenery, to break up the light and contort the very shape of things. It was all recognizable if one looked carefully, but if taken on their own these images were abstracts of colour, swirls of hills and churches and seascapes, elongated limbs and restructured faces. A cross between cubism and funhouse mirrors.

"It's possible, and even desirable," said Algis sagely, "to look at life with a fresh eye. Not to worry if it's true or real. There's nothing that is totally true or real. Everything's what you make of it. Am I right? It's all about what works for you, and most important for someone like you, how much you're willing to give up for it."

Next, he showed me pictures of myself. They were all taken when I hadn't been looking, when I was going about my normal pursuits, shopping, having coffee in the village square, walking on the beach. He had done me in his special method, and while they were obviously pictures of me, they were distorted me's: long swanlike necks, two heads, thin short legs carrying a belly much bigger than a human belly could ever get, faces with several noses and mouths and eyes. These were me's that were transformed and reassembled, me's that only he and I could know for sure to be me.

"From what I witnessed both in Fodele and here in Marioú," continued Algis mercilessly, "you're holding on for dear life to this person that you brought with you from Montreal. You're trying to become Greek, but in fact you're totally refusing any change at all. The most important thing to you is your various routines. Your morning has to have all its little elements. The orange juice, the tea, the hot shower, the coffee. You freak out if the slightest detail is out of place. You panic if the TV isn't working just right, and you lose it completely when the electricity blacks out. You want to become Greek but to continue to live like a Canadian. You want to be spontaneous but not give up any of the stodgy habits you're addicted to." Algis shook his head as if to drive his point home. "It's time you took a deep breath and a long careful accounting of where you're going. If all you want is to retire and count out your days until you die, that's okay. Nothin' wrong with that. Happens all the time in Canada, and surely here in Greece, too. But if it's something more you want, something alive, then search for passion. Passion is what's missing back home, and passion is the bottom line in a place like Greece, its only constant, the only sure thing in a culture where everything else is tenuous."

The Greek passion for olives transcends life and even death. The rains, the storms, the snows had wreaked havoc in the Marioú area. Roads had collapsed, electricity poles and TV transmitters were downed, all the houses leaked water, live-stock had suffered, vegetables patches and oranges had frozen, but the olives had survived.

The olives are eternal. They are the life-giver. They are wealth. They can freeze and wither, and still their oil is intact, waiting to be extracted. But the olive is not an accommodating fruit. It flowers in March and ripens slowly through the long summer and fall. It reaches maturity in December and is at its best if harvested right then, January being a backup to complete whatever work has been left undone.

This year, December had been such a washout that almost all the harvesting was left to the last minute. If January were also to be lost, then the whole crop would rot.

Landlords Niko and Erato, owners of a tidy string of olive groves around Marioú and the neighbouring village of Asomatos, went to their properties on dry days even if it was too cold to work comfortably outdoors. The olives demanded their immediate attention; nothing else mattered.

They waited for a somewhat warm, sunny day to invite us to join them. I believe that they fully expected the two of us to work, but I craftily claimed to have caught *stoithi*, a Greek chest ailment related to *laima* and caused by the same cold, wet drafts. I set myself under an olive tree with a Thermos of hot coffee, to suffer without undue complaints.

Algis threw himself enthusiastically, if erratically, into the tasks at hand, though I caught him slacking off several times to take photographs. The family were too busy to notice. They had far too much to do, and it was a battle against time.

Olives have been pressed into olive oil on Crete since Minoan times. Modern paleontological techniques have given us proof that olive oil was not only known to the Ancients, it was a major export of theirs and therefore a source of their wealth and power.

The Minoans would easily have been able to figure out that the olive contains oil: it oozes out of the fruit without much crushing or squeezing. And amazingly, the oil that the olive relinquishes is sweet and flavourful, even though the raw fruit itself is bitter and unpleasant.

It is not known if the Minoans discovered the method necessary to render olives edible, but modern Greeks, beneficiaries of five thousand years of olive culture, certainly do know. Olives are either cracked or scored, and stored in water to shed their bitterness. The water is refreshed twice a day for ten days until a neutral taste is achieved. Afterwards, the olives are either pickled in brine or they are marinated in lemon or vinegar and eventually preserved in olive oil, to become enjoyable in their own right.

Either as fruit or as oil, olives are the common denominator of Crete's economy and well-being. It was therefore no wonder that the landlords, their playboy son Grigoris, their older son Stamatis, the surprisingly proficient Catalan girlfriend Arete, and the two hired hands were so absorbed in their olive chores.

Olives, when ripe, can either fall off the branch to the ground or stubbornly stick to the branch until prodded. The harvest includes both the fallen and the stubborn. Dark green mesh cloth is spread under the trees to prevent fallen olives from rotting in contact with the soil. The cloth also provides a surface onto which the prodded ones can fall.

In the old days the prodding was done with olive branches. Now it is done with slender, motorized threshers that churn the olives off the branches. It's still a muscle-wrenching business, but at least it's speedier and much more effective. Once the olives are off the branches and on the mesh, the leaves and little twigs are picked out by hand and the olives are gathered into burlap sacks to be transported to the olive oil co-operative. There they are pressed into oil by machine, another welcome improvement over the manual presses of the past.

Olive picking, known locally as *pame yia ellies*, might be hard work, but it has elements of fun and celebration. Drinks, including the all-occasion *raki*, flow throughout the day, and the highlight is the essential lunch break. On this day, to mark the presence of Algis and myself, a charcoal barbecue was set up to roast a humongous spitted turkey.

I was fairly sure that this was the same turkey that I had watched Niko handling not long before and that had once tried to peck my eyes out. I hardly minded being assigned the task of tending to its roasting. Suffering from *stoithi* did not excuse me from cooking chores; if anything, it recommended me for them. I sat by the barbecue, enjoying its warmth, turning the big bird on its spit, and breathing in its comfort-food smells, as the skin charred and the meat dripped fat rhythmically onto the spitting charcoal.

The day was mostly done around three in the afternoon, just as the wintry sun started to hide behind puffy clouds, and the turkey was cooked through, its meat threatening to fall off the bones. The olive pickers—including the exhausted Algis, who had exercised muscles he hadn't known he possessed—gathered around me and my barbecue like moths around a flame.

Erato and Arete, as the women of the group, set out a copious picnic on a makeshift table, with pre-baked dandelion pies, homemade goat cheese, steamed vegetables doused with olive oil and lemon, and crusty bread to accompany my expertly roasted turkey.

Niko would have preferred if the women had taken over all the food-serving chores, but he tolerated my turkey carving since it had been I who had roasted it. Many bottles of wine were fetched from secret satchels, and I was even allowed to just sip mine and enjoy it since this was a working lunch and not anyone's name-day party.

The meal ended with a dessert of tiny clementines freshly picked by Erato from trees at the edge of the olive grove. They were a special treat as they were among the very few that had escaped the frost of the big snowstorm.

The women got busy wrapping up the lunch leftovers,

while the younger men returned to their olive work before darkness set in. Niko stayed with me to finish the wine with the last of the cheese.

"This way of life is nearing its end," he mused. "I'm not unduly sad, because I'll never give up my olives, and I'll continue to do what I've always done and what my parents did. But there are lots of others who are selling their heritage to outsiders, to Europeans, for those precious euros, so that more hotels can be built. It's as if there is no end to the people who want to come here in August, and no limit to the sacrifice of our traditions to accommodate their vacation plans." He took a chunk of cheese in his hand and smelled it. "I had a taste of a goat cheese from France. Arete brought it back from one of her trips home. To impress me. Well, it didn't impress me at all. Not at all. It smelled of nothing. Then I found out that the goats who gave the milk for that cheese live on a farm and eat feed out of a box. My goats live on the hill and graze on herbs. Once hotels are built on all our hills, then our goats will have to eat from the same boxes, and our cheese will also smell of nothing." He smiled and dropped the cheese into his mouth. He shut his eyes and savoured the many perfumes of the herbs his goats had grazed on.

I helped myself to some cheese and ate it quickly. In this rapidly changing world it's imperative to act with alacrity. For all I knew some European's bulldozers could sweep down, nip the last of the heirloom cheese out of my hand, and proceed to put up a flimsy hotel right where I was sitting.

Part III

The Passion

Chapter 12

The Project

I am a handy-challenged person. I'm not talking technology—in that domain I'm beyond hopeless, I'm prehistoric. If the functioning of a device depends on electricity, for me it works strictly by magic. If it stops working, then as far as I am concerned it's dead and can be resuscitated only by a magician (read: repairman).

No, no. Forget technology. I'm talking ordinary, everyday construction and renovation chores: hammering, sawing, drywalling, tiling—any and all tasks that require the use of a tool, native intelligence, and/or dexterity. For me these are battlegrounds fraught with danger and insurmountable hardships. Around them I'm not only a drone, I'm a nuisance. To tackle the simplest such job is to invite indigestion, and normally leads to exacerbation of the original problem.

It was therefore oxymoronic, not to mention a pain in the neck, that I should have become an essential player in the mother of all renovations: the reopening of an abandoned restaurant on the beach outside Plakiás. Greek construction on its own carries a certain amount of risk and depends on luck. To combine its vagaries with my own incompetence was to court disaster.

I didn't undertake this task voluntarily. I was thrust into it, persuaded that I didn't have all that many options. Theo had disappeared. I had called him on his cell phone, leaving many messages that he did not return. I had tried several "emergency" numbers he had left me, and finally I had reached someone who informed me that Theo had taken off to an undisclosed location—no, not a cemetery—and that he had left indications he would remain incommunicado until further notice. Now even the remotest possibility of working with him had been erased.

I had reached the stage of "get involved in something, or else," and the "something" sprang up spontaneously during a dinner of Thai-style chicken curry and rice that Algis and I hosted in our room towards the end of January.

It was a sweetly warm evening, full of the leftover joy of an entire week of summer-like sun and gentle breeze, the so-called *alkionides meres* (halcyon days) that halcyon, the great sea-calming bird, accords midwinter Greece to soothe the natives and grant them a short reprieve from adverse meteorology.

The evening was so silken that we served our meal on the balcony under a three-quarter moon, the better to evoke the provenance of our chosen cuisine. The curry itself was close to the real thing, courtesy of the Thai essentials in Theo's Christmas package. Thus I had been able to melt imported curry paste—composed of lethal chilies, dried shrimps, lemongrass, galangal root, and delightfully rotted garlic—in authentic coconut milk, with real *nam pla* (fish sauce), lemon juice (instead of tamarind juice), and sugar, much in the method taught to me by Wandee Young when she and I had worked on our Thai cookery book. The only important item I was missing was fresh coriander, a stranger to Greece, but it was adequately replaced by intensely flavourful local parsley.

Our guests were the Swedish couple, Olaf and Elsa, and the French-African duo, Jean-Louis and Theresa, happily minus all their Greek-speaking, unruly but lovable offspring, whom they had left behind in the care of babysitters. The chicken curry was a great success, explosive with its multiple exotic tastes and flavours unavailable anywhere on Crete, and supremely welcome to our guests' spice-deprived palates.

Over coffee, the four of them—who had been hinting during dinner that they had something important to discuss—started to talk at once, in the manner of all Greeks, even honourary ones, when excited. And slowly, out of the hubbub, I began to get the idea.

What they were saying was that the four of them had decided to start a business for the tourist season, and had toyed with various sorts of enterprises—car rental, a souvenir shop, even daycare for tourist kids—finally settling on the inevitable: a Restaurant. None of them had the slightest experience in that field, and therefore not the least idea of what was involved. However, they all had vast experience eating out, paying good money for little bits of food, and they imagined that being on the receiving end of those restaurant bills would make for a nice change, like being issued a licence to print money.

They had already, and behind my back, recruited Algis—who espoused the idea enthusiastically—because he did know something about the business, having had to occasionally cook professionally during photographic dry spells. He had been lucky to always work in successful establishments that functioned smoothly and profitably for reasons he was oblivious to, since he had never had cause to leave the confines of the kitchen.

There they were, five restaurant hopefuls, only one of whom had ever spent more than an hour at a time in one, ready to make the big leap, looking to me to join them. They proudly announced that the project was well under way, with finances from their pooled resources. They had found a prime location and had signed a lease. They grudgingly conceded that their money was "just enough," that the place needed "a bit of work," and that, okay, it wasn't really in the middle of the action, only "close enough," but they had at least worked out a "really good deal" with the landlord.

There were many reasons why they needed me. As a Greek, I would be able to deal with the locals. As a food savant, I could help them with their menu. As a chef, I would cook in the kitchen until the staff I was to train could take over and continue under my casual supervision. And as a past restaurant owner, I could show them how to set up the business. In return, they would make me a full profit-sharing partner even though I wouldn't have to invest a penny or work all that hard after it was all set up and clicking.

I laughed and told them to forget it. I had been involved in far too many restaurants in my life to ever agree to work with anyone except seasoned professionals such as Theo. I had especially sworn off working with rank amateurs since my last entanglement some ten years earlier, which had ended with my partners and me in fisticuffs over stupid issues such as the exact spicing of the meatloaf and whether one busboy or two could handle a workload that required at least three. Our physical fight was followed by a long and costly court battle, which benefited none of us but made our lawyers quite a bit richer.

They took turns badgering, pleading, and convincing me, using Algis's call to "passion," promising absolute devotion to my judgments, never to contradict me capriciously, to make me the boss. But I stood my ground. They hoisted several carrots in front of my nose, irrelevancies like fame, fortune, and a sense of true belonging in Crete, a foothold in my own culture, an enterprise to give meaning to my purposeless existence, the money to subsidize my twilight years. They promised me everything except cash on the line, something they couldn't do since they needed every penny of their puny capital to get the business off the ground. But even that rather concrete something would not have swayed me.

What did win me over—such a simple thing, but the key to a Greek's heart—was flattery. In the heat of the discussion we had neglected to clear off the table completely, and the tureen of curry, whose leftover sauce was now cold and a touch congealed, had remained in the middle of the table. Olaf and Theresa particularly, but the others too, had not been able to contain themselves and had been dipping into it with their fingers until there was nothing left.

"This was the best curry I've ever had," exclaimed Olaf. "And back home I go out for curry at least twice a week."

"Me too!" echoed Theresa. "And I have been known to eat curry almost every day. Haven't I, *cheri?*" she asked her husband rhetorically.

"It's the best, no question," concurred Jean-Louis. Then he lit up in the manner of a cartoon character with a lightbulb over its head. "Hey! That's what we cook! Curries. That's our menu!"

"That's a fantastic idea," chimed Elsa.

"That was my idea," complained Algis, as if left out.

"It's true, I remember you saying that," agreed Olaf. "And now that we tasted his curry, I am with you 110 per cent."

"We will call it Byron's Curry-House. We will name our restaurant after you," proclaimed Theresa generously.

"All you have to do is teach us how to make the curries," said Jean-Louis. "Surely you can do that!"

"And we'll cut you in on the action," added Algis.

"Yes. We will," Olaf said cautiously.

"Not a full share," interjected Jean-Louis, "but a good share."

"Yes. A good share!" insisted Algis, betraying his allegiances.

They all stopped talking at once, and looked at me expectantly. They needed me, there was no doubt. I let several pregnant moments elapse. Then I burst out laughing. They laughed too, unsure why.

"If I were to be involved—" I paused. "I say 'if'—then I'd have to be involved totally." I paused again. "And I'd want my full share for the amount of work you discussed, and you never come to me for money. I'm a non-investing equal partner, with specific duties. And if you put all that in writing . . . then I say yes."

They didn't hesitate a moment. Out came the *raki*, and little glasses were filled to the brim. They picked up their glasses in toasting mode and waited for me. I raised mine, and we clinked.

"*Aspro pato!*" they cried in unison. "To Byron's Curry-House!"

We drank the *raki*, bottoms up for them and a meaningful sip for me, and the deal was set. And that's how I found myself the very next morning, a sunny paradisiacal start to another halcyon late-January day in Crete, sitting opposite

Kirios Petros, owner of the premises that my newly formed partnership had rented. The intended purpose of the meeting was to finalize the plans and schedule for the upcoming renovations, Greek to Greek.

Aside from being reno-incompetent, I also suffer from CTS (construction trauma syndrome), a particular disease of my own whose chief symptom is a relentlessly upset stomach during the entire duration of a building project, its only cure a steady diet of Maalox Plus in its discreet, chewable tablet form.

I had popped a pill when I had seen just how far out of the centre of Plakiás the place was. And another when I had looked at the damaged, obviously leaky roof, the diseased plumbing and mangled electrical wiring, and even the floor, which had ample evidence of Crete's edible greens growing out of its generous cracks.

I took a third antacid upon meeting Mister Petros, who preferred to be called Pete, one of those hardened Greeks who had jumped ship at sixteen with all of twenty dollars to his name in Providence, Rhode Island, and had proceeded to work his butt off in restaurants and gambling dens—and God knows where else—and in his late forties had returned to Crete to bury his father, inherit the family properties, and act the king rat.

A shyster in the making, if not in fact, Pete, who had once been handsome and a ladies' man, was now bloatedly overweight, flatulent, and unspeakably arrogant. Upon reading through the lease I had found out just how really "good" the deal my guys had signed with him was.

The rent was about half the going rate of central Plakiás locations, but to make up for it Pete had extracted 20 per cent of the gross of the future restaurant's sales. My partners had understood that he was to get that same percentage of the net profits, which in itself was exorbitant, and I had come prepared to negotiate that down. Twenty per cent of the gross sales was sheer madness, as it usually represents the entire profit of a successful restaurant. In effect we would all be investing money and time, and then working for him.

All this was on top of having to rebuild his place at our expense. To make things truly ridiculous, Pete had got them to agree to hand over the construction budget to him so that he could hire people he trusted and have his valuable building restored according to his own standards.

This last bit was equivalent to burning our money since we would have no guarantee that the work would finish before the funds did. It was the stupidest arrangement I had ever heard of, and apparently it was based on a total trust of Pete, instilled in Jean-Louis and Olaf over a long night of *raki* drinking prior to signing.

Now much as I hate being part of a construction site, I revel in the haggling of a good negotiation, where, I learned long ago, he who is underestimated always wins. Pete was obviously assuming that I was as much of a sucker as the rest of my team, and we had barely started sipping our get-acquainted coffee when he lunged into his concerns about our money: he wanted all of the renovation budget up front, not in two halves as had been proposed. This way, were he so inclined, he could easily fix up this restaurant while he bankrupted us, and then operate the business himself.

I dropped another Maalox, took a deep breath, and drew the signed lease out of my pocket. I smiled sweetly, and proceeded to tear the document neatly in half. Pete's eyes bulged, his face flushed, and he passed some evil-smelling wind.

"This deal stinks," I said to him in Greek, even though we had been speaking English.

"I have real copy! They sign!! They love me and they trust me!!! I deal them good," he spluttered, showering me with half-chewed potato chips, droplets of coffee, and chipped English sentences.

"Kirie Petro mou," I placated him. "The waters of the bay will have to freeze over before these people make any money out of this restaurant. You made an excellent deal. You're a very smart man."

"You think so?" he said, no longer in English, and smiled.

"I can also tell you're very sensitive. An aesthete. A romantic." I peered at him. "I bet you're a poet. You write *mantinades*, don't you?" An easy guess since everyone in Crete writes *mantinades*, plus I'd noticed a notebook under his other papers.

Pete opened his swollen eyelids in wonderment. "You must be the most perceptive *xenos* on the island."

"I'm not a *xenos*. My great-grandparents were from Crete," I lied. "I'd love to hear your poetry." The fourth Maalox had finally settled me. I was ready for anything.

"You're in for a treat. These verses are better than the *Iliad*, maybe even the *Odyssey*. And I'm famous for my recitations." He opened his notebook and recited endless rhyming couplets in a melodious but pretentious singsong rhythm. His themes were Unrequited Love (his own), Grief (his own), Corruption (of others), and Thirsty Flowers (who knows).

I listened respectfully, patiently. I applauded, I exclaimed, I nodded my head appreciatively and knowingly for over an hour until my neck hurt, but I never let him know how trite and repetitive I found his poetry, not even after the last refrain had been recited, and I finally had him where I wanted him.

He was so mellow and wistful, so grateful to have had a receptive, knowledgeable audience, that when I turned the conversation back to the "deal," poet to poet, fat man to fat man, he listened, because I didn't give him much of a choice. I told him that the whole business was off unless he reconsidered and offered us fairer terms.

To wit: same rent as before, but only 10 per cent of the profits as bonus, instead of the ludicrous 20 per cent of the gross. As for the renovations, we would definitely seek his approval of the plans and hire people he trusted. But we would control our own budget and spend the money as needed. Also, even though we would pay up front for all the repairs to the building ourselves, we would expect some money back from him for structural repairs, to be paid out of his 10 per cent profit share once the profits became substantial.

It was the best deal he could get, and he knew it. And it was a much better deal than I would have offered him had there not been a far worse deal already signed and sealed.

Pete peered at me out of the slits between his puffy cheeks and eyelids. I had no idea if he was poised to shoot me or simply to sit on my face and gas me to death. Instead, he fished among his documents, found the one-sided lease, and tore it in half as I had done with mine earlier. He added the torn pages on top of mine.

"For the fire," he suggested, and laughed out loud. "It was such a good deal, wasn't it?"

"The best," I reassured him.

Pete set up *raki* in little glasses and pointed to them. "Let's drink to our new deal," he sighed. I picked up my glass, clinked his, and downed the contents without a word.

"One condition," he said.

"Anything," I agreed without hesitation.

"Of all your partners, you're the only one I trust completely. Not only are you some sort of Greek, you're also fatter than me, and this makes me comfortable with you. So I'm putting you in charge of the workers, so that I don't have to do it. You'll come here every day, and you'll watch them and make them work instead of loafing off. Then every evening you report to me. By phone is okay. We put this in writing into the contract. If you miss even a single day, even if you're sick, then the whole deal is dead, and all of you go home, great-grandparents from Crete or no great-grandparents from Crete. Understood?"

Chapter 13

The Blessing

It took several days to smooth out the new contract, particularly the clause about Pete's repayment for some of the structural work. He had, since our handshake, reconsidered that bit, reasoning that the work was needed solely for the purposes of the renter and that therefore the renter should pay for all of it. Our argument that it was his building that was being rebuilt and that normally when one rents a store to conduct business in it one has the right to expect that the store should have proper walls, roof, and floor didn't get us very far.

He finally relented when I pointed out that he would be the owner of a solid building out of the deal, paid for partly by us but belonging entirely to him, to re-rent at a higher rate after we had served our last curry. This, of course, had been the case all along, though it had its pitfalls since there would be wear and tear on the building during our time in it, but I presented the facts as such a revelation—crafty me!—that he nodded greedily, as if he were getting something for nothing.

That final hurdle out of the way, the new deal was signed to the accompaniment of as many bottles of *raki* as the original deal had inspired. If nothing else, we were all getting properly soused during the wheeling and dealing.

The next day, a warm February 1, we were invited to our newly acquired premises to meet Pete's fabled workers and get the ball rolling so that the place could be ready by mid-March, the start of the early tourist season, when the relative warmth of the Greek spring draws winter-weary northern Europeans, looking to defrost their iced behinds.

The partners, their children, Algis, and I arrived bright and early at eight o'clock, dressed in our festive best, with Elsa and Olaf in matching Norwegian bright red cardigans and Theresa splendid in a silver and gold djellaba, opened in the front to reveal a sapphire blue silk dress.

Also in silks were Pete and his Hellenized American wife Thelma, known as Mrs. Pete; they were already there, waiting for us. With them was a young priest in flowing, austerely black robes, who answered to the highly Byzantine name of Theocritos, and who was tending to the incense-burning brazier with nervous, staccato movements. The non-Greeks had no way of knowing this, but I saw right away that we were to have an *ayasmo*, a holy blessing, a ceremony without which no Greek enterprise is advised to begin work.

"I'm glad you're here," confided Mrs. Pete. "We were about to start the *ayasmo* without you. The priest is in a great hurry; he has three funerals today, all those people who got *laima* and *stoithoi* during the snows."

"Everyone gather around the entrance, but no one going in," shouted Pete in English. "No one before the priest finishing the *ayasmo*. And after, wait! Okay? Must go in the special way, or we are having the lots of trouble!"

The partners were amused, and I was happy that none of

them laughed. I didn't so much believe in the *ayasmo* as fear the consequences of its misfiring. I figured that one either stays strictly clear of the mumbo-jumbo or does it by the book. It's not that I was superstitious, only Greek.

The priest, a touch devilish with his jet-black beard, his tall, lean figure, and his incomprehensible prayers accompanied by much incense, took his sweet time with the blessing, though he was meant to be in such a hurry. I guessed that he was trying to give Pete his money's worth, chanting all thirty-three psalms of the *ayasmo*, until all of us, and especially the children, were on the verge of fainting—which could also have been the result of all the incense.

The essential prayers at long last over, the priest entered the edifice right foot first as stipulated by the rules of *podariko* (first step); untold catastrophes would result if one led with the left foot. He proceeded to bless the interior, incensing and chanting each corner, beginning with the eastern.

The ritual now required that the rest of us enter the building, always with the right foot first, and in my case, as a Greek Orthodox, while crossing myself. Pete fixed his eyes on the door stoop, much like a foot-fault umpire in tennis, to ensure correct *podariko* observance, not trusting heathen brains to take it seriously—or worse, not to left-foot it on purpose just to be funny and un-Greek.

Despite his vigilance, Pete missed the dart-like dash of the youngest Swedish child, the angelic but precocious three-year-old Gustav, who rushed his mother Elsa's entrance, causing her to temporarily lose her balance and come in left foot first. Pete was speechless.

"Oh, my God," moaned Mrs. Pete. "What are we to do now?"

"Thass it!" screamed Pete. "Deal is off! Forget it." He was exasperated. "The left foot from the partner-lady. This—this—this is the abomination!"

The priest rushed out from the interior. "Wait. The child. How old?"

"Only three," pleaded Olaf, shielding his youngster from the collective wrath of the assembly. "Barely born! How could he know how important this is?"

"This is true. He's not responsible. He's too young and innocent," declared the priest.

"But it was the mother who walked in left-footed," whimpered Pete.

"But he caused it," reasoned Elsa while hugging young Gustav, who had broken out in tears to obviate the punishment for whatever he had done wrong.

"That is correct," agreed the priest, and he sang two psalms of appeasement just for insurance.

"Left foot is devil's foot. Not happy me!" Pete was not convinced, but he was outvoted. He went out to the courtyard to sulk.

"Let's hope nothing bad comes of this," warned Mrs. Pete as she exited to calm her husband.

"I am satisfied," said the priest, and exited also to join the Petes, leaving us alone to ponder the metaphysics of the situation.

"Nonsense," scoffed Jean-Louis. "I never heard such nonsense. Left foot. Right foot. *Merde!*"

"Oh, I believe it," said Theresa, subdued. "We have much more than this back home, and it always comes true."

"So what do we do?" asked Elsa desperately. "Abandon ship? Forget all about it? Are we asking for trouble?"

"Maybe not," Theresa placated. "I know some powerful antidotes for things like these. I'll call my mother to make sure. We'll do something. Don't worry."

We stepped out into the sunlight, hangdog and confused. A bad omen at the very first moment of our business. Pete and his wife were sitting at the balcony table handing the priest various samples of their own produce—olive oil, cheese, live chickens, wine, and an envelope thick with cash. In our opinion the priest had more than earned his booty: he had managed to soothe Pete, who was now smiling radiantly, tiny eyes glinting.

The priest left, and all of us sat at the table to find out what came next. It was the usual *raki*, but this time catered by Mrs. Pete with all manner of ultra-Grecian snacks. Mini dandelion-cheese pies in homemade olive oil crust, snails in tomato-wine sauce, fried salt cod with potato-garlic dip, and a deep pot of labour-intensive vine leaves stuffed with rice, onion, and pine nuts. How a woman of a New England Irish background had seamlessly picked up Greek cookery can be explained only by the power of love.

Mrs. Pete, who at fifty-three was just older than her husband, was a petite replica of him, complete with her own pot belly and puffy cheeks that invaded her eye sockets. She was devotedly and furiously in love with Pete, and, as I was to learn later, had beaten a Lefkogeian divorcee to within an inch of her life for daring to suggestively touch lover-boy on his pudgy arm for one whole second.

Luckily for us, we were not in the least interested in seducing her husband, so Mrs. Pete relaxed and, unlike a truly Greek wife, she had enough *raki* to laugh ringingly at the antics of young Gustav. Pete himself quickly became jolly and thought better of scolding his wife publicly, probably making a mental note to have a row with her later.

Jean-Louis, an architecture school dropout, had drawn up detailed plans for the proposed interior. In reality, since this was meant as a tourist hangout to operate only in the warm months, the interior was academic and only really useful for its kitchen, toilets, and storage space; all the seating would be set up outdoors facing the sea. Nevertheless, Jean-Louis's meticulous plans for a cozy restaurant with an elaborate kitchen drew applause.

To compound the unnecessary and expensive plans for the interior, Olaf and Theresa next presented their joint design for its decor, combining Scandinavian detached simplicity with African immediacy and warm colours. This was much lauded by Mrs. Pete, while Pete shook his head, dubious that Olaf would be able to find the zinc bar, the pinpoint spots for his lighting scheme, or the Russian maple for his trims and tables. He was also sure that Theresa would despair of locating her preferred ornaments and that both of them would inevitably settle, like everyone else in Crete, for whitewashed adobe with Greek artifacts and ugly tungsten bulbs inside knit lampshades.

Algis stepped up to the podium with a complex concept for the outdoor space, one of his specialties. It featured an extension of his rock sculptures, to be placed inside and around uprooted trees that had come undone during the storms and that could now be claimed from roadsides. He had a mock-up of his concept, and we could all appreciate its brilliance, but we couldn't help noticing that to fully dignify it would mean surrendering most of the space available for those all-important beachfront tables.

Elsa's contribution was the most tangible, and the most welcome to Pete since it had to do with money. A working accountant who was supporting her family by doing clients' taxes back in Sweden via the Internet, Elsa had formulated the financial side of the business, with a detailed study of the renovation budget based on figures she had gleaned from Pete as well as from major contractors in the area.

Pete perused the figures quickly. "You are the smart cookie." He nodded his approval. "You have the money, where?"

"In the bank," smiled Elsa as if to a slow accountancy student.

"Good. Now go to your bank and get the cash, and give it all to the Byron."

"Why!?" Elsa was shocked.

"Because workers get the cash every night, after one day work. But they do not want the cash from the woman. It must be from the man, and it must be the Byron, because I want it like that." Pete had spoken, and he didn't seem willing to be swayed, but Elsa tried anyway: "I think this very not good. We change. We pay only on Saturday for one week. In cash, like you want." She articulated this in a Greek of her own manufacture, the result of one year of determined Viking self-instruction.

"Is not your business to think stupid things like that," interrupted Pete in English. "We pay the cash every day, like always, and the man, the Byron, give the cash. Not you. Okay?" Pete smiled drunkenly, and it was settled. Elsa helped herself to a stuffed vine leaf and a shot of *raki*, obviously plotting revenge. One wins arguments with accountants at one's own peril.

Before long, the various workers started to drive in for a

look-see at the worksite, and to meet us. First off was Spiros, the operator of the heavy equipment that we would need to reopen the driveways and cart off all the unseemly debris that had accumulated around the building over the two years of its disuse. Spiros was a quiet, burly man, but he was no ordinary hard hat. I noticed a blue notebook open on the passenger side of his vehicle. On the pages were two-line writings, obviously *mantinades*. Another poet!

His entrance was followed by the three Yannises. Big Yannis, a macho fop who knew he was good-looking, was the master mason. The others were his assistant, Little Yannis, an unassuming youth with empty, dolorous eyes, and Water Yannis, the plumber, who Pete had told us was a family man, father of four at the age of twenty-six, and terminally religious, crossing himself and secretly stealing glances at the sky, praying under his breath more or less constantly.

"Should've been a priest," snickered Pete, "but there's more money in water."

Raki and snacks were served, but no business was discussed until the last trio of workers made their appearance, casually, half an hour later. The leader of this contingent was Aristoteles, nicknamed Onassis, a magician of wiring, just the man to set up our power in a country that agrees with me that all matters electric are wizardry.

Behind Onassis were the final two, Stavros and Pavlos, two interchangeable fellows, tiler-painter-carpenters, timid to the point of invisibility, a condition that malicious gossip was to later inform me was natural since they were suspected of being a gay couple. There appears to be no end to Greeks' vehement homophobia, a vestige from their Moslem conquerors, who superimposed their own fears of sexual expression on a nation whose Ancients legitimized and glorified homosexuality. Whatever the cause of the persecution, it is prudent for gays in Greece to maintain a low profile.

The most recent arrivals were duly served their *raki* and food, and then all seven workers were led en masse to the building, Elsa following on their heels. Pete didn't need to warn any of these Greeks to enter with the right foot, but he waited on the stoop to watch just in case.

Elsa made a big show of entering with her right foot, which must in itself have been an affront to the sacrament of *ayasmo*, because Pete crossed himself three times before entering left foot first, explaining over his shoulder that *podariko* refers only to a person's initial entrance.

The work crew examined the site excitedly, everyone talking at once, asking Pete questions, drowning his answers in their own noise. Elsa watched in amazement, justifiably wondering how anyone could understand what was to be done if no one listened. She had no hope of decoding the communication methods of a querulous, know-it-all culture.

Pete led them out of the building and introduced me as their crew boss. He unnecessarily reminded them to be at work at 7:30 sharp, and dismissed them rudely, as if they were errant children. They filed out, not at all cowed, waving cheerful farewells to all of us and casting slightly respectful glances at me.

"You'll have to be rough with them," Pete instructed me in loud Greek, while they were still within earshot. "I'm counting on you to make them work hard. You have to shout, and it helps if you can be angry at them, even if you don't feel like it, even if they're working flat out."

"I promise to whip them into shape with the utmost ferocity," I said, laughing.

"I'm not joking," scowled Pete.

"No, he's not!" echoed Mrs. Pete.

"But why did you tell all of them to be here tomorrow?" asked Elsa.

"Well, to work." Pete shrugged.

"Half of them will have nothing to do until the structural work is finished," said Elsa.

"You'd be surprised," answered Pete.

"So will you. As it happens I haven't allowed for seven salaries per day. Take another look at my budget. I have them coming in when they're needed, according to standard renovation procedures."

"Standard? What is the standard?" Pete mouthed the word like it tasted of rotten onions. "This is the Crete. They are now hired to do the job. Like the team. That's how the work is here. They can't wait. They need the cash. If we say don't come tomorrow, tomorrow they get one other job, and pouf, they are gone. Are you understanding now?"

"I understand, but there is nothing I can do. We'll have to take that chance. If not we'll run out of money before we can finish the work."

"How can you run out of money? You are Swedish!"

Elsa laughed bitterly. "Not anymore. Now I'm Greek. I live here. So do Jean-Louis and Theresa. We are all Greeks now. And we have as little money as all other Greeks. Barely enough."

"Really?" Pete seemed incredulous.

"We told you this at the start," said Elsa patiently.

"I didn't believe you."

"Well, it's true." Elsa held Pete's eyes and didn't blink until he averted his gaze in discomfort. Thus, he let her think that she had him, to ease the tension and lose what was at best a moot point. In reality the work would evolve as it was meant to, but Elsa need not yet know.

She was such a fearless negotiator, I wondered how she had failed to catch the iniquities of the original lease. Long-range planning was obviously her weak point, and she was valiantly trying to make up for it now.

"Okay, okay," smiled Pete good-naturedly. "I agree. Tomorrow all of them. But after tomorrow, only as we need them. And if they run out of the job, it is your big fault."

"If they run out on us, we'll get in there ourselves and finish the work," said Olaf, as if this idea had not already been roundly vetoed by Pete.

"Not allowed. Not even think the thought. None of you, only the Byron allowed here. I told you already, for God's sake. Only the professionals."

Jean-Louis's Gallic temper, fuelled by his consumption of half a litre of *raki*, flared. "I'm not an amateur! And it doesn't take such professionals to build a brick shack. *Mon dieu*, you talk as if we're renovating Chartres Cathedral!"

Pete clamped his jaws shut and folded his arms across his chest. He punctuated his position with an audible fart, a penetrating gust of rotting onions from the previous night's delicious rabbit *stiffado*.

"Have another *hortopitaki*," urged Mrs. Pete, brandishing the platter of dandelion mini-pies menacingly in Jean-Louis's general direction.

Chapter 14

Moving Heaven and Earth

In practice, Elsa's carefully staggered work schedule was totally unenforceable. The crew followed an idiosyncratic path that was based on random occurrences, where the services of the plumber and the electrician could be required even during ostensibly unrelated operations like moving rocks and dead trees away from the back garden or repairing the bricks of the balcony parapets.

The whole place was a mess of old electrical wiring and rusted plumbing pipes, which had been patched into and diverted repeatedly, and which would have best been ripped out and a new network installed. But that was not how our guys did things. For them it seemed sacrilege to throw out anything that was already in place, even if reviving it meant much greater expense and labour.

The only employees who were not in the least necessary at this early stage of the work were the finishers, Stavros and Pavlos, but they showed up every day anyway, in matching all-white starched coveralls. They did odd jobs to help out the others, nothing much really, but they lined up for their full cash payment every evening nonetheless.

Elsa did some quick recalculations, her victory over Pete having been short-lived, and finally had to reach deeper into her own family's resources, as well those of Jean-Louis, Theresa, and Algis, to raise the additional money that was needed, ruining her "we're as poor as all other Greeks" credibility permanently.

I steered clear of all the haggling and fundraising, not only because it didn't concern me as a non-investing partner, but also because I had my hands full waking up all too early every morning, coping with my construction trauma syndrome, and maintaining the upper hand in the power struggle with the workers and with Pete.

Luckily, I never had to challenge anyone to toil harder and to do things my way—I had no idea how speedily and with what means anything needed to be done in the first place. And, as it turned out, all the workers were indeed conscientious and professional; in a very few days the smoke began to clear, and even I could see where all the confusion of mortar and brick and piping and wire was leading.

In a mere three days, they had cleared out the rubbish, knocked away suspect walling, torn off errant vine branches that had grown through windows and onto the roof, and removed broken glass and rotting wood: we were ready to proceed with the fortification of the walls, and then fix the roof.

Water Yannis's wife and their oldest son, a spry eight-year-old named Lefteris, short for Eleftherios ("the free one"), brought us lunch. As the only wife in the mostly unmarried crew, it had become her duty to feed all the men. She had made a big pot of pork and wild greens stew in the traditional

way, overcooked to meltingness, seasoned only with a sprinkle of black pepper and free-hand salt.

As usual, she had set us up under the plane tree in the front
garden. The sun shone its unseasonable best, and the tiny
breeze carried the happy sounds and sweet smells of pre-
empted winter in intermittent gusts. Spiros took his lunch to
his truck to eat it there while he composed his next *mantinada*; the rest of us settled on rocks and broken bits of para-
pet with our plates.

Little Lefteris had brought his lyre. He had been chosen to
attend the special music school in Réthymno, where gifted
youngsters were given scholarships. "They pay for the bus
every day to take him there, and a taxi to bring him back at
lunch," boasted his mother, while his father sent several
urgent prayers to the Almighty, presumably to bless his son's
musical aptitude.

It turned out that prayers were redundant. The boy played
like an angel, like a Pan of the mountains, with clear, lingering
notes that spoke of the rich history of Crete, notes that
bounced playfully off the wavelets of the shimmering sea.

Onassis the electrician listened with half an ear and with
palpable displeasure. During a break in the music he stage-
whispered, loud enough for the boy to hear, "I don't know
why we waste money and time on this old stuff. No one gives
a damn for the lyre anymore. Electric guitar, yes!"

"Shut up, you!" shouted Big Yannis. "Let the boy play!"

"What did I say? I didn't say anything," exclaimed
Onassis, happy to have been of disservice.

"Play, my son," pleaded Water Yannis as the deflated Lefteris nervously packed his venerable lyre back into its silk ker-
chiefs and velvet-lined case.

"As it happens, I already know how to play the electric guitar. And I'm getting one for my name day. Isn't that so, Daddy?" Lefteris's lower jaw was perceptibly quivering, and he ran off to the beach to cry on his own.

"If this job works out, I'll get you the biggest electric guitar ever made!" shouted his father after him, and he looked up at the sky to make sure God was listening.

Onassis stood up and took his empty plate to the sink, where Mrs. Water would eventually wash it. "I just made an observation," he muttered. "And you all know I'm right!" He wandered off to have his cigarette by himself.

Little Yannis came and sat near me. "When I die," he confided, "I want them to play only lyre music. So that people cry for me the way they should."

"Aren't you a bit young to be thinking of your funeral?" I asked.

"Oh, no," said Little Yannis wide-eyed. "I've been thinking of my death since I was five. It's possibly the only thing I think about. I can't help it. I feel that the longer I live the closer I come to death. Life is the worst disease we have. Death is the only cure for life."

"Can't argue with that," I said pensively. A pessimistic assistant bricklayer had just reduced all of life to a sickness, death its only joy.

"Stop infecting Mister Byron with your morbidity," interjected Big Yannis, who had come over with a coffee for me: cold Nescafé, shaken with sugar to become the frothy Greek favourite, frappé. "Me, I'm only interested in women. That's because I drive them crazy. I don't have to do a single thing. Not move a muscle. They're drawn to me like I was fresh blood, and they were sharks."

"So how come you're not married yet," mocked Onassis,

who had forgiven himself for the irreparable damage he had caused the young musician and had sauntered back to join us.

"Limit myself to one woman!?" Big Yannis was aghast. "That would be very cruel for the rest of them, don't you think? To crush their hope that one day they'll win me and I'll be theirs. Many women live and breathe because of that one tiny possibility for supreme happiness to give meaning to their empty lives. It would be inhuman. I can't do it to them. Ever." Big Yannis had managed to say all this in total earnestness. He was not only manhood's great gift to womankind, he was also a committed humanitarian.

Stavros and Pavlos, who had eaten in total silence, finished their last bite simultaneously. They stood up in tandem to take their dishes to the washing area. I could see that they had to fight off the urge to wash up, as this would be interpreted as a homosexual trait instead of as a small gesture of thanks to Mrs. Water for bringing us our daily lunch.

I took my own plate to the sink and turned on the faucet. Instantly, Water Yannis made a yelping noise and his missus rushed to the sink. She subtly elbowed me out of the way. Not only was I the wrong gender for dishwashing, I was the crew boss.

So let's hear it for the boss! I walked down to the water's edge to breathe in the iodine in the salty air and to unwind. In any case, work was suspended until Pete and Elsa could arrive, as per their telephone instructions. Something to do with a new plan for the roof.

Soon enough, the two of them thundered in on Elsa's vintage German motorcycle, she driving in her shorts, spandex sweater, and antique aviator's goggles and he hanging on for dear life behind her, huffing, cellulite extending over both sides of the seat, probably farting.

Elsa was beaming. Pete had allowed the company to save some money by agreeing to take another look at the roof. They hoped we would be able to leave it alone, maybe just patch it up.

The workers became agitated all in one breath, including Mrs. Water and Lefteris, who had come back from the beach where he had been hitting big chords à la Keith Richards on a phantom Stratocaster. For them, not remaking the roof was twice a double-cross: it would not only deprive them of promised work days, but also jeopardize all the backbreaking renovations, and their artisans' integrity, if the roof collapsed somewhere down the line.

Those most affected by a collapsed roof would be Stavros and Pavlos, and for once they shed their timidity and found their voice. They argued vehemently with Pete, in unison and in turn, completing each other's excited complaints. They didn't let up until Pete screamed at them to shut up and started explaining: "We're here to test the roof. Elsa is going to . . . I mean, Elsa and . . . I, the two of us together, will go up on the roof and jump around. If it holds, we leave it alone. If so much as one new crack appears anywhere, we make a new roof. If it holds, we patch it, and we save some money for poor Elsa."

Poor Elsa nodded her agreement like some victorious Viking Valkyrie, stretching her magnificent long legs for all to admire. A ladder was fetched, and the two of them, the long-limbed northern blond and the chubby Greek with legs far too short and skinny to properly propel his bulk, climbed to the roof and jumped around as promised, while the rest of us cautiously stared at the ceiling underneath them.

There were already so many cracks and breaches that if

they did create new ones we wouldn't have been able to tell. They climbed back down triumphantly.

"Spread some cement on top and some on the ceiling, and we should be all right," shrugged Pete.

"One rain, and it'll leak all over," remarked Onassis knowingly.

"Put plastic underneath cement," suggested Elsa.

"That is the brilliant solution. Ah, the First World and the beautiful brains," marvelled Pete as he concentrated his gaze somewhere in the region of Elsa's bare midriff.

"We sincerely do not recommend this. Rain can penetrate plastic," declared Stavros and Pavlos in unison.

"Enough!" shouted Pete. "Now. Everybody! Back to work! We're not paying you to discuss rain." He walked away towards Elsa's motorcycle. "Make them work!" he said to me over his shoulder. "They're not worth the air they breathe unless you push them. Beat them if you have to."

Elsa and Pete sped away in a cloud of dust. I settled back under the plane tree to laze in the shade, an age-old Greek tradition. Mrs. Water packed her dishes, her son, and his belittled lyre and drove away in her three-wheeler.

The crew, having lost the roof argument, returned to work cheerfully, displaying another age-old Greek tradition: holding onto one's *kefi* despite endless adversity. They worked with gusto, paying close attention to Jean-Louis's exacting plans for the kitchen, for which German equipment had been ordered and was expected imminently. Jean-Louis had insisted that the kitchen be finished first so that the equipment could go in the moment it arrived.

They did their best with the roof, but we all knew it could never be perfect. Ever the spoilsport, Onassis proved to us how completely imperfect it really was. He took a pail of water up the ladder and emptied it on the newly refinished surface. We waited for a few minutes and sure enough, several spots of the new ceiling plaster darkened with penetrated moisture.

As a result, Onassis remade his electricity layout to include no wiring at all on the ceiling and wire only along the walls. Lacking overhead lighting would be an especial hardship in the kitchen, but we accepted it by practising yet another of the age-old Greek traditions: making do. Or, as Mick Jagger has said, "You can't always get what you want." I guess some things have no borders.

And so by Saturday at lunch, great progress was in evidence; the basic building was done and ready for its kitchen and its cosmetic work. Some outside work was still needed, including getting rid of a mound of dirt that had been pushed off the driveway on the first day and had stayed there ever since, making driving over or around it difficult for all but the largest vehicles.

Pete and Elsa appeared at two o'clock sharp, the designated mealtime, their first appearance since their mid-week divisive roof mission. This time they drove in Pete's brand new pickup truck with a couple of cases of booze: many bottles of Pete's own wine and *raki*, as well as a few of Scotch.

"Those two are becoming quite inseparable," hissed Onassis loud enough for Pete to hear and answer him with a clutch of the genitals.

Close on their heels followed Mrs. Water and all four of her children, each one as charming and obviously talented as Lefteris, who had been convinced again that his lyre was indeed a fine instrument and would probably outlive the electric guitar by a good millennium. He had brought it along in case we wanted him to play after lunch. Water Yannis greeted his family with many grateful glances up to heaven, so very thankful for their sweet presence in his life.

Mrs. Pete drove in a few seconds later in a car loaded to the gills with festive foods, including an entire lamb, meltingly baked in a wood-burning oven. The two women busied themselves laying out the goodies under the tree for all to drool over.

The lunch began as soon as the other partners and their children had trundled in. The various youngsters and the workers, including me, were invited to first digs while Pete took the partners into the building to inspect it.

"The roof, she is perfect!" exclaimed Pete, looking up in admiration.

"She leaks like an old man with a bladder problem," shouted Onassis from outside as he chomped into a succulent chop from one of Pete's own private-stock, specially fed lambs.

"The leaks only when the rains," laughed Pete, pointing at the baby blue sky and its bright sun.

"Yes. We'll be just fine," agreed Elsa smugly, neatly side-stepping Pete, who was about to hug her in celebration of the saved money.

We ate and drank for over three hours, each of us wrapped in our own dreams of the glory, money, and good times that were sure to be generated by this restaurant, which we all felt was as good as opened. Towards the end of the afternoon, with a sky reinventing itself in pastel, Pete got a phone call on his mobile. He listened without saying much, and then clicked off with a howl.

"My niece is having the shotgun wedding tomorrow. Her father, my cousin, he catch her with the baby in the belly, and she is only fifteen. The boy is sixteen, and he agree he must to ask her to marry, or else! Ha, ha. The women do the cooking all night, and we have the feast tomorrow. All, everyone, invited. We having the good time. Oh boy, wedding!!"

We raised our glasses and clinked to the happy couple-to-be. Pete cracked open the Scotch, and I took this as my cue to walk down the beach feeling a little taller. Renovation? CTS? Piece of cake.

Chapter 15

Wedding

For many centuries and until a generation ago, village weddings in Crete were arranged by the families. A highly sheltered young woman, still a teenager, would marry a young man of the same age who had been her intended since birth. If some reason—such as the untimely death of the boy, or an unscheduled recent feud between their families—obviated the wedding, then the girl would be married off to the highest bidder, regardless of his age.

Now, in the era of television and globalized lust, young people often choose their own partners, and sometimes have premarital sex. Yet modern courtships are as supervised and orchestrated as the old-fashioned ones. The families still organize the finances of the future-marrieds, and all hell still breaks loose if a young woman is jilted, especially if it can be proven that her integrity was breached during the courtship.

There was little doubt that young Sophia's sexual innocence was a thing of the past. Slim and fresh-faced, she was five months gone, and already an incongruous belly bulged from her slight, otherwise symmetrical frame. Her hasty, off-the-rack wedding dress was of skin-tight satin, white of course, pleatless and rigid in the front, accentuating the anomalous bulge. It was as if she were saying, Yes, I'm pregnant, and proud of it.

Much less proud, visibly tormented by the surprise nuptials, was the equally diminutive groom, the as-yet-beardless, pimpled Pantelis, son of the upstart Socrates, who had risen from humble beginnings in his parents' tiny grocery shop to become franchisee of the village's shiny new supermarket. "Kickback," evil tongues had hissed, angered by Socrates' co-operation with a corrupt foreign chain of supermarkets.

Sophocles, the bride's middle-middle-class farmer father, had in the past kept his distance from the suspect Socrates, along with the rest of the villagers. However, now that Fate and the caprices of human reproduction had thrust them together, and Socrates had offered his in-law-to-be top eurodollar and ample shelf space for his produce in the supermarket, the farmer and the super-grocer were locked in a permanent embrace.

The wedding might have been announced only the day before, but somehow the same two thousand guests who would have been expected to attend a well-organized event had gathered in the village square. Most of them were from neighbouring villages within fifty kilometres. The others were blood relatives who had moved away and now lived in points all over Crete, some as far as a four-hour drive away.

Our group, dressed festively, had had to drive almost two hours into the mountains to reach the village, the Petes leading the way in our six-car convoy. Neither the partners nor I had ever attended a wedding in Crete before. We were anxious that we would be intruding on festivities to which Pete and his wife were the only official invitees, while twenty-two of us tagged along.

We parked our car well outside the village, where countless other vehicles had been left in all available nooks of the road. We joined the long queue of wedding revellers filing through the village towards the source of a great deal of noise.

Finally inside the claustrophobically crowded central square, we lost all fear of intruding. This apparently typical wedding was an exuberant free-for-all with live music, a huge buffet, and much posturing by drunken armed-warrior types, dressed in all black with knee-high leather boots, flaring trousers, long-sleeved shirts, and fringed headbands.

The ceremony inside the church was finished. The couple, who had just been joined in the eyes of God and their wide-smiling parents, made their appearance on the front steps of the church. The groom was awkward in an ill-fitting black suit and badly knotted emerald green tie, still traumatized by the gun barrel he had stared into the day before. The bride was radiant in her tightly fitted satins and undisguised pregnant belly, with freshly coiffed and dyed short platinum hair to contrast with the olive of her skin and the jet black of her eyes.

The warriors sprang to action upon seeing them, and like *Star Trek*'s Klingons, whipped out their pistols and their rifles to fire many loud rounds of live bullets into the sky, butting each other on the shoulders in jubilation, laughing menacingly, and overwhelming the square with the stink of their gunpowder.

"How barbaric," sneered Onassis, who sensed that I enjoyed his sardonic observations. "Next thing we know they'll be playing soccer with the head of a ram for a ball."

"It is these customs that define you, that make Crete as great and unusual as it is. You'd be miserable if they were lost," I said.

"Maybe miserable, but at least not embarrassed. I'm mortified that Elsa and everyone are watching this. It's as if we were barbarians or something." Onassis took a deep drag on his cigarette. "This whole wedding is a sham. What does that stupid boy know about being a husband? Look at him! I bet he still shits his pants."

I looked at him, and sadly I found no grounds on which to contradict Onassis. The groom seemed on the verge of tears, or at least in dire need of the potty. "What would you have them do? Force the girl to have an abortion? Or to have the baby out of wedlock? Which?"

"Either of those choices is better for her than this. It wouldn't seem so, but we are very modern on Crete. We have the same 50 per cent divorce rate as the rest of the Western world. Those two will be divorced within five years, that's for certain, except that they will have to put up with each other and with being married during the best years of their lives. It's criminal."

Big Yannis sidled near us and interrupted our conversation. "Pretend we're talking," he said. "Three vixens from Koxaré are after me, but I don't want to talk to them. Their fathers and their fiancés are here."

I looked over. He wasn't exaggerating. Three girls, not yet twenty, absolutely marriageable, hanging on the arms of three good-looking young guys, were unabashedly staring at our master bricklayer, each one desperate for a wink or a smile. Onassis cleared his throat derisively and walked away to the buffet. Little Yannis joined us, white as a sheet as if he had just seen the Grim Reaper.

"Ten people died during January. I missed ten funerals. I didn't know. I feel so ashamed."

"It does you good to miss funerals. I'm thinking of forbidding you to ever attend another," said Big Yannis, his mind already off his ardent admirers.

"That's ten families who have a right to refuse to attend my funeral. That's close to a hundred people!" Little Yannis shed a tear for his much-diminished funeral.

Water Yannis and his family had found a table and were piously drinking toasts to the newlyweds. They waved me over, and I found my excuse to walk away from the romantic and mournful problems of the two brick Yannises.

Mrs. Water was overjoyed by the wedding. She was a big fan of love matches, having married Water Yannis when they were both teenagers in love though not officially "intended" for each other, and now being blissfully on the positive side of the 50 per cent statistic.

"The only celebration I enjoy more than a wedding is our church Ste. Papanti's name day. You know the church, don't you Kirie Byron?" she asked me. "It's the one at the entrance to Marioú, built into the rock. And all the important priests come there on that day, even the archbishop of South Crete, and they sing a long service, which you can hear and observe from the front yard. The faithful from the nearby villages attend with their entire families. And after the service, there's food for everyone, boiled goat, just like at weddings, and blessed bread, and wine. It's such a nice holiday. February second. Exactly forty days after Christmas, when the Theotokos [God-Bearer] takes her baby to be blessed at the temple, and He, though only an infant, in turn blesses old Simon, allowing the poor man to die in peace now that he has met the Messiah in the flesh."

"What a lucky man," added Water Yannis.

The partners, led by Elsa, swooped down on me and urged me to follow them. They had met the women who had worked all night to cook the massive feast, and had promised that I would interview them for a newspaper travel piece that Algis had dreamt up on the spot, without bothering to consult me. Apparently, he felt that he had finally found the "angle" he had been searching for as our story idea: "How to Cater for Thousands Overnight." He was already with them, taking pictures.

The four women, two aunts each of the bride and the groom, had worked in a makeshift outdoor kitchen behind the church, grateful that it hadn't rained. Normally shy and measured, today they were energized and voluble, adrenalin rushing, eyes crazed from lack of sleep, giving it one last push now that the bulk of the work was done and all that was left was to put out the food in stages.

The cooking had all been accomplished on army-size propane-powered burners with proportionately oversized pots of thick blackened metal. They had boiled forty goats all night until the meat softened and the boiling broth was rich and flavourful. The meat was removed from the pots to be eaten just as it was. The broth was used to cook the risotto-like *gamopilafo*, rice so redolent of goat essence it seemed ready to scamper up the hillside unless one spooned it down as quickly as possible.

On the side, they had blanched whole mountains of mixed wild greens, which they dressed with vinegar and oil as a salad. Close to ten thousand snails were stewed with herbs and white wine. Two thousand cheese pies, one per guest, were concocted out of their homemade olive oil dough and barrelfuls of sweet *myzithra* cheese. The showpiece *Chaniopita* meat pie was started but never finished for lack of time.

But they had found time to bake several not-for-eating wedding *koulouras*, decorated with symbols of fertility and happiness, hard-glazed to last the lifetimes of the happy couple.

The chefs were busy with gargantuan serving chores when I stepped into their kitchen, Algis's flash going off every two seconds as he captured them in action. All activity ceased when they saw me. Now they were ready to talk and be immortalized in a newspaper article, with their names and everything. Ah, the power of the Fourth Estate.

I listened to them with due respect, going through the paces of tape-recording their statements and taking copious notes in my little book. Frankly, however, I had reaped more of a story from merely watching them work for ten seconds than from the combined facts of their lives that they were detailing for me now.

The rest of the story came with a heaping plateful of their food: the shortgrain rice, plump and juicy yet still textured, not mushy; the chewy goat meat; the faintly bitter, perky greens; the comforting, thick-crusted cheese pie.

Overfed and slightly dizzy from all the attention, I led the partners back out to the festivities. The lyre music, amplified electronically, was fortified by the singing of the plenty-drunk guests, one enormous harmony voicing the too-human complaints of unrequited love, unreciprocated passion, unrelieved suffering. There was a long, snaking line of dancers expressing the same emotions in agile rhythmic movements.

We found Pete at the head of a large table orating to a number of his kin, the bride's side of the family. He was giving them instructions on how to deal with Socrates, the groom's father, a man who could sully them all with his suspect reputation. Mrs. Pete added little noises to punctuate her husband's proclamations.

"Yes, we shop at his store, but we accept no unnecessary discounts," Pete was cautioning. "We invite him to major holidays, but we leave him out of our name days. On the street, we limit ourselves to friendly salutations, but no cheek kissing, and no lengthy conversations. We accept invitations to his house, but we call up at the last moment and cancel due to illness or whatever until he gets the message and stops inviting us. And we never, never get drunk or sing *mantinades* with him. Our Sophocles, in his role as the father-in-law, must have the kind of contact that he must. But the rest of us will show restraint, even coolness, without, if possible, offending him."

He should've been a diplomat, I thought. And just as I was ready to discount him as a big talker with no real power, he did something that amazed and even scared me. He gave some sort of blunt signal, and all his relatives stood up from the table as one to make room for all of us to sit down.

Once the changeover had occurred and Pete was in charge of his business group instead of his relatives, he abandoned Greek for his own particular brand of English. He talked only of me, in the most flattering terms possible. He praised my performance as crew boss, my know-how, my focus, my authority, the respect in which the workers held me, and the kudos I deserved, because, he said, it was I and I alone who was responsible for the excellent progress of the work in the restaurant. With the great omen of this most festive of weddings, he was convinced we would enjoy the greatest of luck, clear sailing until our opening party.

I love being praised, and I adore good omens. I put away my amazement and my fear of Pete, and I replaced them with unswerving devotion bordering on love.

Chapter 16

Smooth Sailing

The widows were out early this morning to gather their wild greens. Collecting greens has rules all its own. During the rainy season, the greens shoot out at the slightest sun and can be picked at any time of the day. But when the rains stop, they glean their water from the night dew and are at their best soon after sunrise.

The women, somber in their permanent all-black mourning-wear, were bending in a lush green field airbrushed with buttercup-yellow flowers. The widows' large black behinds wavered side to side in slow, determined gyrations. The picking is in the hand movements: a shuffle through the ground foliage to uncover the moist, tender leaves, a deft incision just above the roots to claim the plant from the soil, a left-handed transfer of the prize into the bag while the right hand is already searching for the next.

A single widow can clear an entire field of its greens, safe in the knowledge that the alchemy of nature will replace the plenty the next day. It has been calculated that there are twelve hundred edible life-sustaining greens and herbs that grow wild on Crete at different times of the year, so that the tables of the island are graced with at least one kind at all times.

Wondering if seeing so many bereaved women in one place could possibly augur well, I drove into the restaurant's driveway, my little car complaining as it struggled over the mound of dirt, which was quickly turning into a cumbersome bump. Making a mental note to have that smoothed out today, I arrived on a scene that couldn't help but bode well.

A gleaming delivery truck with French licence plates was backed up to the rear of the building, and out of it were being lowered all manner of German-built shiny kitchen gear: an imposing eight-burner stove with double ovens; three major refrigeration units, including one with a long counter space with detachable metal shelving and warm-up lights for serving the plates; a complex machine with attached sinks, the latest word in dishwashing; and smaller items such as a stand-up mixer, an extra-capacity food processor, boxes of the finest chef's knives and stainless steel cooking implements, and case upon case of professional top-of-the-line china, stemware, and cutlery.

There was a sufficient quantity of equipment and serving-ware to furnish a major restaurant in a big city. A bit of overkill for a casual curry-house on the Plakiás waterfront, but Jean-Louis had insisted on them, mostly because he could obtain them less than what ordinary things cost locally. Something to do with a contact of his in the south of France who specialized in name-brand merchandise that had recently fallen out of trucks during transport.

An oven that has been acquired at gunpoint on a European highway is no more dodgy than a wedding expedited by a similar gun in a village on Crete, and it'll cook curry a heck of a lot better. However, I immediately demanded that my name be removed from all official documents, even though the partners insisted on their right to call the place Byron's.

Legally purchased or otherwise, there was no denying the beauty of this equipment. We would have the finest kitchen in the area, its equal not to be found outside Crete's jet-set complexes.

"They'll be willing to pay admission just to visit this kitchen," I remarked to Jean-Louis, who had driven in at top speed when he had heard the truck had come. He missed my sarcasm—he was too busy caressing his new toys, relishing the industrial sheen.

"A good machine is as pleasing to the touch as a beautiful woman," he said with Gallic sensuality. Then he reconsidered: "Don't tell Theresa I said that. She'd cut me off for a week." He winced at the mere possibility of such deprivation.

The workers rolled in just as the delivery truck was backing up at a bit of an angle on our driveway bump, getting ready for its long drive back to Marseilles. Jean-Louis was in the cab with the driver, handing him a doctor's case stuffed with euros.

The three Yannises, the clean-as-a-whistle, starched-white Stavros and Pavlos, and even the reclusive poet Spiros approached the machinery with reverence, running their fingertips over its surfaces, making appropriate noises of approval. Only Onassis was skeptical. He examined the sides of the heavier equipment carefully, and then uttered a satisfied grunt. He took out his measuring tape and took dimensions and then measured the entrances to the kitchen. He shook his head in mock pity.

"Just as I thought," he said dryly. "Not a prayer of getting these things inside the building. We'll have to tear down a wall."

The information squashed our collective well-being. We waited, speechless, for Jean-Louis to finish his business before we discussed our options. Onassis, having played out his usefulness, settled back on the balcony with his Thermos of morning coffee and his victory cigarette.

Jean-Louis didn't even flinch at the news. He shrugged, "Let's tear down the wall then, and quickly!" He rushed off to buy plastic sheets with which to cover the valuable gear; no one could guarantee how long it would have to wait outside.

Within an hour, our beautiful, all-but-finished construction site looked like Kabul once again. The designated part of the wall was demolished cleanly enough, but the missing support had caused a chunk of the kitchen ceiling to collapse, and now the whole place was covered in dust and broken bricks—exactly the sort of spectacle that upsets my stomach. I chewed two Maalox tablets in quick succession and watched helplessly as the situation went from bad to worse.

The whole crew, carpenters and bricklayers alike, worked tirelessly, barely stopping for Mrs. Water's lunch, but by evening only the more cumbersome of the debris had been removed. Then Spiros backed in a bit too close and gave the building a friendly nudge, causing more of the wall to fall and even more of the roof to rain down.

The next morning, and every morning for the entire week to follow, I drove to work without even a glance at the greens-picking widows, vainly hoping that overnight the building would have repaired itself.

Elsa, meanwhile, was in even stormier turmoil. The unforeseeable expense that this downturn represented was catastrophic for her carefully drawn budget, and she had nowhere left to turn. Algis had already invested more than he could afford, while Jean-Louis and Theresa were tapped after buying his kitchen equipment and ordering her special artifacts and decorations from her home in Tunisia. Elsa had no choice but to fly to Sweden in search of new funds, furtively so that the Greeks would not be alarmed.

And it was a good thing she did, because the worst was yet to come. Overnight on Friday, when the kitchen area was more or less fixed and steel piles had been secured to hold up its roof, a tempestuous wind travelling at a million k.p.h. from some hellish southern desert, ripped through Plakiás. Several trees buckled, including a proudly perpendicular ancient cedar, which came crashing down on our building, boring through the roof and the supporting wall of the toilets.

Somehow the catapulting rocks and bricks missed the sinks and toilet bowls, but they broke through the floor and seriously damaged the sewage system and the antique cesspool underneath. Water Yannis inspected the damage gravely. "Now we must replace. I had hoped to save the old system, but now we have no choice."

By lunchtime on Saturday we were swamped with unpleasantness. Forlorn kitchen equipment was sitting wrapped in terminally dusty plastic outside a kitchenful of messy cement and upright piles, next to a vile-smelling muddy hole, while ungainly sewage ducts were accessorizing the balcony.

So much of the place was upside down that none of us was able to enjoy Mrs. Pete's special lunch, which was admittedly rather tasteless since the poor lady had cooked it under the duress of extreme construction headaches.

There was some kind of plan for a group party on Sunday, but I passed on it, feigning illness, just to get away from everyone, most of all from the spectre of at least another week of the same unbearable mess at the restaurant. I went to Réthymno harbour and had several coffees while sitting outside in the stolen February sunshine. I stayed through sunset, when the yellow stones turned to gold and the sea a witch's-brew crimson.

I must have stayed outside in the sea breeze too long, because I woke up on Monday with a ferocious case of *laima* as well as an attack of *stoithoi*. I could barely talk from the sore throat, while my chest hurt as if the old bronchitis was ready to make yet another of its comebacks. Algis, though uncharacteristically pessimistic and deflated about the project lately, offered to supervise the workers in my place to give me a break. I agreed instantly, prepared to suffer Pete's displeasure at my absence.

I spent the day in bed, watching Greek TV with its relentlessly melodramatic soap operas and its current events programs on which fast-talking panelists all spoke at once, in the school of debating where whoever shouts loudest wins.

Algis returned late in the evening to find me asleep with the TV blaring, exhausted from the debates as well as from the battle of viruses inside me. He brewed me a cup of a cure-all exclusive to Crete, *diktamo* tea, made from an herb that grows only along the cliffs of the highest mountains and has been famous for its curative powers since antiquity.

"Drink this," he advised, waking me up to hand me the tea. "It will help you, no problem. Even Aristotle used to recommend *diktamo* for all sorts of sicknesses. And there's a nice surprise for you in the morning."

❨ ❨ ❨

It was a religious experience. A sight for my watery eyes, the only flu symptom the *diktamo* had failed to cure. Through a miracle of efficiency and superhuman effort, all the major construction faults had been corrected during my day of illness.

The kitchen had been whipped into shape, its equipment unwrapped and brought into its proper slots, its ceiling repaired; even its new wall was well on the way to completion. More gratifying than that, the new sewage pipes and cesspool had been installed, the old smelly garbage had been removed, and a serious effort to repair the floor and ceiling was underway. The crew, led by the tireless, conspicuously re-enthusiastic Algis, had worked extra hours for free, motivated by a desire to beat the Fates.

I was very pleased, but I reached for my Maalox anyway. My overriding problem had not gone anywhere: our money was practically finished. We had had to pay out so much for new building materials and plumbing that there wasn't enough left in the kitty to pay the workers past this day.

But right on cue, Elsa returned, with a suitcase of cash in tow. She had found a sun-worshipper in a suburb of Stockholm who was now our brand-new full-share silent partner. This made eight people who would be drawing percentages out of this restaurant. We'll have to sell a lot of curry, I mused, as I dropped another antacid.

The next few days were smooth sailing, and by the end of the work week the interior was ready for its close-ups and ornaments. The driveway had a whole slew of new mounds of dirt that had become permanent bumps, an accepted and familiar part of our landscape.

Theresa, a true princess who was no particular fan of cooking, invited everyone over on Sunday for an heirloom couscous, to be adorned with authentic harissa hot sauce and real *merguez* sausages, which had been airmailed to her along with the wall hangings and other items from Tunisia.

Having sampled her reluctant cooking before, we had low expectations, but she proved us wrong with a monumental mound of exactingly buttered couscous, a fiery, flavourful sauce, charcoal-broiled irresistible sausages, and caramelized onions to decorate the top.

Prudently, Mrs. Pete had brought a large casserole of lamb with orzo, knowing that the Greeks, famous for eating only what their mothers had fed them when they were children, were bound to have scruples about tackling a dish they had never even heard of. This party-saver did not require any gustatory leaps from our workers, while it allowed the rest of us seconds and thirds of Theresa's excellent couscous.

We were a happy group, feeling as if we had really accomplished something. Pete, as uncharitable as ever, obliquely chastised me for missing a day of work simply by omitting me from his praise. He went to great pains to lionize Algis for his spectacular leadership on the day of my illness, practically neglecting the roles of the workers in the achievements of that miraculous day. I was hoping he'd insist that Algis replace me as crew boss, but no such luck. When his encomia of Algis were over, he turned to me with a dire warning never to dare get ill again.

Pete next addressed an issue that was on everyone's mind. He put forth the notion that our barrage of bad luck could very well have been the unfortunate but predictable result of Elsa's left-footed *podariko* on the day of the *ayasmo*. To ease concern over this issue he pointed out that the *podariko* effrontery was bound to have been absolved now, since she had suffered most from the adversities. He knew well how painful it was for an accountant to have to revise a budget upwards and, even worse, to be obligated to go out on a limb and find new money.

Many bottles of *raki* made their entrance at this point, and in no time at all, none of the cast and crew of our little comedy was feeling any pain. I took this opportunity to effect my escape. Somewhat deflated by Pete's disapproval, I drove into the darkening hills of Marioú, gunning the gas pedal of my Hyundai as if it were a Ferrari, into a snaking line of blind curves, accompanied by Vangelis's heroic *Mythodea*, convinced despite everything that the worst of it was over and that soon—oh please!—soon . . .

The following week was pure joy. Stavros and Pavlos, finally in their element, tiled the floor in finely veined marble and fitted handcrafted window frames in which they mounted stained glass of their own design. They painted the interior an apricot yellow with lime highlights and the exterior a brick red that could be seen a kilometre away even though it mirrored the colours of the rock head at the edge of the beach.

Olaf had been able to buy a zinc bar. It came from a defunct pub in the godawful resort of Mália, east of Heraklion. Mália, the opposite of a gentle, low-key area like Plakiás, is the kind of resort that has given Crete a bad name. Home to cheap package tourism for the young rowdies of Britain and Germany, it is made up of a country mile of beachfront drinkeries with the ambience of pubs near a soccer stadium on game day. The object of a fortnight's Mália holiday is to get involved in blind drunk fistfights twenty-four hours each day.

The establishment from which our zinc bar had been purchased had been closed down after a double death that resulted from the favourite holiday pastime of its Liverpool habitués. It's called "butt-head," and it involves two equally strong and stupid thugs, terminally drunk, charging at each other head first at full speed. The player who remains conscious after the head-on collision is declared the winner. On that particular evening, the fans, disappointed by the double frailty of the participants, declared the match a "draw" and continued drinking several rounds before they realized that their buddies were not simply unconscious, they were stiffs.

It was a beautiful zinc bar, muted and friendly to the touch, just the right length for the designated bar area. It would separate the dining room from the kitchen with a definitive, metallic apostrophe.

Olaf had also uncovered a quantity of fine maple wood, albeit Canadian and not Russian, originally imported by a Greek Canadian who had returned to Crete triumphantly to recreate his highly successful Bloor Street *burgeria* in the heart of Heraklion. Inopportunely, he had chosen the exact moment to open his enterprise as the McDonald's megachain, which had franchised an outlet right across the street. The Torontonian lost his backers, who didn't have the heart to compete with the minced-meat behemoth, forcing him into an early bankruptcy well before he required his prize lumber. It had been sitting in a warehouse ever since, priced to sell.

Our restaurant space now turned into an elf's workshop, with much hammering and chiselling. They installed the bar and carpentered the tables and chairs, the whole crew chipping in and allowing Olaf to work alongside them despite Pete's warnings that all the partners steer clear of the premises until the renovation was finished.

This phase of the work, with its essential and extremely dangerous tools, such as the electric saw, the nails, the screwdrivers—instruments that can become painful agents of death and dismemberment with someone as clumsy as I even breathing around them—prompted my exit from the work-space.

I spent many happy hours under the plane tree reading about London's cultural goings-on in the *Sunday Times*, occasionally lifting my eyes off the pages to watch the graceful posturings of the Plakiás swans, who normally live in the built-up part of the port, but who had flown over to our side to check us out. There is something noble and sad about swans, as if they really are princesses in white tutus cursed into a life in feathers by a capricious sorcerer.

The swans made for an appropriate segue into the next chapter of our project, the entrance of Theresa and her orna-ments. Like the princess that she was, she waited for the dust to settle from the carpentry, and all the sharp instruments to be removed, before bringing us her Tunisian treasures.

Theresa, the radical daughter of a very proper and tradi-tional North African land-owning family, had escaped the rigidity of her heritage by marrying the decidedly lower-class Jean-Louis, but she had retained all her fine upbringing. It was understood, for example, that in her presence one behaved with civility and held back the profanities. It was also taken for granted that she would rise from her easy chair for her own children's emergencies, but for no other chore what-soever, unless she felt like it.

Twice lucky for us, she had first become inspired for the exemplary couscous of last Sunday, and now she was gung-ho for the decor. She enlisted the willing Stavros and Pavlos, and in exactly two days, ending promptly in time for Saturday lunch, the place had been transformed into a mythical spot in a kasbah, worthy of the star-entrance in a Hedy Lamarr film.

Thin woven tapestries, depicting pre-Crusades Moors' curlicuing geometrics in natural colours, punctuated the walls and extended to corresponding strips on the ceiling. Similar designs were on the upholstery of the custom-made maple wood chairs, and the puffy cushions of the lounging banquettes in the corners. To counterpoint the fabric, she placed shiny metal artifacts, candle-holders, and trays on various surfaces around the room. Giant carved-brass circular tables on low chestnut legs accented the banquettes. And a master touch, a beaded twinkling string-curtain, was installed to separate the toilets from the dining area, forever lazily swaying, shooting back prisms of multicoloured rays.

Mrs. Water and Mrs. Pete teamed up for the week's end lunch, and it was a special meal with oven-baked free-range rooster and a celery-scented fish soup. Hungry as we all were, the meal took a back seat to our appreciation of Olaf and Theresa's interior decor. We all sang their praises and those of Stavros and Pavlos, who beamed in tandem. Then we got to actually sit in the room to eat, delighting in the colours and the textures. Everyone, even Onassis, was unreservedly pleased.

There was precious little left to do. Final details of electricity and plumbing. Connecting the kitchen to its sources of power. And then the landscaping of the outdoor space, and hopefully the elimination of the various bumps of leftover earth. It had taken a little longer and cost quite a bit more money than originally projected, but we had done it. It was over.

Now it was time for the business details: the licences, the

menu, the hiring and training of the staff, the all-important opening party. We'd be ready to go if not precisely mid-March, then soon thereafter. Nothing could stop us now. Nothing ordinary, that is.

Chapter 17

Roof Over Our Heads

A celebration of our splendid progress was held in the house of Mr. and Mrs. Pete on a wintry Sunday. The warm sunny weather of the past several weeks had become cold and windy overnight. Ominous storm clouds were flying by, allowing only brief, rather hazy sunny moments. Had we been in the least superstitious, we could have worried about the many potentially negative effects this weather could rain on our heads. But we did not, because we were beyond superstition. We were all-powerful.

In any case, nature was doing her best to be compelling on this overcast day. The dramatic skies contrasted sharply with the patchwork quilt of the fields, now in blazing colour with wildflowers and poppies aplenty shivering in the breeze amid the almond trees, which were dressed in cream-and-claret blossoms like young girls in a costume drama. I would have dearly loved a long drive into the countryside.

Instead I found myself inside the Pete residence. A rambling, rich person's farmhouse, one of the oldest in the area, it was on the hillside halfway up from Plakiás to Marioú. It was a mini-village all its own, with a chapel, a barn, a wine-making shed, a still for boiling wine sediment into *raki*, an ancient but now unused olive oil press, and ample residential quarters for the extended family.

Like all Greek homes, it was dark and shaded, designed to stay cool in summer and therefore always somewhat dank in winter. Mrs. Pete had done her New England best to make the musty old house cheerful with extra lights and bright-coloured furniture, but her efforts were compromised by this day's inclement weather.

I settled into one of Pete's fat-person chairs. It was large, obviously, had good back support, and was the proper height off the floor. He had been sitting in the other chair when I entered. He made to rise, but I rushed to pat him back down. There are certain advantages to being overweight. Always being offered the front passenger seat in a car is one of them. Not having to stand up to greet a guest is another.

We looked at each other for a few minutes, and then burst out laughing simultaneously. Mrs. Pete, who entered from the kitchen at that moment with the coffees, gave us a quizzing "What," thinking we were laughing at her.

"Mr. Pete and I just realized we are one and the same person." I winked at her.

"Well, yes, you are both equally silly," observed Mrs. Pete, depositing the coffee with the most *kaimaki* by me, the guest, and the second, almost as foamy, by her husband. She put the third, from the bottom of the *briki* and practically foamless, to the side for herself.

"When we grow up, we'll turn serious and adult like you," sneered Pete.

Mrs. Pete made a funny face and sat down on a rickety, uncomfortable "wife" chair next to her self-sacrificingly flat coffee. Was I witnessing a rift in this rock-tight marriage? Was that a truly venomous glance I had caught Mrs. Pete shooting at Elsa during yesterday's lunch? Was Pete becoming too obvious in his infatuation with the blond charms of our Nordic partner? We had certainly caught him ogling her more or less constantly and touching her as often as she'd let him.

As if to mock me and tease the gods, Elsa arrived right then on her motorcycle, ahead of Olaf and the children, who were bringing up the rear in the van. She was luminously curvy, wrapped in futuristic silver spandex, her rich blond hair flowing loosely. She was glowing with contentment, happy that she would not need to raise any more funds now that the heavy expenses were done with. She walked into the dark house like a blinding light and the room instantly sizzled with Pete's longing. Mrs. Pete winced painfully as she stood up to greet her.

Elsa, unaware—or was it too aware?—of the turmoil she was capable of causing in the Pete household, kissed Mrs. Pete on each cheek and then extended her hand for a warm but businesslike handshake with Pete, who had struggled out of his chair when she had entered.

Pete remained standing because others began to show up before he'd had a chance to sit back down. In no time at all there was life in the old house. The children's Greek mingled with a Babel of conversations in a pan-European mix of languages: more Greek from the workers, excited French from Jean-Louis and Theresa, who seemed to be in the midst of some spat of their own, guttural Swedish from the blonds, and English between Algis and me.

"I came here to discover Zeus and the Minotaur," Algis smiled, "and they captured me instead. I guess I'll have to lose my return ticket and stick around to cook curry."

"Hey, Al, it could be worse," I laughed. "They might have forced you to stick around and eat your own curry."

"I happen to make terrific curry," he said.

"Terrific, almost terrifying, yes," I replied, remembering an incident back in Montreal when Algis, fresh from India, had invited guests for a truly "authentic" curry. Three of his victims had had to undergo psychotherapy, so traumatic had been his excessively hot curry's effect on their fragile minds.

"Those three should've been in therapy long before my curry," he shrugged at the memory.

"This'll give you a chance to spend a summer in Greece," I teased him. "If you thought that curry was hot stuff, wait for August on Crete."

"I have things I want to do here and that's really why I've agreed to be part of this business," Algis countered. "The weather is incidental to me. The work is everything. I would never go to a hot place just to laze around. I can't laze. It bugs me. Here, I'll have the curries, and I have my other plans."

There was a call to order by Pete before I had the chance to hear about Algis's other plans. Our host had poured shot glasses of *raki* for everyone, even all the children (except for little Gustav and even littler Triantafilitsa, Mr. and Mrs. Water's youngest).

"This is the good day," shouted Pete. "Let's drink so that more the good days come the every day!" We all raised our glasses as one, and shouting "*yassoo*," drank down the *raki*.

The searing alcohol exploded in my stomach, but in a pleasant way. It didn't make me reach for the Maalox, it made me want to eat. As if reading my mind, Mrs. Pete shot back into her kitchen and returned in a flash carrying a loaded tray of homemade *maratho* (wild fennel-leaf) pies.

Maratho grows just about everywhere on Crete, lining

property boundaries with its profusion of emerald leaves, slender and soft in cottony wisps, catching every little breeze, swaying in one direction then the other. Baked in a pie it imparts a sweet licorice flavour and a crisp yet soft texture.

It made a tasty prologue for the gargantuan meal that was to follow. Always a generous person, Mrs. Pete had stinted on neither labour nor expense for this feast, the first in her house for our group. She had prepared three separate stewed meats, all of them overcooked in proper Greek manner: pork, lamb, and rooster to represent the three sorts of livestock in the family barn. With the meats she presented lemon potatoes sprinkled with oregano and thyme, steamed broccoli with vinegar and oil, boiled chestnuts turned in butter, deep-fried zucchini with yogurt-cucumber tzatziki, and, for me the prizes of the menu, a heaping plate of wild artichoke braised with broad beans, and an abundance of the elusive *ascrolibri* (radish) greens, tart, spicy radish roots attached, lightly steamed and sparsely dressed with oil and lemon to accentuate their natural flavour.

While the eating and the drinking were still in gluttonous progress, Pete switched to the business at hand, starting with an update on our operating licence. It was, he said, very much in order, as assured by a judge friend of his who was handling the case. The only element missing was the results of the personal-record police checks on each of the partners. This was a new European Union–recommended procedure, which the Greek police were pursuing ultra-diligently.

"So if nobody from you is the criminal, then the no problem," said Pete. I hoped it was only my imagination, but I thought I heard Jean-Louis swallowing hard.

"And now, speak!" ordered Pete. "This the curry. This the menu. What is? What's cooking?!"

We spent a good half-hour explaining curry, but it was

beyond him. Finally Mrs. Pete came to our rescue.

"Look, I told you. It's like *kokinisto* [tomato-reddened stewed meat]. Except with more spices."

"The spices?" Pete asked suspiciously. "What spices?"

"No spices you've ever heard of before, I told you," Mrs. Pete repeated patiently.

"Greeks like these spices?" Pete was trying to compute this difficult information.

"I told you," moaned Mrs. Pete.

"Tell me again!" shouted Pete.

"No Greek would touch these spices, okay?" said Mrs. Pete, as if happy to deliver the unfavourable news. "They have never eaten them before."

"Hmm," grunted Pete. "This is not the good thing then, is it?" His question was to all of us. "Look, make the curry for the tourists, okay. For the Greeks make moussaka and *horiatiki* salad with the tomato and the feta, and most important, make the *bifteki*. Everyone loves the *bifteki*."

"The dreaded burger," whispered Algis, remembering Theo's tribulations with the same. However, none of us, including me, were hampered by Theo's high standards. We agreed to the *bifteki*, promising to offer the best damned burger Plakiás had ever seen, and we agreed to the tomato salad, because we all loved it anyway—Greek tomatoes and local feta were two of the most compelling reasons the partners had moved to Greece in the first place—but we drew the line at the moussaka.

Pete, not being fond of partial victories, was revving up to defend moussaka, after which he was no doubt intending to push *pastichio* (noodle casserole), souvlaki, and fried *marides* (whitebait), when we felt the house shake—not with any force, but unmistakably.

Everyone, even the youngest children, froze. Earthquakes have a sobering effect on exuberance. The follow-up tremor, which we all knew was to come, delayed itself agonizingly. To fill the gap, the sky suddenly burst into pieces with piercing lightning, loud thunder and a monsoon-like downpour of big, tear-shaped drops that lashed at the windowpanes, driven by a wind of tropical intensity.

The storm lasted only minutes, drifting off as speedily as it had come, the last of its violent tears bouncing loudly off the roof. And just as it had stopped altogether and little wet spots began to darken patches of the Petes' ceiling, the second tremor made itself felt, quite a few points on the Richter scale stronger than the first, shaking the table, rattling the china in the wall cabinet, causing bits of plaster to come undone from high corners of the walls, widening a crack on the floor, and drawing screams of terror from all of us.

Pete crossed himself three times, while the entire Water family fell on their knees, chanting a prayer of repentance and supplication to the mercy of God.

"Is okay. Is okay!" shouted Pete. "Is over now. The Crete have this many times. This not too strong. Only is problem if roof is no good . . ." Pete gulped and turned pale. "*Christe kai Panaghia mou* [Oh, my Christ and Holy Virgin], the roof!"

He let out a pained wail and stormed out of the house to his car. Everyone started screaming at once as we rushed to our own vehicles to drive to the restaurant.

The aftermath of the fleeting storm had swept all the oppressive clouds from the sky. It was now clear, with the sun already golden in preparation for setting. And it was in this soft yellow light that we surveyed the destruction.

At first we had dared to hope that the building had escaped

largely unscathed. It seemed untouched from the outside except for one gash on the front wall beside the large stained-glass window, which was very much unbroken.

But when we opened the door, it stared us in the face then punched us in the gut. The entire roof of the dining room had collapsed, breaking tiles, slicing the zinc, ripping the wall hangings, crushing the brass tables and flattening the wooden ones—destroying everything, with the miraculous exception of the windowpanes, which stared at us mockingly intact.

The rebuilt parts of the roof over the kitchen and toilets had held, but the dining room and everything in it, all those handsome design elements—all of it was a write-off.

Theresa, regal to the end, made a gesture of disgust and uttered a series of terse, well-bred curses. Then she turned around and walked away, Jean-Louis on her heels to console her.

The rest of us didn't need to display any emotion because right after Theresa's restrained outburst, Stavros and Pavlos did it for all of us. They broke down in loud, sobbing, uncontrollable, pointedly unmanly tears, clutching at each other, looking at the heavens, wondering how they had sinned to deserve this calamity, weeping for all their lovely, meticulous work on the walls, the floors, the tables, the chairs, which now lay in total ruin.

Pete shook his head and crossed himself three times. "This is no more a *podariko* problem," he whispered to me in awe. "This is now the *matyasma* [eye curse]. Somebody has put a hex on us. Somebody's eye is cursing us. Tomorrow we go for a *xematyasma* [undoing of the eye curse]!"

Chapter 18

Chapel in the Cliff

Many societies fear hexes, and there are documented, rather painful cures for them, known in their extreme Christian forms as exorcisms. The Greeks are unique in their relationship to hexes in that hexes don't necessarily have to originate from complex or even ill-intentioned sources. A hex in Greece can come from a fleeting glance, an involuntary pang of envy, even from a heartthrob of well-wishing that is motivated by sincere friendship and love.

It's all in the eye. That "mirror of the soul," the lens that lets us focus on what we want to see while blanking out the rest, can with a single peek bring the worst of bad luck to even the most innocent and benevolent of entities. To *mati* (the eye) is all-powerful because it controls us, we have no defence against it. It sees, it disapproves, it covets, it loves, it hates. Its forces are formidable and unravellable. For reasons all its own, the eye can imprint anything it touches with an evil that can infect a lifetime.

The *matyasma* that is born out of the fateful *matyà* (look) can come from any direction: a childless aunt admiring her newborn niece, a close friend visiting one's new house, a cynic sneering, and most decidedly a rival fearing unfair competition from a business better than his own. A *matyasma* can, in the extreme, be caused even by someone whose own interests suffer from the ensuing adversity.

In our situation it could have come from anyone, not only from fellow citizens of the Plakiás area, but possibly from one of us, our workers, even our children.

Pete and I drove deep into the interior, to Patsós and the blessed chapel of St. Anthony, famous for its miracles and its effective *xematyasmas*. Reportedly, praying to St. Anthony had undone countless ruinations caused by the "evil eye."

Pete had insisted I travel with him so that he could have someone "who understands" him, and does so in Greek, on this stressful journey. He told me that he feared everyone because each of us had reasons to be the one. Onassis and his non-stop troublemaking. Little Yannis and his obsession with death. Big Yannis and his vanity. Water Yannis and his incurable fear of God. Jean-Louis and Theresa and their ongoing lust for each other despite being husband and wife. Elsa and her worship of money. Olaf and his unmanly house-husbandry—a man doing the family laundry! Elsa and Olaf's oldest son Eric and his green eyes—the most dangerous colour of *matyasma*, and Pete had noticed that the boy was feeling neglected because of his parents' preoccupation with the restaurant. Ultimately, even me and my pathological fear of construction.

Pete drove quickly and in silence. Buried in his fears, he was oblivious to the potholes that the rains and snows had carved on the cheaply paved road that climbed the mountain to forgotten villages not targeted for tourism. Gamely keeping up behind us were the partners, their children, and Mrs. Pete, the only ones who had been invited to the outing. Pete had ordered the workers to start clearing the rubble from the site, albeit unsupervised.

Pete had planned this supremely important mission as if it were a military expedition to battle the forces against us and bring back on course our sadly compromised enterprise. *Xematyasma* is risky business. Total unswerving faith and absolute observance of the rituals are givens, but the slightest oversight can reverse the undoing, and there is always the possibility of failure if the original curse was simply too powerful.

"I wrote a new *mantinada* about this," muttered Pete to break his own silence. He recited a gruesome rhyming couplet that dripped with venom at whoever it was who had brought disfavour into his life.

"That says it all right," I agreed. "And I'm sure St. Anthony is listening and will help us."

"Don't be so cocky," he cautioned me. "My father once needed grace on an inheritance matter. He went to do a blessing and an offering to the saint, but his resolve must have been less than adamant because he ended up having to kill his own brother."

All I could squeak out at this casual disclosure was "Really?"

"This shocks you?"

"Well . . . Yes."

"It shocked us as well, but it was inevitable. Our greatest crimes happen inside the family. It has been so since the old days. Have you never seen Sophocles? Those family tragedies were all based on fact, and they've been a curse on the Greeks for thousands of years. I guess it is because we have the most to gain from harming those closest to us." Pete

stated all this matter-of-factly, astounding me with his literary
allusions.

"Were there repercussions?"

"Aren't there always? Oedipus watched his mother kill herself and then gouged out his own eyes."

"I meant for your father. For killing his brother."

"It's not for you to discuss this," said Pete sternly. "My
family's most sacred drama is none of your business. But
since you are so curious: no, there were not. The law was not
involved. It was obviously a private matter, inside the family.
The dead man had no children to avenge him, he was unmarried. My grandfather was dead, that's why the inheritance
was an issue. My grandmother, bless her soul, was mercifully
never informed. She was sick and bedridden, and my father
told her that the brother had gone off on the ships. He even
brought her fake letters from him to keep her happy. She died
longing to see her dead son, but she was pleased for him,
believing he had disembarked in Argentina, married a Greek
girl, had many sons, and stayed to make his fortune."

"And your father. He was able to carry the burden? He
could live with himself?"

"Of course. Because he was right. The brother had wanted
land that was not his. He was greedy. He wanted to sell the
land to a German, to an ex-Nazi who had fallen in love with
our village during the Occupation in the war. Anyway, my
father repented and gave him a grand funeral that everyone
from all the villages this side of both the gorges attended. And
then he revisited St. Anthony and did a heartfelt *xematyasma*.
After which he got married and had one child. Only one, but
an excellent one. Me." Pete laughed at his own immodesty,
and the matter was closed. We had reached the parking area
of the chapel. "We walk from here," he concluded.

The chapel was inside a nature preserve, a small but interesting gorge, home to hundreds of species of birds and plants. Tumbling loudly through the gorge was a river that thinned out to an orderly stream in the dry months but that had become an unruly torrent after yesterday's freak storm. Water appeared to be gushing from everywhere, falling onto the walkway, making it slippery and muddy as it wound its way to the chapel.

All of us, except the surprisingly nimble Pete, slipped and fell in the mud at least once, the children several times, so that by the time we reached the chapel covered in mud, we looked properly, thoroughly chastised and direly in need of saintly assistance. Pete refrained from mocking us, needing to concentrate on the intricate task ahead.

The chapel was chiselled into the sodden heart of the cliff, jagged rock its ceiling, smoothed rock its walls, an uneven floor of porous flat stones. The structure was divided into two parts, an enclosed cave and an antechamber open to the elements, where we found all the accessories for self-performed blessings, as well as the collection box for our donation.

There were wax candles, oil and wicks for prayer lamps, frankincense and self-igniting charcoal, and votive charms to hang on the saint's icon if mere candles and lamps and incense were no match for the enormity of one's affliction. Pete took no chances. He collected thirteen of everything—candles, incense, charms, oil lamps—one for each of us. He deposited several medium-denomination euro notes through the slit of the donations box, and turned to face us.

He told us that he would be going through the full ritual of smoke and fire and incantation thirteen separate times, once for each one of us, doing himself last. He warned us that it would take a long time. Thankfully no other penitents had bothered to show up on this muddy day, so we could take all the time we needed.

However, he admonished us with finger erect like some preacher of doom, if anyone dared to snicker, shuffle, fidget, moan, faint, or die during his service, the whole thing would be nullified and we would have to start all over again. Young Gustav, too innocent to matter, could do as he liked, except run around, which might cause a big spill and start a fire that might then kill all of us and send us to eternal hell for burning down the saint's chapel.

Before any of it could begin, we would have to enter the enclosed part of the chapel to offer individual prayers, single file since the tiny space had enough room for only one person at a time. A hidden door in the rock, slim and flimsy, led into a natural cave that was inexplicably moisture-free. Icons were painted directly on its walls. Shielded from sunlight, the room was aglow with hundreds of still-flickering prayer lamps left there by previous supplicants.

Prominently in the centre of the cramped space, raised on an easel, was the jewel-like glassed-in icon of the chapel's patron saint, outlined in embossed silver in the Byzantine style. The prescribed prayer to St. Anthony, as taught to us by Pete, started with a sincere atonement for all our sins, past, present, and future, to be followed by a pleading for his absolution. It concluded with the kissing of the icon, lips not touching the glass if we were squeamish.

Pete watched us closely from the doorway as we all went through our paces, singly, except for Gustav, who did it in the arms of his father. The Muslim-born Theresa had no misgivings observing the rite, recognizing its affinity to prehistory rather than to Christianity. Jean-Louis and I, both of us some brand of atheist, had the most trouble putting enough conviction into our actions to please Pete, while Elsa and Olaf's barely disguised Calvinist deprecation of this heathen practice had Pete silently regretting that he had ever brought them to this holy spot. Algis made up for all of us with his usual open-throttled piety, ecstatic as always to worship at altars to the bizarre, hoping that the more exotic a religious observance was, the more mystical it would be, and the more likely to grant his wishes.

Satisfied that we had done our best to arouse the saint's interest and pity, Pete lined us up in front of him in the chapel's antechamber to proceed with the lengthy fire and smoke ritual. He set fire to a mound of incense, then lit the wax candles, asking each one of us in turn to anchor one upright in the sandbox beside him. He measured out anointed oil into shapely glass vases and set wicks afloat on the oil. He lit the wicks and let them flicker beneficently. He dipped the tip of the votive charms into the flaming oil while chanting ancient psalms. He touched the hotly burning charms to the appropriate foreheads, and sent each of us into the cave to hang our own charm on the skirts of the saint's icon.

It took about ten minutes to do one individual, more than two hours all told. Two hours of standing under a dripping roof, breathing in the fumes of burning incense and charcoal and paraffin and oil, being scarred by scorched metal—a holy torture that was meant to exorcise the most persistent devil within any of us, and to also gouge out the evil eyes of the devils gunning for us from outside. We had no idea if it would work, but if it didn't we were truly doomed because it was all we had.

When the last of his high-priest chores had been performed, Pete turned abruptly and walked down the long path to the cars. He was even more nimble and quick than before, invigorated by his communion with the beyond, full of resolve, in charge of his own destiny once again.

The same could not be said for the rest of us. We all took turns tumbling in the mud, now more treacherous since we were moving faster, trying to keep up with the speedy Pete. By the time we reached the parking area to find Pete already inside his car, the engine on, the radio switched to a lyre-playing, *mantinada*-singing station, we were soiled and cursing, surely and rapidly undoing whatever good the rituals had done.

Pete and I once again led the pack, each of us lost in our own reflections. Mine were almost uniformly grey. The new renovation crisis meant that I would be stuck inside a construction site yet again.

"Don't worry," said Pete, sensing my fears. "I wouldn't dream of having you as the crew boss anymore. The odds have gotten too high. The situation is too critical. From now on, I sit with the workers myself, because from now on I am the one spending the money. Elsa has a small amount left to her name, and she'll need that to purchase supplies for the opening. To fix the damage of the earthquake is my expense, and of course, this'll mean a brand new deal."

Chapter 19

New Deal

Elsa was furious, but she had no ready recourse. Pete was demanding a 50 per cent share of the restaurant's profits and its ownership, on top of his rent, to agree to subsidize the work that was now necessary. Our own funds, controlled by Elsa, were, as he had correctly guessed, insufficient to cover the new damage, and the only alternative was to throw in the towel and withdraw from the project altogether, losing all hope of ever recouping the capital.

In truth, even though the collapsed roof appeared catastrophic, the actual cost of the work and materials needed to restore order amounted to far less than what the partnership had invested so far, and it wasn't exactly fair to demand half of the business for it. Then again, there isn't much that's fair about business. Pete had been given an opportunity by the forces of nature, and he was grabbing it.

"They should be grateful," he complained to me after a highly emotional confrontation with the partners. "I could've decided to forget about the whole deal, and then where would they be?"

So it came to pass that the partners, disgruntled and feeling cheated, had no choice but to agree to Pete's terms, the only casualty of the wheeling and dealing being Elsa's erstwhile chumminess with Pete. She now hated him, and pointedly avoided being anywhere near him. Mrs. Pete was finally able to relax; she now smiled a lot, humming happy tunes under her breath.

The workers, the cement, the bricks, the girders, the piles, Spiros's big truck, the whole shebang returned to the site, creating a need for cartfuls of Maalox, blissfully no longer mine to chew but Pete's. This time around I was barred from the construction site, welcome back only when Pete needed someone to hear one of his recently composed *mantinades*.

I was free. Free to wake up late and to enjoy my inviolable morning routine at leisure. Free from breathing in plaster dust. Free from having to tolerate the sights and sounds of hammers and saws and uncut lumber and loads of bricks.

It meant that my promised non-investing profit-share was reduced by half, but it also meant a liberating, exhilarating reprieve from the renovations, for which I was indeed grateful.

Now I finally had time to walk around and look at the flowers. Myriads, in all colours, had sprouted on all available surfaces, even in the cracks of road asphalt, while I wasn't looking. Spring, bolstered by early March heatwaves, was here to stay. This was no temporary "halcyon days" reprieve, this was the harbinger of the long hot summer.

The flowers, better than ever this year because of the unusually excessive rains, seemed to primp and pose, flaunting their beauty, savouring their moment, all too aware that once the upcoming dry heat had its way they would die off and become weeds, then thorns.

The most surprising was the *maratho*. Two-metre-tall stalks had sprouted from the middle of the fern-leafed bushes, with fragmented lime-green chrysanthemums decorating the crowns. Where the roads had been bordered by edible wisps of emerald brush, now there were fluorescent crystal-etched clusters that grew in three directions at once.

I walked on, as if stopping to rest would be a betrayal of the extraordinary effort nature had undertaken. The landscape of this area was so varied—the vistas studded with little and big hills, hidden valleys, surprise plateaux, jagged cliffs, stunning views of the sea, and dramatic chutes into forbidding gorges— that it defied jadedness while it challenged the imagination.

It was like the finest of music, the most gripping of tales. It wouldn't let go until the final note, the very last page, except that unlike any music or tale, this land had no ending other than one's own endurance to continue exploring it. My senses overloaded, warm and sweaty, I arrived at Niko's olive grove, even though I hadn't set out to go there. Niko was lying in a lounge chair, eyes half shut.

He saw me and made to stand up, but winced with pain and extended his hand instead. He seemed dazed, but not from drink.

"I cracked my rib reaching for an olive branch," he explained. "They have me on so many pills that I don't even feel like drinking. Get me a *raki*, if you don't mind." He pointed to the supplies in his bag. "I'll give it another try."

Reluctantly he drank a couple of shots to one of mine, and another two to top up. His infectious smile hovered around his lips but stopped short of lighting his face as it had before.

"It's such a surprise for me. This . . . this getting old. I don't like it. I've reached for millions of branches in my time. I've climbed thousands of trees. I never cracked a rib before.

And if I had, it would never have stopped me from drinking, it would never have made me lose my *kefi*." He looked scared. "Do you think this is it? Tell me. Am I dying?"

I returned his gaze earnestly. "Yes, I'm sure you are."

"I knew it!" He reached for his glass and I refilled it for him.

"I give you at most thirty years." I winked. "No more than forty, no way."

"Then I better hurry up and live every minute to the full." His smile finally broke through. The booze was working its magic. "And what makes you so happy?" he asked me.

"I just lost a whole bunch of money." I smiled contentedly.

"That'll do it!" He slapped his thigh, then yelped and contorted his face. "That hurt! I don't understand. How can slapping my thigh hurt my rib?"

"Everything is connected," I explained authoritatively.

"And after pain comes pleasure?" he asked, groping for hope.

"Occasionally. Usually just more pain."

"More pain . . . You're right, damn you."

"The trick is to enjoy the pain," I said in consolation.

"That's funny," he remarked. "Normally I'm the one who says things like that. I guess it's easier when it's the other guy who's sick."

"It's always better for the other guy to be the sick one," I agreed.

"It would be nice if no one ever got sick," he tested me.

"Just eat your greens," I concluded. I continued my walk, leaving him to suffer alone.

Back at Marioú, I found Algis in a state of feverish creativity.

"My plans are on," he announced triumphantly. "I'm

building rock sculptures on the side of the church. I asked Erato-landlady and she thought it was a great idea!"

He was referring to an as-yet-unfinished church on a remote bend of the road to Asomatos from Marioú. This was an affectation of the Marioú parish priest, and it was proving to be a controversial ecclesiastical addition to an area already inundated with churches. I had heard that the building of this church had dipped into the municipal budget at the expense of sorely needed road repairs and had been opposed by leading socialists in the town council. But the conservatives had won the day, and the church had been started. Now there was a new row because the original budget had proved inadequate and more money was needed to complete the work, apparently a familiar refrain when it comes to construction.

Algis had spied a pile of attractively shaped stones in an orderly heap beside the church, likely meant as materials for the eventual pavement of its courtyard. But they had called out to be used as the fabric of sculptures, totem poles of sorts, stone sitting on stone rising above the edge of the hill, stark against the distant meniscus of sea and sky.

He hadn't dared to begin his project until he got sanction from someone important, and so he had approached the nearest authority figure, Erato, a card-carrying Conservative, leader of the Plakiás Ladies' Auxiliary, and perennial honourary vice-president of the area's Chamber of Commerce.

I don't know how he had made himself understood, but I knew she had a soft spot for him, so lily-white and youthful. He had driven her to the church and explained with gestures what he intended, and she had laughed merrily. He had interpreted her mirth as approval.

Now it was too late for her to change her mind. Algis had

spent several days with the stones and had erected some twenty humanoid shapes, reminiscent of Stonehenge and Easter Island, proudly primitive, provocative and solid, a swath of stone idols adjunct to the church.

He took me there in the late afternoon, when the sculptures seemed like charcoal drawings against the orange sky. He photographed them from many angles, breathlessly running around them to look for the best perspectives. He outlined his further plans to create more than one hundred of the figures, an entire community of stone, endlessly in muted movement, shifting images that changed as one drove towards or away from them and also as the rays of the sun lit them from different directions at various times of the day.

This was an evolution of his ongoing personal mythology for Crete, an island of ethereal mystery to him. Marioú was especially important as the most likely landing spot of extraterrestrials in a time when Kronos and Zeus were involved in a familial power struggle across the reaches of the universe.

Algis had invited the other partners to the church so that they too could share in the excitement of his installation. Theresa had had enough of all of us for the time being and refused to attend, choosing instead to pack her family in the car for a trip to the deluxe resort of Porto Eloúnda, with its private-swimming-pool rooms and full-body Swedish massages. She had grandly announced that she needed to forget the disturbing image of her beautiful decor in ruins, not even trying to hide her conviction that we were all somehow to blame for this affront against her.

Elsa and Olaf did come, a little drunk, plenty frustrated, almost sad. They viewed Algis's art work with Nordic detachment until they saw how much their children enjoyed the pieces, running around them in circles, striking poses to echo those of the sculptures, enjoying them without having to intellectually justify it as only children can.

Algis threw himself into his creation, working at it daily, adding some new pieces but mostly repairing precariously built ones that the wind could knock down. He was modifying his technique, choosing stones that fit into each other and couldn't easily be budged.

He was in fact reviving an age-old practice of the Greek Islands, where rocks and stones are the easiest-found construction materials and were used exclusively to build walls between properties. The trick to ensuring durability of stone-only structures is to stack complementary rocks on each other in just such a way that they grip and "stick" together.

Algis's perseverance and tireless industry piqued the curiosity of the villagers, who were making a point of slowly driving past the church, pausing to watch him work, and honking their encouragement as they drove off.

Left to fend for my own diversion, I once again began to question my place in this unreal land with its fragile infrastructure that broke down at will, its aspirations to big tourist business, and its achingly beautiful natural features. It was dawning on me that I was becoming one with its problems and its shortcomings as well as with its beauty and its promise of the good life. I was making this my home, and it was debatable now whether I would be able to survive without it.

A total commitment to this new truth necessitated cutting myself off completely from the rest of my world. Montreal, New York, London—cities that I had in the past felt I could never live without—would have to become abstractions for me. Actually settling down here would have to involve buying a house, an investment that would eat all my meagre funds, making it impossible to keep travelling back and forth.

This, of course, would have had to be the case in any scenario that involved retirement in Greece. It was just that I had secretly hoped I would never find the proper location to entice me to move here definitively and force me to give up the life I had lived until now.

I guess what I really needed at that point was either an all-consuming project like Algis's or a visit from Theo. And the great one showed up just in time to help me celebrate my existential crisis. This time he was driving a vintage convertible MGB, an early fifties model, slick and svelte, with a flat-nosed front bumper and a scarlet low-flung body straight out of a cartoon.

I stuffed myself into the passenger seat, a snug cavity clearly not designed for corpulence, and Theo flew us to Chania as if he were driving in a big-money race, which he said he had once actually done in Monte Carlo.

Chania is Crete's most aristocratic town. Its inland nineteenth-century avenues are lined with neoclassical mansions in the manner of Provençal *manoirs*. They feature square architecture with porticos, columns, tall windows, and creamy, though slightly crumbling, pastel-coloured walls encircled by wrought metal fenced, French-style manicured gardens.

Chania's port, dating from the Renaissance, is the crown jewel of the Venetian period. An extended curl of sea-fronting, flat and narrow three-storey houses bank a cobble-stoned corniche, which becomes the long, harbour-enclosing jetty with a slender, handsculpted lighthouse at its tip.

On the western edge of the port, watching over the safety of the citizens, its air still ringing with the clanging of swords and the screams of invaders boiled alive with cauldrons of scalding oil flung at them from the ramparts, is an immutable castle, a garrison for a large contingent of troops to defend an imperial outpost.

Chania is the one town in Crete that I had known well in the past, and I had originally meant it to be the starting point of my current trip. It had taken five months of adventures elsewhere, but I was finally there. This was a town where doing absolutely nothing is itself a full-time occupation. Here one never questions the purpose of life, one simply eats it. The meal on this special day was in Mathios's seafood taverna at the far end of the port.

Once seated, facing the sea, Theo explained his two-month disappearance. He told me that he had finally decided to quit trying so hard to improve the cooking of his native land, and he had gone into his seclusion refusing all offers for restaurant-doctoring ever since the New Year. As a result his marketability had soared, and when he had recently resurfaced, he had immediately been invited to work for a private think tank assembled for the purpose of deciding how to properly feed the multitudes of foreigners expected for the 2004 Athens Olympics.

The job, though temporary, carried an obscene salary, and he was rolling in the bucks. He had bought the sports car and had brought me to Mathios's to spend some of the money with him.

He ordered the entire menu, starting with sea-urchin salad that had been missing from our Yuletide feast. The spiky, dark sea creatures had been harvested less than an hour before, and had been cracked open while still breathing.

Apostrophes of their orange roe had been arranged on a plate and dressed with a simple lemon-oil sauce.

The only way to eat sea urchin is on its own by the spoonful. It tastes as good as beluga, and exudes the same kind of life force as any caviar but with less of the Caspian's hard-to-digest fat. It is the definitive luxury food: tasty, lean, rejuvenating, imperfect and expensive away from its habitat but cheap and addictively astonishing in the Aegean—a Grecian recompense for my total failure as a renovator.

The urchins were followed by a cavalcade of sea dishes, served one by one as per Theo's instructions so that we could savour each one properly. The ubiquitous fried whitebait and *calamarakia* were next, prologued by an order of pulsating, just-steamed wild greens before the tiny fish, and a vinegary salad of seaweed prior to the baby squid.

A trio of slow-cooked dishes landed on the table, each in its turn, to raise the level of the meal in stages: cuttlefish braised with dandelions, octopus stewed in wine and capers, and lobster baked with sweet peppers, onions, and bay leaf. They were all overcooked, softly textured, and minimally flavoured, but slurpingly good. They were the triple overture for the star of the lunch, the royalty of Greek fish, *barbounia* (red mullet).

It was a very long meal, and by the time the mullets made their entrance, the sun had begun to set and a chill breeze was blowing from the north. We were too full to move inside though. We stayed at our seaside table, on the crest of the lengthening shadows from the old buildings, flaking off pink-tinged mullet flesh to let it slowly evaporate in the mouth. True to Theo's theory, we fully enjoyed the fish because we were not in the least hungry.

Theo and I hadn't found much to say during the meal, not only because we were too busy eating, but also because we had said it all during Christmas. After it was over, and a large wad of Theo's money had been handed over to Mathios, we moved indoors to a smoky, rickety-chaired café for some warmth and a couple of strong Greek coffees. I gave Theo the short version of the curry-house saga, including the various disasters, setbacks, personality clashes, items of sexual gossip, and menu details.

He snickered at the adversities, declaring them normal for building a restaurant in Greece, and quizzed me about Elsa. He expressed an interest in meeting her—he was a fan of her brand of motorcycle, having once owned one when he lived in Hamburg. But when he heard I had agreed to include *bifteki* on our menu, his mouth dropped.

"Shameful!" he growled. "I leave you on your own for a couple of months because I need to spend time on improving my own life, and look at the mess you get into! Getting involved with poor partners, agreeing to make burgers. Jeez!"

Chapter 20

All but Ready

Theo stayed overnight, and early the next morning he ushered me back into the narrow confines of his sports car to take me into the hills for one of his favourite pastimes: goat-watching.

Goats, singly and in small herds, are a staple of Crete's countryside, climbing perpendicular cliffsides to find the tastiest leaves, the rarest herbs. It is said that they alone know all the edible leaves and are acquainted with the exact benefits of each, partaking of them as they need them. They are known, for example, to seek out the therapeutic *diktamo* when they are ill or injured.

Bearded haughty billy goats, often-pregnant submissive nanny goats, and their playful kids are a nuclear family that hasn't changed its ways since the Minoans and that has retained its native hold on the island throughout the ages.

For Theodoros, goats are the foundation of Crete and therefore of its music. Their songs come from their bleating and also from the chiming of the small bells goatherds attach to the animals' necks so that they can locate them when they stray. Each goatherd uses a slightly differently toned bell that can be recognized from a distance.

"Imagine bells of ascending tonalities ringing in random syncopation and unmelodic harmony. There is no way someone as middle-class as you can appreciate such confusion," Theo said, "but if you defuse your innate smugness, and listen—I mean really listen—you'd hear wondrous music, blending and bending every musical idiom ever invented, without, obviously, belonging to any of them. This is nature singing her own story just for you. It won't sound the same to any two people standing on the same hill. Listen and tell me what it says to you."

I listened very hard, but what I heard were occasional trills of bells mixed in with insect-buzzing, bird-chirping, wind-whistling. All it did was remind me that I hadn't had time to finish my cup of morning coffee, inarguably the most sacred cup of the day and from which only a Theo could be so insensitive as to rush me away, in order to go listen to some bloody goat bells.

Happily, I was not required to pass Theo's goat quiz; the exegesis of what the goats sang to me would have to wait another day. A phone call from Pete came at exactly the right moment, demanding my immediate presence at the restaurant. Theo drove back like a fiend as I sat cramped, dreading what the emergency could be.

The driveway of the restaurant was now like a slalom course, with several awkward mounds of earth drying into moguls, while a new and deep cement-mixing pond was so prominently in the way that the only hope of crossing it lay in straddling it at great risk of at least one wheel falling into the muck. Theo parked his fragile car away from all the obstacles, and we walked through the garden up to the balcony.

Pete was sprawled on a bench, poring over his latest *mantinades*. Oh, great, I thought, the tyrant had summoned me to read to me. Well, he'd have to read to Theo too, and Theo would doubtless prove a much harsher audience than I.

But it wasn't the *mantinades*. It was a real problem, and in its way just as thorny as everything else that had befallen our ill-starred enterprise. The police searches of the partners had come in, and it had been discovered that Jean-Louis had amassed a mile-long juvenile record of petty offences while a wild teenager in Grenoble. The worst of it was that his farewell gesture, breaking open the cash box of a public telephone, had occurred on the inebriated afternoon of his eighteenth birthday. This had earned him a slot in adult court, which our hero had impulsively avoided by running off and getting lost in Paris. He had been sentenced in absentia, and there was an open warrant for his arrest.

"I was only a kid," screamed Jean-Louis, who had just driven in and barely escaped being stuck in the cement. "And I've been paying for that one stupid action all my life. I travel on a fake passport. I'm afraid to return to France. And now I am to be persecuted in Greece? This is too much! There were only eighteen francs in that damned payphone."

"Oh, like Jean Valjean," said Pete with open contempt. "And why no finish the problem? Why you no buy off the jail time?"

"In France you cannot buy off a sentence like you can here. In civilized countries you have to do the time," whimpered Jean-Louis, pacing nervously up and down the balcony.

"And in the Greece, foreigners with the criminal in the brain are not welcome!" Pete grunted while passing wind. He caught Theo wandering into the restaurant out of the corner of his eye. "Hey, you!" he shouted in Greek. "Get your ass away from there. Not allowed! Stop!"

Theo turned in slow motion to face Pete. Two king rats about to square off, I thought excitedly despite myself. By all rights I should have been devastated now that we had a legal problem to exacerbate our structural woes, but the prospect of Theo and Pete going at each other was thrilling me.

Theo sauntered back neither chastened nor sorry, simply respectful of another's private property. With his gaze riveted on Pete's eye slits, he said with deliberate menace, "Theodoros from Anógia."

"Petros from Marioú," answered Pete steadily, putting out his hand. Theo let the proffered hand hang in the air for a few seconds while he scratched his chin thoughtfully. Then he extended his own for a brief, limp handshake.

"What goes in Anógia?" asked Pete.

"Not much more than in Marioú," answered Theo, taking a seat opposite Pete uninvited.

Jean-Louis was not impressed by the posturings of rival-village honchos. "Look," he pleaded. "We have to cover this up. No one knows about it. Not Theresa. Not the children. It'd destroy me."

"This is a trivial matter that need not interest any civilized person," Theo shot off his shoulder without looking at Jean-Louis. "Only the police. And the Greek police are interested in you only because you never showed any remorse for your crime."

"Remorse. Yes. The remorse is good. The very good," agreed Pete, looking at Theo with respectful admiration. My two king rats were bonding. There was not going to be a showdown. I was disappointed.

"What kind of remorse?" Jean-Louis asked dubiously.

"We'll have to figure it out," Theo said dismissively.

"Yes. Figure out!" Pete said impatiently. Then, in Greek to Theo: "So, what do you think of this curry-house of Byron's?" He enunciated "curry" as if it was about to bite him.

"I love curry," smiled Theo. "All curries, but especially the Indian ones, because they have more flavours than the Thai ones. And generally, except for the Gujarati, they are not as sweet. I once spent two weeks in Hyderabad sampling the lamb curry of various restaurants, and no two of them tasted alike. In Thailand all the curries taste the same wherever you are, be it Phuket or Chiang Mai. Thai palates have no subtlety. All they care about is that each curry possess all four tastes at once. Give them sweet-salty-sour-and-bitter in the same stew and they don't give a damn about anything else."

Pete was completely lost. But his admiration for Theo had now escalated to reverence. He turned back to Jean-Louis and addressed him as if he were a servant: "I'll speak to police assistant chief, and he will the decision for the remorse for you. We fix, forget it. Go home."

"And face Theresa?! I'd rather go back to Grenoble and face jail."

"Then have a *raki*," suggested Theo as Pete laughed out loud, and the two of them punctuated their new friendship with piercingly loud, satisfyingly liberating farts. A strong odour of wet goat slowly permeated the balcony; it attacked my sensitive nose so ringingly, I finally smelled the music of the goat bells.

(((

Algis had streamlined his sculpture project. He had had to concede that one hundred pieces was beyond his means, especially since each one required much rebuilding to get it just right and prevent it from falling over. He decided to keep to the original twenty, trying to perfect each one. So there he was all day long, for days on end, stacking rocks, restacking, buffering against the wind, bolstering the bases so that the slender upper sections could withstand the wind's gusts.

As he reworked them, the figures took on ever more human forms, finally resembling a group of pilgrims walking down the slope. The most imposing of them, a three-metre-tall high priest with a conical headdress, was behind the main group, as if he had paused to enjoy the view while the others walked on.

The villagers had continued to drive by and honk their approval, until the Marioú parish priest, the engine behind the building of the church, stormed onto the site and confronted the sculptor. He screamed several choice phrases that Algis could not understand, but his disapproval was unmistakable. The villagers, thereafter, sped up when they drove by and no longer honked. Algis took this as his cue. He photographed his work once more and declared it complete.

On the same day, Pete invited us to visit the restaurant, which was also declared complete. There was apparently a new roof and new decor all done, in only two weeks since the fateful earthquake. We drove over the moguls, carefully straddled the cement hole, which appeared to have become a permanent fixture, and entered a room that was recognizable only as a grotesque parody of the original.

Two small salvageable sections of the battered zinc bar had been mounted in muted, unattractive corners of the room, serving no function whatsoever, certainly not as a bar that anyone would want to drink on, or as a divider from the kitchen.

The caressable maple wood of the custom-built tables and chairs had splintered into matchsticks. It had been replaced by new tables of cheap pressboard made of wood shavings and glue. The tables were shaky and covered in vinyl to hide their ugliness. The loathsome green-brown motifs of the vinyl, the cheapest Pete could find, were just as ugly as the wood, and they already felt grimy.

The new chairs were of the sadistic, straw-seat, bottom-of-the-line variety found in all the neighbourhood cafés of Greece. They are torture for anyone with less than steely buttocks. Pete was very proud of them; they were so consummately *paradosiaka* (traditional), he said, and oh, yes, so very inexpensive.

The floor tiles had not been replaced: a useless expense, we were told. Unnecessary, and they tended to chip and break, didn't they? A cement floor would have to do.

The walls were hideous. Theresa's lovingly chosen and artfully hung tapestries had been irretrievably damaged. In their place Pete had stuck a garish painting of the Parthenon (intact, with its original statuary and painted columns) on one side, and opposite it a huge wallpaper illustration of some generic beach. The paper had been badly mounted by the inconsolable Stavros and Pavlos, and was already coming unstuck at the corners.

The formerly glittering beaded-string curtain from the kasbah had been recovered from the deluge. It was a little the worse for wear, but it had been rehung in its original location in front of the toilets. It now swayed there, injured and forlorn, unrelated to the rest of the room, irrelevant, an eyesore.

The only improvement in this renovation was the lighting. A new and safe roof on which to work had inspired Onassis to properly wire the room with outlets on the walls as well as the ceiling. The kitchen now had the kind of overhead illumination that Jean-Louis's excellent equipment deserved, and the dining room boasted the pinpoint spots and indirect splashes of light that Olaf had originally conceived.

Ironically, the good lighting illuminated the ugly room far too clearly, making the sorry spectacle appear even sorrier. Theresa gasped when she saw it. Finally losing the cool of her fine manners, she burst into a torrent of French and Arabic, none of which needed interpretation: she was swearing like a sailor.

Pete, who feared her as much as the rest of us, farted discreetly and spoke soothingly: "Kiria Theresa, please," he tried to reason with her. "This is the summer business. The customers not care for the inside. They like the outside. The nice air. The looking at the *yallo* [water's edge]. Why spend the money two times? One time, okay. And now, this is the okay." He took a deep breath. "Now we are ready. Now we have the big party, and drink the *raki*, and the Byron cook the curry. Yes? All right? All right! Now we have the fun. Yes?"

But as a number of famous *mantinades* could have informed us, before the fun there is always the pain. This time around our pain had a legal hue. The Jean-Louis issue had created a tremendous rift in his relations with his family. Both Theresa and the children treated him like a pariah, forcing him to repent with a cruel sequence of humbling penances.

He had been kicked out of the conjugal bed, relegated to the clunky, so-called fold-out bed—another of Greece's torture contraptions, whose hurtful metal supports crunch the ribs and afford no comfortable sleeping position.

He had also lost all his privileges. He was broke after purchasing all that kitchen equipment with his personal money, and it was Theresa's parents' stipends that were now sustaining the family. As a result Theresa had stripped him of the car keys, forcing him to walk or hitchhike everywhere. She also demanded that he take care of all the chores, such as the inevitable laundry, sweeping, and dishwashing, in return for feeding him.

Jean-Louis felt humiliated and emasculated in front of his neighbours, and it was no consolation at all that Olaf was happy to be a househusband to the wage-earning Elsa, good-naturedly bearing his own Greek neighbours' scorn. Olaf, after all, was a limp northerner, a Swede, and Jean-Louis was a hot-blooded Latin, a small step removed from the terminal machismo of the Greeks.

As if all this was not unbearable enough to his volatile temperament, Jean-Louis also had to suffer the indifference, the near contempt, of his young children, whom he loved with a passion. They left for school in the morning without kissing him, they no longer giggled merrily at his jokes, they squirmed away when he tried to hug them, and they took to calling him "Father" instead of "Papa," a formality he read as a slap in the face.

He was so shattered and desperate that it was easy to persuade him to undergo the stipulated remorse that Pete had worked out for him at the police station. It amounted to an inquisition and an apology—demeaningly in front of minor officials. The second assistant police chief, the lower-echelon members of the town council, a retired judge, a senile war-hero general, and a career politician who hoped to become mayor and who considered himself far more influential than he actually was constituted the committee, which was put together not so much to hear the case as to point out to Jean-Louis exactly how unimportant he was.

It was another slap in the face, but the accused was beyond caring. He just wanted his nightmare to end, and he promised to adhere to the letter of Pete's instructions. The idea was for him to act self-effacingly meek, to put himself at the mercy of these unworthy accusers, and to shed as many heartfelt tears as he could muster during his apology. That and obtain some money for the fine that the committee was bound to impose.

"The fine will be a huge problem," Jean-Louis moaned. "But the tears, don't worry. I have many." He planned a trip to Preveli to seek divine assistance—and the courage to ask Theresa for a loan.

Meanwhile, at Algis's church, divine justice was already being meted out. The ornery Marioú priest, citing the Big Guy as his source, had served Algis holy notice to tear down his "idolater" sculptures from the courtyard of the House of God or face eternal damnation.

And so, on the same day that Jean-Louis was scheduled to offer remorse for his past sins at a makeshift courthouse, Algis was up on the hill undoing his exhibition, taking apart his meticulously fixed rocks, creating a void where there had been substance. True to his tenacious artistry, he was making an event out of the dismantling, photographing the phases of the fast-action reversal of a construct that had been created slowly and laboriously. His camera recorded the demolition down to the last image, when there were no longer pilgrims trekking down the slope, only piles of rocks.

It hadn't taken long for the word to spread around the villages. And soon a large crowd timidly approached by car and motorcycle and on foot to witness the deconstruction in silence and with a certain measure of sadness. When it was all over, no one cheered, and they all dispersed quietly. Algis brushed the dust off his clothes and walked away from the site without looking back.

Sometime late that afternoon the appointed dignitaries assembled in Plakiás harbour. It was a nice day, and no one felt like being cooped up indoors. They chose the seaside terrace of Plakiás's best coffeehouse at which to hold the event. The judges installed themselves at an extended table right next to the lapping wavelets and ordered coffees, the better to enjoy the upcoming show. The hearing was meant to be closed to the public, but many of the curious had sidled beachside to be within earshot. Though technically off the café's territory, they too were able to order refreshments, even if they had to sit on the sand.

Jean-Louis was brought in not in chains but in the barbed wire of his repentance. He had fasted for two days, to appear gaunt and pitiable. He was accompanied by his wife and children, in truce for the occasion; they were dressed in black, already in mourning for their patriarch. And behind him were all of us, including Algis, who had rushed down from his hill, all the workers, and the Petes, everyone somber and suitably penitent.

Jean-Louis delivered an admirably impassioned speech composed of a few well-chosen Greek phrases that he had rehearsed to perfection and now repeated in rotation, all on the same obvious themes: how fathomlessly sorry he was to have tampered with telephone company equipment; how he had learned his lesson; how he could never again contemplate, or even dream of, insulting society with any thoughtless, selfish, criminal actions.

He nuanced his speech throughout with minor, controlled

sobs, but when he repeated the last of his refrains he broke down in a veritable flood of tears, which were echoed by supplicating, blatantly rehearsed wails from his wife and children.

The judges sipped their coffees pensively and conferred in stage whispers. They were favourably disposed, that was obvious. But the law was the law. Blah-blah. And it would be unwise to cause diplomatic ripples with our Euro-partner, France. Blah-blah. But what about the lovely children and the poor wife? Tra-la. Who would take care of them, leaderless and vulnerable if he were sent off to jail . . . ? It went back and forth for a while, and then they reached their verdict.

The proceedings were called to order, just like in a real trial, and Jean-Louis was made to stand in front of them with his head bowed. They warned him—in formal Greek that he had no prayer of understanding—that from now on he was under advisement—or did they say "probation"?—that they—well, someone—would be watching him day and night, that he would no longer be able to get away with anything, not even offences that are taken for granted in Greece, like swearing in public and driving drunk.

However, they had agreed that what had happened in Grenoble twenty years ago had caused him enough grief to date, and they didn't see the usefulness of any other punishments since he was so obviously sorry for what he had done. They decreed that he could proceed with his restaurant business, and they didn't even mention a fine, probably because none of them were powerful enough to be able to pocket any of the money.

Pete sprang out of his chair, surprisingly smoothly for his girth, and thanked the judges profusely, inviting them all to the opening party. He promised to smack Jean-Louis personally if he so much as forgot to brush his teeth in future, and he grandly announced that no one, not even the kibitzers on the beachside, need worry about paying for their coffees since the bill was already settled. He discreetly motioned Jean-Louis to the cash register to pay for the "settled" bill, itself a hefty fine as this was one of the most expensive cafés in southern Crete and there were, all told, seventy-three coffees to pay for.

The matter agreeably resolved, Pete ordered *raki* for the head table and sat with them to party. A few *aspro patos* later, he had dug out his notebook of *mantinades*, and acting the ersatz Homer, he read them sample after sample of his unworthy versifying.

If anything could have undone their sympathy for our partnership, it was these endless affectations of Pete's. Happily, there was indeed a poet in our group. The truck-driving loner Spiros took pity on our beleaguered enterprise and decided to save us from this new calamity.

The under-appreciated Spiros, accompanied by little Lefteris's sweet stylings on the lyre, took centre stage, pre-empting Pete, to sing his own *mantinades*. These were lovely haikus about nature and the deep emotions, and about our puzzling existence in a firmament teeming with unhappiness. He finished to great applause with this:

The bells of billy goats, music of my heart,
crying, laughing, yearning divine smiles,
flowering blossoms from lips breathlessly apart.

"Breathlessly apart," "breathlessly apart, my heart," sang everyone in chorus, as the lyre played on like so many goat bells, nature's own music. "Breathlessly apart." As if they had been singing these words at parties all their lives. An instant classic.

Chapter 21

Party

Throwing a party in such a closely knit community as the Plakiás-Marioú area means you don't invite anyone in particular, you invite everyone. Much like a wedding or baptism, our restaurant's opening party soon became a free-for-all, both for the Greeks and also for a parallel universe of year-round resident foreigners, people we had heard about but never before met, who started greeting us in the streets, promising to come and threatening to bring everyone they knew.

Pete estimated that we would have close to two thousand guests. He made a list of all the important people, the minor honchos who had sat in judgment of Jean-Louis, but also some real big shots, friends of the Mayoral Hopeful, rich farmers, business leaders, and the area's most important person, a godfather of sorts, the wheel that propelled the region's economy: the owner of the local olive oil factory. The list of these men and their wives would number about fifty, and they would need special attention, assured seating, and most decidedly an excess of food.

We concluded that it would be best to set up Pete's captain's table in the spanking new and hideously ugly dining room—"They love it. Forget it!" he assured us—and cater everyone else on the balcony and the garden, having prayed for a dry, warm afternoon—"End of March? Never the rain. Forget it!" scoffed Pete. But we had been bitten once too often to take any good luck for granted.

Algis and I, the only kitchen-savvy partners in the lot, put on our aprons and retired to Jean-Louis's dream kitchen to determine the logistics of cooking for a couple of thousand people, a major chore even in a kitchen of this magnitude.

Algis expressed grave concerns that we wouldn't be able to handle such a big job. He threatened to quit unless we reduced the numbers, but since that was beyond our control, we cajoled him, appealed to his sense of adventure, promised him bribes—such as Jean-Louis's scanner on which to digitalize his photographs—and then we begged him on our knees.

The fact was, we couldn't possibly do without him, as we hadn't been able to recruit kitchen help during the relentless renovation problems. Now we were stuck with a parade of candidates that Pete had hastily assembled, young men and aged women, none of whom had ever cooked professionally and the best of whom (the aged women) would need far too much training to be of any real use for the party.

The person I would have most loved to have help us was Theo, but he had absolutely refused to heed my desperate phone pleas to come back from Athens—not only because he was busy, but mostly to punish me for getting into business without consulting him. The fact that he had been unavailable for consultation during both January and February did not weigh in my favour.

I did finally persuade Algis to give it a go as my co-chef, and then I risked further chaos by asking the partners to be our helpers because, if nothing else, they would have to be enthusiastic, having so much at stake. Even so, I got only two of them, Jean-Louis and Olaf, who in any case had fully intended to learn the ways of the kitchen. Elsa begged off, arguing that she'd be much more useful playing hostess and schmoozing with the heavy hitters on Pete's list. Theresa refused to consider any position whatsoever. She had no intention of being anywhere near an event of such low standards as to be open to everyone.

We haggled over the menu for a while, finally conceding that it was beyond our means, financially if nothing else, to feed the masses properly. The bulk of our guests, those who were consigned to the outdoors, would be given the old standby, burgers.

Well, *biftekis*, naturally, made the Greek way with the addition of chopped onion and parsley—but minced meat nevertheless, and that's a burger by any other name. To please the foreigners, who were potentially our best customers, and to introduce them to our curry-house concept, we proposed a generic curry sauce as an optional dressing for the *biftekis*. Bread and a giant salad would round out the meal.

Burgers were a far cry from the fare intended for the titans in the dining room. For them nothing was too good. Pete, more imperious by the moment, instructed us to prepare a full roster of our curries for them, though he promised us none of them would ever consider putting them in their mouths. But at least they would know we had made the effort. Pete proceeded to inform us—he saw no grounds for debate on this issue—that Mrs. Pete would cook the best of her Greek specialties so that the guests could have something to eat instead of starving to death. That none of those items were supposed to be on the restaurant's permanent menu didn't concern him in the least.

With only three days to go, we became a whirlwind of confusion and exaggerated activity. Restaurants are like pieces of theatre. And just like a play, three days before opening everything comes unravelled, seems impossible to correct on time, yet somehow, through sheer determination or Dionysian intervention, it all works out in the end and the curtain rises.

Onassis, with much grumbling and gloomy sarcasm, wired the outdoors with extensive lights, because we all knew that our midday party would extend far into the night and would turn into a melee if a huge crowd had to circulate in the dark among live-charcoal barbecues.

The outdoor cookers themselves were manufactured from metal barrels sawn in half horizontally and propped up precariously on skinny metal legs. There were four of them, one in each corner of the garden, with a total capacity of eighty *biftekis* at once.

Algis calculated that it would take over five hours of continuous grilling to produce the minimum of two thousand pieces, which would also require about a thousand kilos of charcoal, four cooks to operate the grills, and two swing-assistants.

Now that he was into it, Algis was unstoppable. He persuaded all three Yannises, Spiro, and the demonstrably willing Stavros and Pavlos to become the cooks- and assistant-cooks-for-a-day. He intended to train them in the heat of things since there was no time to do it before. Only Onassis refused to participate, declaring that he had better ways to burn his fingers than flipping burgers for a bunch of freeloaders.

My old nemeses the power saw, the hammers, and the nails made a comeback with only two days to go when Pete had a sudden flash of panic and rushed the carpenters to make tables for people to sit in the garden, it being offensively un-Greek to expect guests to eat standing up.

I survived the carpentry, didn't even need a Maalox, because I was swamped in the kitchen, where I was effectively working alone, Algis being mostly outside with his barbecues. Jean-Louis and Olaf were proving to be terrible assistants, as they were too overwhelmed by the unfamiliar work to be of any help.

My most urgent chore was to mix and shape the *biftekis*. The idea was to prepare batches of them and freeze them, to get them out of the way so we could concentrate on the complexities of our curries. On the other hand, those curries could very well never materialize, since the all-important spices and curry pastes, on order from a wholesaler in Athens, were dangerously overdue with less than forty-eight hours to go.

The industrial-size stand-up mixer was to be my saving grace: kneading four hundred kilos of hamburger meat by hand is no joy. I put the first thirty kilos of meat into the gleaming virginal bowl and added two kilos of minced onion, one kilo of chopped parsley, a hundred grams each of salt and pepper, and two dozen raw whole eggs, as per a Constantinopolitan recipe of my mother's. I was just about to flick the switch when Pete yelled for me.

This time it was a matter of olive oil. We had let it slip that curries are better with a lighter oil, such as safflower, and it had been a thorn in his side ever since. Now he had upgraded his concern to panic level, claiming that we would surely be boycotted by the locals if we refused to use olive oil, the area's highest-profile product. It would be a matter of pride and also of economics, as the olive farmers would view our lack of patronage as a personal affront as well as an attack on their purses.

He had, without warning and without consulting me, removed all the safflower oil from the premises and replaced it with local olive oil. He had called me out simply to tell me, not to argue the matter. I had no idea how I was meant to respond, and anyway I had trouble concentrating on the issue with all the table-carpentry going on at full swing around me, plus my mind was on the *bifteki* fixings sitting in the mixer at Jean-Louis's and Olaf's mercy. A loud double cry from the kitchen confirmed my fears.

Pete and I rushed in to find both of my inept assistants covered head to toe in bits of meat and onion and parsley, drips of blood and runny egg. Just as I had feared, the dolts had decided to "help" me and complete the interrupted mixing by cranking the control to maximum and pressing the "on" button.

Professional mixers will invariably attack with a tidal wave of whatever is in the bowl when they're turned on at high speed. These machines are so powerful that turning them on, even at the lowest speed, is best done with caution. They are like young and excitable horses: they take off with abandon, they buck and kick and toss, before they settle down to a measured trot, a steady beat of the revolving blade.

Jean-Louis and Olaf were covered in the entirety of the *bifteki* components; they had been unable to reach the "off" switch when the surprise attack had first hit. They had then shielded the rest of the kitchen from the onslaught by leaning over the wildly rotating machine. By the time they were able to disable the lethal churning—after some ten seconds—every last speck had flown out of the bowl and onto them.

And so started my Plakiás cooking adventure, and it continued in the same slapstick fashion: cut fingers, overturned bowls of curry, numberless burns, a succession of screams and loud expletives, shouting, recriminations, more shouting, many cups of coffee, debilitating frustration—the whole sequence of disharmony and unhappiness without which professional cooking could never really work.

In the middle of it, the towering uncertainty of our spice delivery tortured me with three-antacid anxiety. But in the end it all worked out too. The spices got to us in plenty of time, and the preparations were completed just ahead of schedule.

By two in the afternoon on the day of the party, a brilliantly sunny, warm Sunday, when even the village grouches and recent widows couldn't help but smile with contentment, we were in workable if slightly imperfect order. The cement hole had been mostly covered but was still an open invitation for a child to run into it and fall in; the outdoor lights, which we had tested the previous night, gave our place an Anatolian-wonderland feel, even if all their connections were exposed and could electrocute our guests if it happened to rain; the garden tables were not in the least solid, but at least they were standing, covered in the same awful green-brown vinyl as the ones inside; Algis had placed his barbecues out of harm's way, and though far apart, they were all ingeniously close to the kitchen for fetching and restocking—although no one had been able to locate proper grills, and the cooking surface was Algis-unapproved pieces of flat metal that would buckle if nudged and spill the burgers to the ground.

On my side, over in the kitchen, my mauled partners and I had managed the impossible. Some three thousand *biftekis* had been kneaded and shaped, stored in all available spaces of the freezer. Two hundred litres of curry sauce had been concocted and now waited in the fridges to garnish the burgers. A truckful of tomatoes and cucumbers had been sliced and sealed in plastic, and were also in the fridge.

For the master table we had pulled out all the stops on curries that they would never eat: Thai seafood curries from Krabi province with red chilies and an excess of curry leaf; fiery green curries with eggplant and mutton from the north of Thailand; multi-aromatic vegetable curries from Tamil Nadu in southern India; thick-sauced chicken curries from the *karahis* of Bengal; silken fish and coconut-milk yellow curries from Laos; curried goat and chickpeas from Jamaica; a million spices, a kaleidoscope of chilies, all shapes, all sizes, all hot enough to scorch the mouths of the uninitiated.

The first drink was served at one minute past two in the afternoon, and the last one just before sunrise at three minutes to six the following morning. What exactly happened in between is anybody's guess. I noticed very little, working harder than I had ever done in my life, even harder than on that impossible, unending day when I was catering the filming of *Once upon a Time in America* and the director, Sergio Leone, kept shooting the same "death on a wet street" scene over and over again, going into overtime and an unscheduled second meal to feed two hundred disgruntled cast and crew, soaked through by artificial rain, smelling of grime and cold sweat, impossible to please with my lukewarm emergency quiche and last-ditch iceberg-lettuce salad.

There were no deaths at our party that warm spring Sunday in Plakiás. There were many people, that's for sure, even more than the predicted two thousand; but they came in staggered groups, the last one arriving at three in the morning, and there were never more than a manageable few hundred at any one time. And the burgers were popular and they lasted, and the foreigners really, really loved the curry sauce, so starved were their palates for flavours other than the same old oregano, lemon, onion, and judicious garlic that pervades the native cuisine of Crete. And there was plenty to drink, and live music right through the eighteen hours, as everyone who played a musical instrument brought it and joined the tireless Lefteris for a lyre session that jammed its haunting melodies straight up to the heavens to sing the praises of all the heroes who ever climbed the craggy mountain paths of this fiercely loved homeland.

It was like a wedding and an orgy all at once. The Greeks came in force with their children and their elders, everyone dressed as if for a holiday. They came out of their winter shells to celebrate the start of the tourist season, Plakiás's "other" life, which our opening, the first of the season, came to represent. Within a month, the entire bay would be open for business, with a festive stretch of seaside restaurants and cafés, a necklace of diversion-for-profit, but on this day our place was it, a microcosm of what was in store.

The orgy part was provided by the more youthful and libidinous of the foreigners, who came to *kefi* after the curry sauce—made explosively aphrodisiac with Algis's added chilies—and the bottomless cups of native wine and *raki*. They ran down to the beach and threw themselves into the cold waters. The Greeks got goose pimples just watching them. After the swim quite a few of them semi-hid behind little trees and low sand hillocks, supposedly to dry off; but as was obvious to everyone, they were doing more than just lying back. The Greek women averted their eyes, the men pretended not to be watching, and the children stared, but no one complained, not even the ultra-religious, because this was one of the prices that had to be paid for the wealth that these debauched people brought to the area.

I witnessed none of this. I only heard the stories afterwards. My domain during the whole length of the festivities was the kitchen, supervising my gradually drunker so-called assistants Jean-Louis and Olaf while working shoulder to shoulder with the ever-resourceful Mrs. Pete.

Our special guests came en masse at three o'clock in the afternoon, the favourite Sunday lunch hour of well-to-do Greeks. They sat down at their appointed tables, primed by Pete to expect favoured service, and had a typical Greek-style party all the way to midnight. We fed them Mrs. Pete's plethora of party foods in a rotation meant to promote drinking and regenerate appetite.

To start, we had the oversalted appetizers: fried meatballs, extra-cheese dandelion mini-pies, fishy carp-roe *tarama* dip, thinly sliced fried eggplant and zucchini with garlicky tzatziki, soured sheep's milk *myzithra* cheese, acrid smoked herring, inedibly vinegared *apaki* (pickled pork), softly stewed intestines and sweetbreads, rice and lamb dumplings in egg-lemon sauce, plump snails swimming in oil—some thirty dishes in all, with ripe tomatoes and Selliá village goat's-milk feta cheese to accompany each of them.

The main courses, to be savoured Theo-style after the pangs of hunger had been more than satiated by the appetizers, were a lexicon of pan-Greek meat cookery from across the ages. These were the same items my mother and grandmothers had cooked back in Constantinople, and surely the same items that Greek mothers and grandmothers will be cooking well past this third millennium. To wit: roast suckling pig with charred skin and melted flesh; tomato-stewed *kokinisto* lamb alongside lamb-fat-enriched rice; festive turkey stuffed with pine nuts and raisins, with hopelessly overcooked, rubbery breasts; weighty noodle *pastichio* with artery-clogging cheesy *béchamel* and greasy minced beef; rabbit and pearl onion *stiffado*; pork with prunes; veal with quince; fried salt cod with garlic mashed potato; overfried calf's liver, dry as shoe leather, smothered in shaved onion; tomato-sauce orzo with stewed veal shank; and three kinds of potato, lemon-baked, limply french-fried, and mashed-fried into croquettes.

It was a comprehensive Greek meal, which Mrs. Pete had prepared in her own cramped kitchen and which she was now reheating and finishing in our luxurious, German-outfitted kitchen. I could see a glimmer of envy in her eyes, regretting that such a wonderful set-up would be going to waste cooking inedible curries instead of her own beloved delicacies.

I marvelled at her industry and her attention to detail, her ability to craft a truckful of this labour-intensive cuisine all by herself. It gave me great pleasure to work alongside her, to assist her, and especially to keep Jean-Louis and Olaf away from her by assigning them to help with the constant fetching and the salad-making out in the garden.

Our special guests were catered to their complete satisfaction, even though I came close to ruining it for them in a moment of overexuberance, one of my oldest failings. Never happy to let well enough alone, I insisted that we serve them a sampler of my curries so they could at least take a small taste. I put the curries on the table and instantly regretted it. Just as

Pete had warned me, no one did more than smell them. But
even that was too much, causing several women to come close
to fainting, while quite a few men and women seemed ready
to vomit. The crisis was averted when Pete grabbed the curries and returned them to the kitchen, with a stern look that
said "Don't do this again!"

At around midnight, most of them, including all the wives,
thanked us sincerely, burped with contentment, wished us
great success, and took their leave. Seven of the heaviest hitters—the Mayoral Hopeful and his best cronies, the big business leaders and the olive oil godfather—pickled to the core
by the wine and *raki* and put over the brink by several shots
of ill-advised Scotch and vodka chasers, stayed on to sing
mantinades and continue celebrating as Greek men do best,
after their wives have left the building.

It was at this moment that the Greek family party ended and
a more desperate adult shindig took its place. Up to now it
had been women on one end, men on the other, children running around, gossip, some risqué jokes with punchlines so
deeply shaded that no one could be offended, lots of well-
wishing for surviving the upcoming summer's tourist invasion, and quite a few here's-to-our-next-mayor's directed at
the Mayoral Hopeful. There would soon be much less benign
celebrating, with some serious consequences. I remember the
transitional point well, because the guests' near mass exit gave
us a break in the kitchen and a chance to stack our mounting
piles of dishes into the exquisite dishwasher.

My two partners and I loaded the dishwasher up well
enough, but try as we might we couldn't make it start. We had
not found the time to test it, trusting that such a prominently
fabulous machine couldn't fail to work. We were stymied, the
thoroughly drunk Jean-Louis and Olaf borderline frantic,

when like a saviour outlined in an electric aura, Onassis appeared through the kitchen door.

"You haven't plugged it in, you dolts," he said with his famous disdain, brandishing the neglected plug in his hand.

"Oh, that's funny," I smiled, walking over to see where this essential plugging was meant to occur. And it's a good thing I looked, because just to prove he was a real Greek, Onassis had placed the socket in an impossible place, hidden behind folds of plumbing and requiring a nimble crawl to locate.

I watched his contortions in awe as he managed to do the impossible: fit the plug into the little holes in the wall, while Jean-Louis and Olaf were innocently waiting by the open portals of the machine. There was an instant surge of power through the beast, as we had forgotten to switch it off. A loud spray of warm water mixed with soap and bits of plate grease shot out at my hapless partners, drenching them mercilessly in a more benign replay of their earlier mixer misadventure.

They yelped and cursed, but by now they had become used to being attacked by the kitchen equipment. They laughed as merrily as Onassis and I, and Mrs. Pete, who had been watching from the wings.

This wet incident, a mere anecdote outside the kitchen but a memorable moment inside it, happened at midnight. And while it was going on, the dining room had nearly emptied, leaving behind the seven lingering, *mantinada*-singing, far-too-drunk, unbearably self-important Greeks.

Elsa chose that same moment to make a bubbly entrance into the restaurant. Flushed by the certifiable success of the party, future euro signs sparkling in her liquid-blue eyes, the glitter of financial fulfillment cascading down her lush blond hair, she sat down at the table with Pete and his important Greeks.

The presence of a beautiful young foreign woman stimulates Greek men even more than the departure of their wives. They turned into one collective ogle, undressing the sexy Elsa with their hungry eyes, pouring new drinks, toasting the presence of a creature any one of them would risk bankruptcy for to make his trophy mistress.

The last thing that the ultra-independent Elsa would've considered was becoming the kept woman of a demanding, pot-bellied Greek. But at this heady moment, the apex of an opening party we had all despaired of ever having, she became the spirit and the essence of all their insistent carnal desires.

She drank with them and she flirted—body language and alluring looks only, no touching—and she made each one feel as if Fate had brought her to Plakiás just for him. And so when she gave me the "hunger" signal and I brought her a plate of our tastiest curries, they were trapped. She ate with such gusto and so much lip-smacking, that they had no choice but to follow suit; and despite Pete's warnings and his absolute refusal to join them, they requested the same curries for themselves to keep her company.

They must have been half mad with lust and their tastebuds must have been inured by alcohol, because they ate unfeelingly of dishes that represented their deepest food phobias. They were spurred on by Elsa to try hotter and hotter ones, unwilling to back off, determined to persuade her, and themselves, that they were real men who had conquered untold enemies, vanquished all obstacles, survived life's cruel vagaries, and that there was no way something she could eat with such relish and so much ease could possibly defeat them.

Chapter 22

Endgame

It was a red-alert crisis. A catastrophe. It was death. It was too much.

"It's a disgrace! None of us will ever be able to face the public again!" hissed the Mayoral Hopeful. "I'm hoping to be the next mayor, for God's sake! How can I win an election if I can't show my face? Answer me, please, Kirie Petro, Kirie Byron. Please!"

The Mayoral Hopeful was being obliquely rhetorical because in fact he was utterly furious. It was the Monday afternoon after our party, and Pete and I had been having a victory coffee on the "verandah," as the balcony had just been renamed, planning the next weekend, greedily expecting to start making a killing before the rest of the restaurants had even opened, when the M.H. had driven up, cursing as he bounced over our moguls and came within an inch of crashing into the cement hole, which was rapidly transforming itself into a lethal pothole.

He had put on a wide-brimmed fedora, so at first we hadn't noticed the splotches. All we could see was his wincing mouth, and we mistook the seething for a smile, imagining that he had dropped by to thank us for the party and to congratulate us.

Our first indication that something was seriously wrong was the purple sores, raw-liver-like, that had invaded his face like a map outlined in blood and that came into focus as he got closer to us.

Irrevocable proof came with the subsequent story of the awful afflictions of all seven of the late-night lascivious curry-nibblers, but not of Pete, who had abstained, as was pointed out in accusation. Seven pillars of the Plakiás area had woken up this day with the same atrocious splotches, as well as with mouth burns, piles, diarrhea, and *exapseis* (yet another very Greek disease, usually suffered by women, which translates roughly as "hot flashes"), all of them consequences of the deadly curry—he pronounced the word like the second half of *hara-kiri*—cowardly ailments with which their adversaries could impugn their valour, their authority, their worthiness. This display of their inability to withstand hot chilies that a woman could so easily ingest would surely terminate their careers.

"How is Elsa today, by the way?" the M.H. asked us slyly, not really changing the subject.

"She is fine," I started to say, oblivious to Pete's frantic finger-wagging.

"Not so well, actually," Pete concluded for me. "Rather ill, I would say."

"Splotches?"

"Yes. Yes, many splotches. All over her body," I chimed in, catching Pete's drift.

The M.H. had only a few seconds in which to appreciate this good news, when the actual absolutely splotch-free, creamy body and face of the real Elsa showed up, back from her long jog on the beach. The M.H. turned his back to her, screeching, "Get her away from me! She mustn't see my face!"

I rushed down to the garden to ward her off, and took her for a stroll, giving Pete and the M.H. a chance to get in the car and drive off to a summit conference with the rest of the stricken seven, to decide—and then seal—the fate of our restaurant.

Pete took quite a while, but finally he returned, shaking his head. He gave me the details of the meeting so that I could be the one to pass it on to the partners. His story was a frightening one. The seven mighty men had been reduced to snivelling, laughable monsters. He had found them gathered in the dark in the M.H.'s home, shifting their weight from buttock to buttock to ease the pain of the piles, sighing as hot flashes washed over them, smelling acridly of diarrhea drips they had been unable to catch in time.

"Their mouths are so sadly burned, they can barely speak at all." Pete shuddered at the memory. "But when they did speak, their message was unmistakable. It is as the Mayoral Hopeful said. They are thoroughly disgraced. They are disfigured!"

"Oh, come on, Pete," I tried to calm him. "They're having an allergic reaction or something. The splotches will clear up."

"So now you are a doctor, or what? A professor maybe? It's not just the splotches. It's their reputation, for God's sake! They'll never live this down. Can't you understand? What kind of Greek are you? A woman proved to be stronger than them. This is intolerable! This is an abomination!"

"It's nothing of the kind. It's ridiculous, that's what it is. You're putting me on, aren't you?"

"I wish I was. In fact, I wish I had never met any of you at all. I've had nothing but headaches from the start."

"Oh, Pete. You love us! Admit it."

"As it happens, I don't in the least love you or any other human being. I love my chickens, and my roosters, my sheep, even my pigs. But people? No. I'm afraid the more I get to know people, the less I'm able to love them."

He let the heavy sentiments hang in the air for a few minutes. Then he broke the stifling silence with a howl of laughter.

"Of course, they're being ridiculous. They *are* ridiculous. I can't thank you enough for exposing them and revealing them for the silly pretentious buggers that they are, even though you did it unintentionally. Maybe I'll make an exception to my rule and consider loving you for it. We'll see." He turned serious. "Sadly, however, now that you've had your little joke and your victory, there is a big price to pay. These are big, powerful people, and they must have their revenge. Or at least their vindication."

It had apparently taken them over an hour of discussion to come up with an acceptable vindication, but ultimately the course to follow had made itself clear to them. Pete gave me the short version:

"The most obvious first step is for Elsa to get deadly ill from those curries," said Pete dryly. "Much more ill than our guys. It's not necessary for her to die, though that would help, but she must be absolutely bedridden and seek help from some special Swedish clinic, and go there to recuperate. Now, in truth, there is no need for her to go all the way to Sweden. She can go to Athens if she wants. She must leave Crete, that's all. And she must stay away at least a couple of weeks longer than it'll take for the guys to recover. You see, that way she'll have taken longer to recover in a foreign clinic than our people will at one of our lesser clinics. That would be satisfactory. Okay." Pete waved his hand over his shoulder, a gesture that in Greek means the argument is closed and the verdict is final.

He cleared his throat before continuing. I realized that Elsa's punishment was very much the first step. The coup de grâce was to follow.

"Next," continued Pete, with a touch of sympathy in his voice, "it must be announced that it wasn't simply the chilies and the spices. That it was poison. If it is poison, then there is no blame. No man is strong enough to withstand poison. It's no disgrace to get ill from poison."

I stated the obvious: "If we admit the curry was poisoned, we'll never get anyone to eat here anymore. We'll be out of business."

"Exactly," beamed Pete. "I knew as soon as I met you that you were a smart man."

"It's not fair, Pete," I wailed. "We've been through too much to be closed down for a lie."

"Actually, I guess you're not as smart as all that. To be closed down for a lie is much more preferable than to be closed down for the terrible truth!"

"Which is what!?" I was riled.

"Which is," surged Pete unpityingly, "that you people, my Constantinopolitan friend, are the plague! You brought every sort of calamity on our heads this winter. Floods, sliding rocks, earthquakes, curry-pestilence. My God, what are you after? To destroy the entire valley? If you could arrange for some famine and a war, you could be the Horsemen of the Apocalypse. Plakiás and its surrounding regions cannot afford to have your kind around here! If we let you continue, you'll probably cause droughts and Saharan sandstorms and wipe out our olives and our tourists, our everything. No, no. You must be stopped, and this is the best way to do it."

"By pretending we poisoned the guests?" My chef's ethics were shaken to the core. "How about something a bit milder. Salmonella. Trichinosis. Oversalting. But poison, Pete? Please. Have a heart."

"We won't say which poison. And we won't point any fingers. It will have been an accident. Not a problem. And we'll suppress it from the newspapers. We'll circulate it as a rumour."

"No. I can't live with poison." My teeth were clenched.

"How about an unsubstantiated rumour?"

"No. Poison is poison."

"Well, how about this, then?" Pete was about to play his ace. "The men are willing to buy you all out. They are proposing to give you money!"

"There is no amount of money to justify poison."

"Now you are being ridiculous. Of course there is. As it happens, I worked out a good deal for all of you."

"Poison in the food, Pete? My God."

I was appalled, but I was outvoted. The partners were delighted with the chance to get out of the restaurant business honourably. And everyone, most of all Elsa, was tickled pink about the intended subterfuge.

Elsa wrapped her face in bandages and had herself carried through the streets of Marioú on a stretcher to the waiting ambulance—arranged by the olive oil godfather, who was a major patron of the big hospital in Réthymno—to begin her journey to the fictitious Swedish clinic, actually a luxury hotel in Mykonos, for three glorious weeks for her and her family, all expenses paid by the splotchy seven.

The "poison" victims' faces and the rest of their awful symptoms cleared up in less than a week, and they carried on stronger than ever now that they had proven manly beyond the call of duty by overcoming poison so swiftly and so completely.

Jean-Louis and Theresa made up now that he was back in the bucks. They decided to reinvest their money in a Tunisian import shop, along with Stavros and Pavlos, who assured them that there was a ready market for the beautiful artifacts Theresa had originally imported to decorate the restaurant.

Algis took his money gratefully. Being the most sensible of us all, he had known for a while that the chemistry of this partnership gave off the stench of failure, and he had been sure that his money would be lost without a trace. To make his surprise success even sweeter, he had got word from three Greek magazines and newspapers to which he had submitted his sculpture as well as his distorted-Crete photographs that they would be publishing his work.

To celebrate his good luck he packed his cameras and his money and set out to trek back up to Zeus's cave—to bookend his trip—and then to return to Canada and his real life. I felt sure he wouldn't soon forget his adventures in Crete and that he would return, for he'd stayed long enough to let the island get in his blood.

Ah, yes, Pete's deal for our partnership. It was surprisingly generous, considering it came from sons of Crete, a people who are not famous for parting with their money. I guess the situation was drastic, because they paid all the investing partners double the amount of their original investments, a cool

100 per cent return on capital for wreaking havoc on the Plak-iás area for all of two months.

The seven thus became the new owners of 50 per cent of the business, the other half of which already belonged to Pete. They agreed to remain silent partners behind Pete, who would now operate the restaurant as his own.

"Restaurant is in every Greek's heart, you know," Pete confided in me. "I thought I'd never want one, but now that I have it, I'm looking forward to it."

Pete's first task as a restaurant owner was to sell off the most hyperbolic of the kitchen equipment, such as the phantasmagoric eight-burner, two-oven cooker, the futuristic dishwashing machine, and the far too powerful stand-up mixer. He replaced them with a two-element propane stove and a domestic oven, a poor distant relative with dishpan hands, and a wire whisk with a bowl, respectively. He pocketed the profit from the transactions, and charged the salary of the dishwashing relative to the business. Talk about a good deal.

As for me, they gave me 3,000 euros, mostly to silence my objections to the fake-poison scenario. It wasn't really enough to compensate for being branded a poisoner, but it was all they were offering, and I took it.

Three weeks later, I got a call from Pete to come see him at the restaurant. He sounded just as bossy as ever, but I had nothing else to do, so I went.

The place looked exactly as I remembered it, the untouched mounds of earth and wide-open cement pothole on the driveway intact. The only difference was that the old "Byron's Curry-House" sign had been replaced by the laconic, elegant "Pete's."

Pete himself was reposing on a table under the plane tree, his *metrio* coffee full-*kaimaki* by his right hand. "We open in three days," he announced unceremoniously. "But no party this time. Forget it." He farted. "Just like that. Open the doors, warm up the food, set the tables. What do you think?"

"I think, good luck, Pete. What am I supposed to think?" I shrugged. "You're reopening a place that just finished poisoning eight people. Do you think anyone will come?"

"Yes. They will come because people hate remembering bad things. It's like the legend of Pope Joan. Ever hear of it?"

"The woman who fooled everyone and became pope?" I asked, surprised yet again by Pete's extensive knowledge. This was a twisted little story from the Vatican's secret past.

"A Greek wrote her story in a book. He was from the nineteenth century, and his name was Emmanouil Roidis. That's how I know about her," he informed me. "But what I want to say is that after she gave birth in a public square, proving without a doubt that she was a woman, and the people stoned her to death, the Vatican erased her papacy by extending the dates of the popes around her. As if she had never existed. As far as any Catholic is concerned, that's it, she never was. The same way, your curry-house never existed. 'Pete's' has erased all memory of the curry, and you and the poison. Now it's my restaurant, and my wife is the chef, and we wouldn't dream of ever poisoning anyone."

"And that's why people will come? Because they will forget?"

"No. They will come because they remember the one good thing we had here: your *biftekis* from the party. Everyone is still talking about them, and for a good *bifteki* a Greek will cross mountains."

"That's great, Pete," I exclaimed, suddenly very miffed. "Happy to have been of service."

"Look here, Byron," smiled Pete. "You make the best damn *bifteki* in Crete. Maybe the whole world. You make a *bifteki* that makes any other *bifteki* seem second-rate. You are without a doubt the king of the *bifteki*. And I need you. And Mrs. Pete needs you. Come and work with us. Create the *biftekis* for us, and I promise to love you forever. And also to pay you, and to make you a partner. To give you a share. Come on! What do you say?"

Part IV   # The Beach

Chapter 23

A Home of My Own

I'm writing this by the seaside, waiting in the shade for my coffee. It's hot, some ninety degrees—thirty-five Centigrade—though it's already September. It gets a lot hotter in the summer, but I wasn't here. I was in Montreal, miffed.

I left Crete in a great hurry about a month after Pete's "King of the Bifteki" offer. I may be a sucker for flattery, and will buckle under many forms of it, but even I have my limits. King of the minced beef, regardless of how well it's seasoned, is an honour I can do without.

I refused him outright. There was no need to reflect. It was the beginning of April. The region had transformed itself into a perfumery. The orange and lemon blossoms, white with canary-yellow hearts, had flowered all at once, adding their dizzying aromas to the other springtime smells. The resulting cocktail of scents would be far too sweet in a bottle, but on a hillside in Crete it sings of love and well-being. The weather had also turned deliciously hot. Not quite as hot as it is now, but certainly hot enough to plunge into the sea. The water was still too cold for long swims, but I didn't care. I hadn't been in since Christmas.

There are thousands of beaches in this country, many of them on Crete's endless coastline, but only the perfect ones qualify as true Greek beaches. Greek beach perfection is predicated on compounded pleasures. The criteria are accessibility, water quality, food, and shade.

Accessibility means being able to get to the water's edge without any difficulty. It's okay if one can't drive a car to the beach, because it's always possible to get there by boat. But once on it, there must be only a short distance, an easy thirty-second stroll on even ground, between oneself and the water.

Water quality has several rules. Waves are out of the question. They are a huge turn-off. The gentlest of lapping surf is tolerated, but it is best if there is no surf at all. The ideal water does not have even a ripple, is like *ladi* (oil).

Colour is a crucial issue. Blue-green is best, but not uniformly so. The best beaches have water of several shades of turquoise that blend into each other to add visual diversion to a lengthy swim (Greeks have been known to stay in the water for hours).

Even more important is clarity. A Greek will swim only in water that is totally transparent, through which one can clearly see every pebble at the bottom. There must also be soft sand at the water's edge—no painful stones or rocks—so that walking out at the end of the swim can be a pleasant experience. It must get deep gradually, never suddenly. The proper temperature—a few degrees less than the air, to ensure cooling-off—is taken for granted, since Greeks will submerge themselves in sea water only in the warmest months, when the water is guaranteed to be ideally tempered.

Food and other refreshments are beyond essential, because Greeks don't go to the beach just to swim and enjoy nature, they go there to eat. Every beach worth the name has a commodious *psaro-taverna* (fish restaurant) right next to the water, with fresh, albeit expensive, sea specialties, as well as music and a good crowd of other beach aficionados for people watching.

And finally the shade, the cool of *drossia*, without which a beach visit can be hell. Greeks never needed to be informed that the sun can cause damage—the Greek sun in summer is not a benevolent force. It burns, it disorients, it's uncomfortable. In any case, Greeks do not have to sunbathe to get a tan, since their everyday lives expose them to more sun than is safe. Greeks never lie on the sand like silly tourists. They seek out the *drossia* of a tree, or even better, a taverna table under an awning, to look at the sea and develop an appetite.

My choice of beach back in April (it is now in September) was Soúda Bay, a couple of kilometres west of Plakiás. I had sought refuge in Soúda's floral Galini Restaurant all winter, including for my Christmas swim. In March, I had watched the process of its reopening for the new season, with feverish month-long renovations that reflected similar goings-on over the entire Plakiás area.

The very first day of April, Galini opened and I took my seat off to the side, under the plane tree. I had a full view of the serene waters and was within nose-range of fish grilling on the charcoal, potatoes pan-frying in olive oil, and double-strength *metrio* coffee with *kaimaki* foam worthy of a steady customer.

Those April swims and Galini sitdowns were revelatory. This was the Greece I had trekked all the way from Canada to find. At the end of one week I had forgotten all about the record-breaking winter snows and cold rains, the permanent threat of rogue earthquakes, the numbing problems of the hexed curry-house, the squabbles of my temporary partners, and also my own doubts of belonging in this country.

With every succeeding swim, with every seaside meal, with every cup of coffee in the silken warmth of my shaded table, I became more convinced that I should forge ahead to legitimize my foothold in the homeland. The promise of a Greek summer spent entirely outdoors on the beach, on balconies, at café tables, is the very reason Greeks are willing to put up with the cruelties of foreign, as well as domestic, predators, the vagaries of erratic electricity, and fuel shortages. I was ready for it, come what may.

It has been a long time since I ordered my coffee. The waiter approaches me apologetically. There is a problem with the propane in the kitchen. The cooks are frantic: many orders to fill, and no stove. Sorry, sorry. Devastated. I smile, and nod my forgiveness. Could he offer me a *raki* in the meanwhile? No, I'll wait for the *metrio*.

After that idyllic week in April, there was a rude rewakening. The landlords of my prized room had warned me long before that the rent would more than triple as the calendar neared Easter and the "season" began. But I had had so much on my mind that I had forgotten all about this.

The plan had been for Algis and me to find cheaper accommodation during the curry-house summer, when we would be so busy that an inferior room would serve since it would be used only for sleeping.

Now, with no curry-house to occupy my time, no income to defray costs, and no Algis to share expenses with, I was fac-

ing a depressing prospect: unaffordable rent for an inferior
room that I hadn't even found yet. Niko offered me a solution
of sorts: a rundown hut in his olive grove—cheap, but a hovel.

Erato did her best to clean it out for me, but the plumbing
was a museum piece—back to slow-trickle, cool showers—
the kitchen was good for making coffee and not much else,
the bed smelled of goat piss, and access to the place was over
a seriously damaged dirt road best negotiated by military
tank.

At great financial sacrifice I held onto my rented car, a
dainty Hyundai, which I now had to park on the Tarmac a
kilometre away from the hut, a walk of pure drudgery already
in moderate April and probably sheer torture in the upcoming extra-octane heat of summer.

It was becoming more obvious by the minute that I would
soon have to stop being a visitor, shuffling around to imper-
manent abodes. I needed to take the plunge and enter the
real-estate game so that I could have a place to call my own.

Normally I do not involve myself in games that I don't
stand a chance to win, and I should have remembered that.
Buying a house anywhere without proper finances is a mis-
take. Doing it in Greece as a virtual foreigner, ignorant of the
arcane, ungraspable rules and regulations, is at least crimi-
nally stupid, if not out-and-out suicidal.

Nevertheless, on the aftermath of a particularly memorable
swim and a subsequent spectacular meal of red mullets and
freshly steamed greens, I succumbed. I was sitting with
Kosta, a recent acquaintance of no known profession who
became quite funny after a few *aspro patos* of wine and a couple of *rakis*. He heard my accommodation complaints and
nodded sympathetically. "It happens to everyone who
doesn't own a house," he said.

I sipped my post-prandial coffee and let him talk me into a short drive up the hillside, to look. Just to look. No one is forcing you to buy.

Less than a kilometre straight up from the beach, on a good dirt road—which, he said, was slated to be paved before the winter—was a property that astonished me.

A terraced series of interconnected springtime-lush fields, it was awash in greens studded with red and purple poppies, canary-yellow buttercups, golden forsythia bushes, and lapis-blue lupines. The lot, some four thousand square metres of it, appeared to have a little bit of everything. Olive trees, gnarled and wise in irregular rows. Grapevines, alive and raring to grow after all those rains. Fig trees off to the side. Lemon trees, orange trees. A vegetable patch in neatly separated beds, already planted with a greengrocer's list of edibles and herbs. One palm tree. And a small whitewashed house, barely bigger than a hut but welcoming in the clearing of a compact wild-cherry orchard, pink with countless blooms.

There was an outdoor table in the courtyard of the house, and a nice large chair—my size, as if placed there specially for me. I sat in it instinctively. It faced the sea. It was as if I was perched right over the water, and if I wasn't careful I could fall in. It transported me. I felt as if I had been living here all my life. This was my vision of Crete all along, and now it was mine. Or nearly.

I was so wrapped up in its potential for future happiness that I didn't hear him drive in. The owner of the property, Polykarpos, an unsmiling man of advanced years, bent from decades of hard work, scarred and wrinkled by all he had witnessed of man's inhumanity to man, was standing there, watching me. Beside him, Kosta was aglow with his euro finder's fee practically in his pocket. My interest in the house

was as transparent as the waters of Soúda Bay, and my bar-
gaining position was down the drain.

"I'm not interested in selling this land," declared Polykarpos, ignoring Kostas's introductions and my outstretched
hand. "And if I were, you're way down the list of eligible
buyers."

"It's the way things are around here," Kostas filled me in.
"If Kirios Polykarpos wanted to sell this place, he would have
to first offer it to the neighbours, if they wanted it to expand
their own land. Then to members of his family. Then to people of Soúda and Selliá, then to the Plakiás region, then to
people in other parts of Crete, then to Greeks on the mainland, then to members of the European Union, and finally to
someone like you, a Canadian."

"But I am Greek," I protested, laughing. "Can't we bring
me a little further up the queue? Anyway, I never said I
wanted it."

"It's perfect for you," snapped Polykarpos. "What are you
talking about?"

"Then there's the price," continued Kosta, as if he hadn't
been interrupted. "The neighbours and the family is one
price. The villagers and the Plakiotes another. And so on. It
goes up the further away from home the client is. For you,
since you are Greek, I'm sure we can work it out."

"Everything can be worked out, but never easily. Life is a
terrible battle, and in the end we all lose," stated Polykarpos
matter-of-factly.

I should have believed the grouchy Polykarpos and let the
issue drop right there. But I was desperate to get out of the
goat-pissy hovel I was stuck in. "There's obviously no way I
can afford it," I said, "but, just out of curiosity, what is the
price?"

"It has no water, only a well. It has no electricity, but it can be brought in at great expense. The road will probably never be fixed, though they promised. This is not for you!" Polykarpos started to turn to leave. What happened to "It's perfect for you," I wondered.

"It's perfect for him," Kostas chimed in, reading my thoughts. "And he wants it!"

"I didn't say that!" I exclaimed, by now on very shaky ground.

"Please let me handle this," Kosta insisted, shutting me out of my own negotiation.

Polykarpos eyeballed me as if I were a sacrificial victim. He opened his mouth and casually named a frightening sum of money. I sprang out of my chair. "I'm gone," I said, relieved that the dream had fizzled before it had a chance to become a nightmare.

"Be reasonable, cousin," pleaded Kosta. "The man is not an idiot. He's a Greek. The most he'll pay is—" and he concluded with almost as scary an amount, some few thousand euros less.

"I will not!" I said with finality.

"Then, how much would you pay for it?" asked Polykarpos, ready to hit me if my offer was too low.

"I have to decide that I want it before I talk money," I reasoned, trying to regain some kind of upper hand.

"It's perfect for you!" shouted Polykarpos, kicking the ground. "And you asked me for a price. Didn't you?!"

"Okay, fine," I agreed. I stole another glance at the view— the lupines, the poppies, the vines, the all-dressed-in-pink cherry trees. And I blurted out an amount, about half of what Polykarpos had first quoted. I had no idea if it represented a fair price for this property.

Polykarpos cleared his throat noisily and spat out a large gob of phlegm. "I accept," he grunted, and with a hand gesture to Kosta, he abruptly left.

I was even more astonished by this development than by the beauty of the land.

"You drive a hard bargain, boss!" Kosta slapped his thigh and chuckled with glee. I wasn't sure if he was laughing at me or with me. "Now don't you be in a hurry, though," he cautioned. "As I said, Polykarpos has to speak to a number of people first before he can sell to you."

That evening I consulted Jean-Louis, who was now brimming with an excess of confidence in his improved station in life. "You've offered double what a place like that is worth, but it's a volatile market," he pronounced.

I made some quick calculations. I would have to rent out my house in Montreal to meet the mortgage payments, and I would have to lay out most of my available cash for the down payment and the most immediate work needed in the house. All in all, getting involved in this purchase would leave me nearly bankrupt, but I'd own my own Greek house. And I would no longer be able to meet any crises in my life. This would make me more Greek than I could handle. Any which way I looked at this, even from the perspective of the wonderful view and the pink cherry blossoms, it was a rotten deal. Tomorrow I'd call it off.

The next day Kosta found me at my usual Soúda table, and before I could say a word, he slapped me on the back and grabbed me in a drunken bear hug to announce that it was all set. Polykarpos had cleared the way for my purchase! We had an appointment with the notary two days hence. I greeted the news with an icy silence.

"Oh, you can't back out NOW!" Kosta screamed in panic.

"You proposed a price. He accepted. Now it's a matter of honour!" He paused and hugged himself, rocking in place. "He has been known to shoot people who double-cross him," he said in unmistakable fright. "Which means not only you, but me too!"

I shudder at the memory even now. It scared me then, and it does so still. I could really use that coffee, but it doesn't look as if I'm going to get it soon. The crisis in the kitchen has reached the shouting stage.

Our first visit to the notary did not incur much shouting—that was to come later. We arrived amicably all together in my car. Polykarpos was less grouchy but uncomfortable in an ill-fitting suit, Kosta was sober but still chatty, and I was far too jovial for the serious financial predicament to which I was about to commit myself.

The notary, an old communist, tetchy from some sort of chronic ailment, listened with impatience to Kosta's excited recounting of our transaction. When he had heard enough, he put up a bony hand for silence. He addressed me because, as he had guessed, I was a novice at purchasing land in Greece.

"First of all, I recommend you lose some weight. Obesity is the most criminal side effect of capitalism, and an offence against civilization. Next, I suggest you be very careful when you do business in this country, especially if it involves buying land, and even more especially when you're buying from this crafty codger." He pointed at Polykarpos, who pretended he was deaf. "You can't do this without a lawyer. There is much to investigate. This lot has never been registered or surveyed. Titles in this part of the world go back hundreds of years, and for all we know Polykarpos doesn't even own it."

"Commie bastard," hissed Polykarpos under his breath.

The notary was incensed and proceeded to give a controlled but searing condemnation of all landlords, their crooked methods of manipulating the public, their insatiable greed, their immense cruelty, and their despicable collusion with the clerics to undermine all that was decent and humane. Towards the end of his tirade he raised his voice a notch, but still stayed well short of shouting.

Polykarpos laughed mockingly. He told me that the notary charged by the minute, and that this kind of talk was his way of costing more than he was worth. And that I should object, since paying his fee was my responsibility.

The notary stood up and extended an over-long finger, pointing us to the door. "Get out all of you, and don't you dare show your faces around here again until your documents are in order. I don't have time for idiots like you!"

On the way back I asked if we should find another notary. No, I was told. He was the only notary anyone trusted in the entire jurisdiction.

Kosta helped me find a lawyer, who charged me a ridiculous sum to take two weeks to tell me that the title was clear and free. The lawyer had hired an equally overpriced surveyor, who had completed a map of the lot. All that was well and good. But the lawyer had unearthed an unexpected and expensive problem: "The property will be 799 metres from the sea once the road is paved," he said ruefully.

In response to my puzzled expression, he explained that according to the law, any property whose sea-facing border was closer than 800 metres from the water's edge was liable for a significant luxury tax. As things stood now, the lot was 802 metres from the sea, but once the bulldozers got to work, they would shave off 3 metres and add several thousand euros to my expenses. He told me that I could appeal this obviously biased remeasurement, but it would cost a packet in legal fees and take a long time, and I was sure to lose the case since the government would never be denied once they decided to charge for something.

The lawyer's fee, the cost of the surveying, the new tax, the notary's multiple visits—they were all beginning to add up, but it was still not enough to defeat me. Every new obstacle made me that much more determined to close this deal and move into the little house before the cherries were ripe.

Polykarpos, surely guilty of all the crimes about which the notary had ranted, couldn't help noticing my obsession with his property. Well, no one could. It was all I talked of, and everyone in the region was gossiping about the details, the delays, the money. I heard there was a betting pool as to whether I would end up buying or not, and on last count the "nays" were outnumbering the "yeas."

The legal matters out of the way, we scheduled our second, and purportedly final, meeting with the notary. Polykarpos had delayed us by a good week, which could have made me suspicious, but I chose to believe Kosta that the landlord was ill with *laima*. In truth, a new epidemic of the ailment was ripping through the area; there had been a weather relapse in the last few days of April, with a storm and a slight drop in temperature, exposing the citizens to unseasonal drafts and consequent sore throats.

On the last day of April, with May Day and its flowery—or, depending on one's persuasion, its red-flagged—celebrations just a balmy night away, I was ordered to drive to the notary's for the crucial meeting. Polykarpos had refused to drive there with me; he was coming separately, with Kosta in tow. This should have alarmed me no end, but by now I was desperate for my new home and was heeding no warnings at all.

For one thing, I was dying to move out of my hut in Niko's olive grove. Aside from all its other inconveniences, the smell was driving me crazy. Goat bells might be the music of Crete, but goat smells are surely the island's most effective defence against invasion. It is the only animal stench that outdoes the human. The mere thought of it was making me nauseous, and sleeping in it even one more night would have been nothing short of torture.

The notary was in fighting form, even more cantankerous than the previous time. He must have slept badly—maybe a goat had pissed in his bed that night, or maybe he had pissed in it himself—because we had barely sat down when he took off on an invective against capitalism not heard since Trotsky.

He berated everything: Church, family, business, and obviously landlords—nothing was sacred. He was so angry, so reckless, so very insulting to Polykarpos, that I felt certain the two of them would come to blows.

Polykarpos listened to him as if he were an insect; he winced and slapped his forehead, but he never once replied to the charges that were being hurled at him. He seemed to be biding his time for more important matters.

When the notary finally tired of listening to his own voice and accepted the fact that no one in the room was going to debate him, he opened a folder and withdrew official documents written in precise, legible handwriting. He handed Polykarpos and me copies to peruse. Then he started to read his own copy aloud, as the law stipulates.

The landlord put up a hand and made a gruff noise to interrupt the reading. "One of my cousins came to me yesterday," he said. It was a simple statement with far-reaching consequences.

The notary froze and stopped reading. Kosta made a drowning sound and slumped in his chair. I looked at one, then the other of them, already doomed but not yet cognizant of it.

"Does the bastard want the land?" asked the notary irritably.

"Yes," nodded Polykarpos shrewdly.

The notary shook his head with distaste. "I hope you have lots of money," he said to me. "The scoundrel has you at his mercy."

"I don't understand," I gulped, though I understood perfectly well.

"According to our family-based primeval laws, this patently dishonest *copriti* [dealer in manure] is allowed— hell, he is encouraged—to get an idiot cousin of his to claim an interest in this property and effectively block your transaction. Your only remedy is to prove the cousin's interest capricious, which would be impossible for you to do. Therefore, you have to offer more money."

"I don't have any more money!" I whimpered.

The notary raised his eyebrows in plain distrust of me, as of any other capitalist. "How much money would buy off your cousin's sudden desire to acquire this useless piece of land?" he asked Polykarpos.

The landlord turned to me directly. "People like you come back from America, Canada, Australia, and you think you can cheat us with paltry amounts to buy into our heritage," he scoffed. "Well, think again. I told you originally how much I wanted for my land. My great-grandfather worked himself to an early grave to clear that hillside. To terrace it, to plant the trees, to build that house. By hand, by himself. You pay me my price, or you can go to hell!" He clenched his teeth and put his hand in his pocket to clutch a sharp item that was inside it.

"I'm paying you a fair price!" I shouted.

Polykarpos pursed his lips and looked away. Kosta, back from the drowned, spoke in a squeaky voice. "Maybe you can take out a loan," he suggested.

"Shut up, you!" I screamed. And putting aside all of my Canadian niceness, I rushed Polykarpos. Using my weight to advantage, I knocked him down off his chair. I immobilized his hand, and the weapon that might have been in the pocket, with a heavy foot. Then, using the "f" word—the "gamma" word, in Greek—frequently and creatively, I told him what to do with his land, his heritage, his island, and his honour. "And if you so much as lift a finger to harm me, I'll tear you to shreds, you, YOU . . ." I trailed off, not exactly sure how I could tear him to anything were he to shoot or knife me.

I stormed out of the office, but not before the notary could point out that I'd have to pay his bill regardless.

My coffee has arrived. It's lukewarm. It has no foam. It's gritty. It's over-sugared. It's awful. But I'm sipping it anyway. I'm gazing at the sea. A group of children, brown as beans from a whole summer of sun and beach, are frolicking in the water. Their mothers come out of nowhere to call them to lunch.

The propane problem in the kitchen must have been solved. The coffee they made me is terrible, but the family's fried *marides* look so good, rosy-crisp and sea-flavoured, it's all I can do to stop myself from grabbing some. I call my waiter and take the safer route to whitebait satisfaction. I order some of my own.

I left Crete the same afternoon of my outburst in the notary's office. I drove to Heraklion, handed back my car, and then took a taxi to the port and boarded the ferry to Piraeus. I looked over my shoulder the whole way, expecting Polykarpos or one of his cousins to come for me and, with a couple of well-placed bullets to the crotch, leave me to die moaning, bleeding on the deck within sight of the sea.

But no one came gunning for me, and I made it back to the mainland. Thus, on May Day, instead of gambolling with flowers in my hair—or draped in a red flag—on the pasture behind Soúda Bay, I boarded Olympic Airways' Athens–Montreal direct flight. Dazed and unhappy for the ten hours of the journey, wondering how else I could have bought myself a parcel of Greekness instead of losing my temper and starting a vendetta and excluding myself from the Plakiás area, possibly from all of Crete, I arrived back home in my adoptive land.

If a Greek has to live in North America and doesn't end up in Astoria, New York, Montreal is a pretty good choice. Save for the four atrocious months of deep winter, which no sane person could ever get used to, this metropolis in French-speaking Canada offers eight months a year of good, somewhat naughty, European-style diversion.

In the actual summer, June to September, Montreal warms up to a joyous, self-regenerating street party that embraces music, sports, dancing, movies, outdoor drinking, and as much sex as can be crammed into the dull periods between sessions of world-class, mostly free entertainment. The weather gets steamy. The countless lakes—a mere forty-minute drive in all directions from the city centre—are eminently swimmable, if on the cold side. The camaraderie oozes and gushes from a Latinate populace who are addicted to human interaction in all its kindlier forms.

My house, located in a high-energy, low-crime area, is within walking distance from a mini-Greece, with markets, restaurants, music joints, and services where I can function entirely in Greek and can easily pretend to be in Greece itself.

Sadly, it was no longer satisfactory. It had worked in the past because I had had commitments and couldn't feasibly have moved to Greece without endangering my work and my income. Now, however, when I had made a clean break and had actually decided to go and settle in the homeland, being back in Montreal had a tinge of bleakness that I couldn't shake.

Truth is, I never really gave the city much of a chance to draw me back in, because Greece kept returning to haunt me. There were many visits from Algis, for example, with hundreds of photographs to elicit Plakiás and Marioú and Soúda, as well as remembrances of our room with a view of the olive groves and the unbroken horizon of the Libyan Sea.

More evocative yet were the regular phone calls from Theo, who still couldn't believe I had left without consulting him. Now he was dangling carrots to entice me back. Pieces of land, trouble-free and cheap, that I could have on demand. A job with Eftihia, whose revived restaurant would be operative by August and would stay open all winter. Sinecures that kept cropping up from his powerful position in the think tank. He made me feel wanted and welcome back in Greece, but he failed to convince me.

I spent the summer sulking and isolated, uninterested in any of the Montreal goings-on, and yet incapable of contemplating Greece. There are close to seven thousand miles between Montreal and Crete, and each one felt like a mountain that was impossible to scale. I half-heartedly tried to recoup some of my abandoned professional life as a food commentator with radio and newspapers, but I was so tentative during interviews that no one took me seriously.

By mid-August I was in such a slump that on many days I never left the house, preferring to remain indoors in the air conditioning, dreading that summer would soon turn to autumn, with its pretty but foreboding red-leafed trees and its inevitable winter around the corner, to crush me as it always had in the past.

At that point, when I would have welcomed any excuse to escape from my self-imposed funk, came a series of unforeseen events. To begin with, I got an inflated, out-of-the-blue offer to sell my house. The location had been gaining in value for a while, and an estate agent rang my bell uninvited to ask me if I wished to sell, quoting an irresistible price. And almost simultaneously I received a letter from Soúda.

Kosta, my old drunken buddy, had secured my mailing address, and he wrote me in his schoolboy Greek to inform me that Polykarpos had died from a heart attack while haggling over the price of manure fertilizer for his olive trees. His son and sole heir, Telemachus, was anxious to sell me my dream property at my price. To make it more attractive, the asphalt road, which was now a reality, had actually increased the lot's distance from the sea, releasing me from the additional tax.

I had no guarantee that these favourable conditions would endure once I got there, but a third omen compelled me to call Olympic and book a flight. The intrepidly resourceful Algis had, during the winter, approached the mayor of Plakiás with a proposal for an art installation.

The project involved his Québec summer wildflowers pictures, created on the computer prior to his trip to Europe. He proposed to have the images transferred onto porcelain and mounted on a towering cliff face, the Paligremmos, which rises straight out of the sand dunes in a flat, unblemished surface, at the far end of Plakiás Bay. His project required quite a bit of cash investment by city hall, and Algis had deemed the chances of its being approved so slim that he had never mentioned it to me.

Now he had received an e-mail informing him that a commercial sponsor had been found and that a complimentary air ticket had been booked for him. Algis was returning to Plakiás, and he was urging me to join him, albeit at my own expense. He ascribed his good luck to Zeus, and also to St. Anthony of the wet chapel in the gorge, where he had performed the rites with such zeal.

Good luck that comes in threes is not to be taken lightly, whether it includes a free air ticket or not. I expedited the sale of my house and opened a euro account at a Greek bank that just happened to have a branch down the street. I flew off into the late August skies, hopeful that this time nothing would stand in my way. My life as a repatriated Greek was about to really begin.

The lowly *marides*, or whitebait, is a common fish that lives in all the seas of the earth. It has managed to withstand maritime calamities such as overfishing and pollution. It is the cockroach of fishes, and quite likely would survive even a nuclear holocaust.

In most countries it is eaten as penance if one can't afford anything else. In Greece it is also a food of last resort, the fish choice of the poor. But here it combines seamlessly with the mythological landscape, the coruscating sensation of well-being, the birthright of living for the moment because each moment is a treasure and will not be replaced once it's spent, even if it has been spent eating nothing better than *marides*.

My order of the tiny fishes is fried just as rosily as the ones I coveted, and it smells just as cleanly of unspoiled sea water. The *marides* are the gustatory equivalent of diving into the cool sea on a scorching day. These *marides*, today, on my shaded table under the plane tree, are reason enough to take my next breath. Too heavy a burden for such small creatures to bear?

I had *marides* back in Montreal. Those were three days old, imported from Portugal. They were over-fried by a Greek who hated what he was doing, biding his time in foreign lands until he had saved enough money to return home. They tasted fishy and gave me indigestion. I craved them and I ate them repeatedly anyway, just to try to reclaim the sensation of having them in Greece. It didn't work.

Montreal is a storehouse of the world's delicacies. I tasted of all of them during my summer of discontent, but I did not have the capacity to enjoy any of them. I was eating rare and prized morsels cooked with precision in exactingly creative recipes, and yet I found myself missing the overcooked meats and underspiced sauces of rural Crete.

I am a gourmet. It is illogical that I should have been missing bad cooking, regardless of how traditional it is. Obviously what I was missing were the full-flavour organic vegetables, the wild greens, the pure cheeses, the herb-fed lambs, the just-caught fish, Chania's sea urchins, sundried octopus thrown on the charcoal to reclaim its moisture . . . It was nostalgia for Greece itself. And nostalgia can kill, because it can only be palliated, never cured, unless one goes back to the origin.

And so I've returned. I'm here now. And it's a good thing my nostalgia wasn't for the Crete I experienced in the winter and spring. This is the Plakiás of the summer. Not deep summer when all the factories of Europe empty out and millions of partiers descend on all parts of Greece to let off steam and compensate for the fifty weeks a year of jobs that they hate. This is September Plakiás, with a more mature crowd, people who have jobs they like back home and who come to Greece after the big crowds for slightly less manic vacations.

But vacationers, whatever their socio-economic status, are disruptive, especially in huge numbers. They are trampling all over the land, taking off their underwear on beaches they think are deserted, and nightly filling every seat in those countless restaurants that were noisily hammering and sawing back in April, trying to renew themselves and open for business.

I don't mind. I'm back, and that's all that counts. I join the invasion, I become one of the visitors, knowing that soon they'll all go home and the place will be mine once more. And in the meantime, I savour the sunshine and revel in the knowledge that I can have *marides* at their best, I can swim in the crystalline waters, I can sit in the *drossia* of my plane tree. I am back in Greece, and I can have a *metrio* coffee done to a turn—unless the kitchen is going bananas because the propane is faulty, or the electricity is once again on the blink, or the sous-chef has quit because the tourist babe he was wetting his pants to possess chose to sleep with her boyfriend instead.

(((

I walked up to my property yesterday. It is now even more beautiful than it seemed back in April. But it is different. The long, dry summer has burned off the wildflowers and the grass. The hills are now brown-grey, dressed only in the sturdier weeds, the most persistent flowers, timeless olive trees, and tall noble evergreens.

The cherries are long gone, but the figs and the grapes are ripe, and sweeter than honey. Polykarpos's son cleaned out the little house for me and got it to smell of thyme and oregano like the hillside. He has installed a new tank of propane so that I can cook. And he bought a new pump to bring water up from the well for my showers. He let me stay there last night, even though we're closing the sale later on today.

I am happy. The price of the property is as promised. The distance from the sea is firmly established at 805 metres, so there's no tax. I made enough money from the sale of my Montreal house to pay off this one, and have a nice nest egg besides. On top of all the other good tidings, Kosta has organized a group, and it looks like I shall be making some food-money teaching English to adults.

Now that Greece is committed to strive for First-World status, English is the nation's quasi-official second language, and everyone is scampering to learn it. This will be amusing. Greeks simply can't get their minds and mouths to learn and articulate any foreign language. In this regard they are just like the Americans, whom they love to emulate even though they always condemn imperialist ambitions.

Algis came to have breakfast in my new digs this morning. We sat at the table in the courtyard and gazed at the view. There was morning haze, a Turneresque, ghostly watercolour with a barely defined horizon, and distant islands that seemed to be floating in between the sea and the sky.

We drank milky coffee from Colombian beans that I brought from Montreal, and had a typical Greek morning meal of fresh bread, thyme honey, and sheep's-milk butter. Algis, who has been here for more than a week, is going through the Greek-officialdom waltz. He told me that the day before he had spent the better part of three hours in conference with the mayor and three members of the town council out by the cliff.

In a setting of sand dunes, brush, olive trees growing out at impossible angles, and goats (naturally), the dignitaries and Algis discussed a municipal art installation on the face of the ancient rock, arguing about the size of the images and if the work to be exhibited should be re-thought in terms of local flowers instead of those from Québec. No decision was reached, and so many new notions were introduced that the whole affair was further from completion than before it was approved. Algis is such an optimist and so determined that I have no doubt he will out-dance everyone, overcome bureaucratic obliquity, and mount his ethereal flower pictures on that cliff face.

He brought me up to date on our old curry-house chums. It has been an eventful summer for everyone. Most prominently, Pete discovered—to his dismay—that "the restaurants don't roll in the money as if it grew on the trees." It takes hard work, and even if everything else works out, the employees' sticky fingers will lighten the load of the cash register. So Pete had sold the business for a hugely inflated price, keeping his "good deal" record intact.

Elsa and her family had loved Mykonos so much during

their three-week imposed vacation on that debauched island that they had moved there to join the permanent parade of suntanned jet-setters who daily trample the otherworldly whitewashed town looking for each other.

Little Yannis had fallen in love with a mortician's daughter and gotten her pregnant. His wedding was attended by the usual two thousand guests, and now he was working around the clock to make ends meet, far too busy to worry about death and his own funeral.

Big Yannis had left the Plakiás area in an awful hurry when the boyfriends of the three Koxaré maidens had joined forces and come looking for him with carbines loaded. The electrician Onassis had gone with him. When last heard from, they had opened a construction firm in Corfu, as far away from Crete as one can get and still live on a Greek island.

Water Yannis had also fled, to Ayion Oros, the exclusively male monastery complex near Thessaloníki, and had become a monk. *Mantinada*-composing, truck-driving Spiros had moved into the Water household, awaiting the divorce papers so he could marry Mrs. Water. To pass the time until then, he was taping his poems, set to music by little Lefteris, in hopes of a recording contract.

The most uplifting of Algis's gossip had to do with Jean-Louis and Theresa, and their partnership with Stavros and Pavlos. The quartet had moved to Athens, where they had become an instant success with their Tunisian-import artifacts, and even more so with their sideline of restaurant interior design in that restaurant-mad town.

Stavros and Pavlos, emboldened by the marginally more permissive society of the capital, had come out as a gay couple. They had been sighted and photographed holding hands in a gay bar in Kolonaki by a Plakiás local who had stumbled into the place by accident while in Athens on business. The photograph, greasy from overhandling, had made the rounds of the Plakiás region to the accompaniment of much *tou-sou* (pretend spitting to denote disgust) and many *na-sou* (an open-palmed hand gesture to denote utter disgust).

After my breakfast with Algis, I had come down to Soúda to swim, have my imperfect coffee, eat my definitive *marides*, and wait for Theo. On hearing of my renewed house-buying plans, he had insisted on joining me to lend his weight to my efforts and help me avoid any further debacles.

Theo sits down with a moan. It has been a gruelling drive in his newest vehicle, an air-conditioning-free, beat-up Fiat. He claims it's meant to lend him anonymity and humility now that he has been appointed head of a high-profile government agency to formulate some vague new policy for exporting olive oil to Thailand.

"God, it's beautiful out here," he exclaims. "Let's have some coffee to celebrate."

"The propane is giving them problems."

"I don't give a damn about their propane. If I want coffee they can light a woodfire if they have to!" He orders our coffees in his most terrifying voice, melting the waiter's head with dragon-breath fumes.

"My mother came to my dreams last night," I say to defuse his temper.

"Aah, the late and great goddess Despina," he responds with reverence.

"I don't remember you ever meeting my mother."

"I've met every woman worth meeting on the planet," says Theo with a wink.

My mother and Theo!? I banish the thought. "She was smiling in my dream. I think she approves of my decision to buy this land."

"It's a pretty location, and it'll do you good to rough it a little. You've gone way too soft in that Montreal lifestyle of yours."

"I'm installing a brand new shower and a solar water heater. I'm improving the plumbing. I'm also putting in a generator for electricity. I'll be living the soft life before you know it."

"The plumbing will break down. The generator needs fuel, which will be in short supply every other week. Welcome to Greece, and get used to it," says Theo with an annoying snicker. "This is a country of hardship. Things don't just go wrong, they do so tragically. It's not for nothing that we invented Tragedy. Have you not heard our popular songs? Grief and misfortune in every lyric. A true Greek refuses to ever be happy. Forget happy. It doesn't exist. And there is no middle ground. We are a desperate, passionate people, unable to feel things halfway. No one in Greece will ever admit that life is okay though it could be better. No, no! Here, it's All or Nothing. And since none of us can have it All, it is Nothing. It is hopelessness. It is a life of absolutely no rewards. It is unrelieved misery." The coffees, ideally foamy and appetizing, expedited by Theo's arrogance, are timidly placed on our table.

"So I guess suicide is, after all, truly the only viable alternative?"

"Not really," shrugs Theo. "It is too easy. Too effective a release from the misery of life. It doesn't satisfy. The only alternative to suffering wholeheartedly in paradise is to suffer even more. To suffer magnificently." Theo takes a sip of his coffee and sighs deeply with contentment.

Byron Ayanoglu is the author of four cookbooks, including the bestselling *The New Vegetarian Gourmet*, *Simply Thai Cooking*, and *Simply Mediterranean Cooking*. He is also the author of three restaurant guides, 14 stage plays—all produced internationally—and a critically acclaimed novel, *Love in the Age of Confusion*. The former restaurant critic for Toronto's *NOW* and Montreal's *The Gazette*, he has written for numerous magazines and newspapers. Known as "food god" among movie and television stars, Ayanoglu has catered many film shoots, and was once Mick Jagger's live-in chef. He lives in Montreal and will be retiring to Crete.